ANDRÉ GIDE

ANDRÉ GIDE:
his life and art

BY WALLACE FOWLIE

The Macmillan Company, New York
Collier-Macmillan Ltd., London

THE MACMILLAN COMPANY, NEW YORK
COLLIER-MACMILLAN CANADA LTD., TORONTO, ONTARIO

Library of Congress catalog card number: 64-20739

Printed in the United States of America

CONTENTS

1. Introduction   1
2. Childhood and adolescence: 1869–1891   10
3. From Mallarmé to Africa: 1891–1895 (*Paludes*)   19
4. The earliest quest: *Les Nourritures terrestres*
   (1897)   34
5. *L'Immoraliste* (1902) and the problem of
   freedom   46
6. The prodigal and the saint: *Le Retour de
   l'enfant prodigue* (1907) and *La Porte
   étroite* (1909)   57
7. The gratuitous act: *Les Caves du Vatican* (1914)   68
8. The art of the *récit: La Symphonie pastorale*
   (1919)   76
9. The art of the novel: *Les Faux-Monnayeurs*
   (1925)   85
10. 1925–1945   98
11. The heroic myth: *Oedipe* (1931) and *Thésée*
    (1946)   107
12. At Gide's death: 1951–1953   121
13. The journal and the autobiography   134
14. Gide's marriage   147
15. Gide and Catholicism   158
16. Gide and the vocation of writer   175
17. Gide today   188
Selected Bibliography   209

INTRODUCTION

By no means the first writer of confessions, in the history of French letters, André Gide is undoubtedly the most persistently autobiographical, the most determined to use his skill of a writer as a method of self-exploration and as a way to an understanding of himself. No matter what form of literature he used: the *récit* or short novel, the *sotie* or ironic tale, the long novel of *Les Faux-Monnayeurs (The Counterfeiters)*, the play, letters or essays, each work turns out to be a portrait of André Gide or at least the examination of some moral problem central to his very existence.

Throughout his long career as a writer, which extended from the first entry of his journal in 1889, to the last entry, six days before his death in 1951, Gide was fully aware of the vanity which many twentieth century writers see in a literature of confession. One of his closest friends, Paul Valéry, reproached him for this tendency toward self-portraiture. Pascal, three centuries earlier, had reproached Montaigne for the same excess, and on several occasions Gide acknowledged his approval of Montaigne. The method of self-analysis used by the author of *Les Essais* (Gide once estimated that one-third of the writings of Montaigne is autobiography), was appropriated by Gide with a twentieth century consciousness of the infinite complexities of psychological analysis and of the attacks that would come from his attempts to establish an individual morality in contradistinction to orthodox morality.

The character analyses of the seventeenth century La Bruyère (*Les Caractères*), in their directness and honesty, give a clear portrait of what men are, but Gide claims that they never tell how the men become what they are. This is what interests Gide, this is what appears important to him: the multiple forces, both obscure and visible, which have made a man what he is. In some of the outspoken passages of Gide's autobiography, *Si le grain ne meurt*, passages which appeared scandalous to many of the first readers, and in certain passages of the *Journal* where Gide makes intimate revelations of his thoughts and behavior, he moves beyond the degree of frankness reached by such writers of confessions as Saint Augustine, Cellini and Rousseau. Repeatedly Gide claims that this kind of confessional writing in which he indulges is an effort on his part to understand the laws of his own development, the influences that made him what he was.

To Valéry's scorn for biography and for mere factual information concerning a writer's life (he dismissed this type of writing by saying that the biographer counts the socks and the mistresses of his subject), Gide would answer that a literary genius is not created spontaneously or easily. His story is often obscured by physiological secrets, by anomalies, by deep-seated dissatisfactions. When Gide stated that he had been formed by a solitary and ill-humored childhood (*mon enfance solitaire et rechignée*), he indicated a belief that the drama of his life as well as the accomplishments of his art are to be found in his earliest years.

No contemporary has had a more fervent sense of literary vocation than Gide. From late adolescence through maturity and into old age, his life was consecrated to literature, to the art of expressing himself by means of the written word. He would be the first to acknowledge that everything has been said about man. His originality is not found in the mere revelation of his weaknesses and imperfections. Montaigne did this admirably long before Gide's time, and in a language as elegant and suggestive as that of the *Journal*. Gide's originality lies rather in his belief that when everything has been said about a man, very little has been understood, or indeed, everything remains to be understood. This is the premise of his writing. A physical illness, an anomaly, a tendency to schizophrenia—

any such defect or threat may cause serious disquiet, but in time may lead to spiritual growth, to that kind of acuity and perception which characterize a genius. It is a familiar thesis, but one on which Gide insisted: an inferiority in the character or in the physical nature of a man may be the leading factor in his attainment to a marked superiority.

Especially in his critical work on Dostoevski, Gide analyzes the system of compensations which seem to account for genius. At the genesis of a reform there is usually a dissatisfaction or an illness or a discomfort. Gide remembers the mote in the eye to which Saint Luke refers, and the sense of void Pascal knew (*Pascal avait son gouffre*) and the signs of insanity in such writers as Rousseau and Nietzsche. The particularized private problem of one man may help lead him to the creation of a universal thought, of a reform which will be felt by countless others. A work of art may have its beginnings in the illness of an artist, but when it is achieved, it will represent a new kind of health. Such a theory of transcendence, implicit in the creation of a literary work, and the belief that a writer is inevitably depicting his own life and character in his work, would appear to be among the principal tenets of Gide's aesthetics. Gide felt obliged to tell the truth about himself. His Protestant forbears in the north and the south of France had instilled in him the serious demands of rectitude.

In one of the earliest entries in his *Journal*, January 1892, when Gide was twenty-three, he comments on the fact that his life will be spent in giving that kind of self-portrait which is ineffaceable. He was worried, at that early age, about who he was to become, because he did not know who he wanted to be. Countless possibilities solicited him. (*Je sens mille possibles en moi.*) But he was determined to force himself to speak the truth, as he understood it. This trait of honesty is difficult to prove and measure in any man, but it would seem to be applicable to Gide the writer who gave in his first book, *Les Cahiers d'André Walter,* a truthful analysis of an ascetic's fear of life and love, and in one of his last books, *Thésée*, an account of inner spiritual peacefulness reached after a long life of search and self-criticism.

The adolescence and young manhood of Gide coincided with a period of European civilization when the conventions that had protected and reassured men's peace of mind began to collapse. During the last decade of the nineteenth century, and well into the twentieth, individual man found himself much more alone than in earlier periods because moral and social values were being questioned more, and some were found to be lacking in any real significance. In many ways the personal crisis which Gide went through in his twenties, and which, from several angles, is meticulously recorded in his writings, was to be raised to a level of universal meaning during the next twenty years. The dilemma seemed to be insoluble because it was based upon a conflict between an imposed moral order and a personal moral order in opposition to authority. Sincerity of action would mean revolt. Obedience to authority would mean hypocrisy.

The early years of the century were characterized by a fairly widespread lack of faith in rationalism. This was apparent especially in the new writers who tended to express a marked defiance with regard to the dependability of man's intellect. Rather than relying upon the more stable, the more classical rationalistic approach to man's problems, the new writers, among whom André Gide was to figure more and more conspicuously, presented a new philosophy. It was a belief in a more spontaneous, more immediate kind of living, where the value of a single existence was found in the degree to which it differed from every other existence. This is fundamentally the thesis of *L'Immoraliste*, published in 1902. No longer is man defined by the universality of his dreams and accomplishments, but rather by his originality, by those characteristics which make of him a separate personality. Each individual destiny has its own truth, distinguishable and infinitely precious.

After the years of the late nineteenth century, when

among intellectuals the theories of Renan and Taine prevailed, confidence in universal reason diminished and was replaced by an almost prophetic mission among the newer writers. Each individual writer inhabits his own universe and lives by his personal scale of values. The word "adventure," with its implications of risk and unknown lands and exoticism, is one of the key words of the new century. "Adventure" applies not only to an experience of peril and exploration and physical prowess, but to experiences of spirituality and art. The word will be used by travelers to Africa and the Orient, as well as religious writers and surrealists. A life of adventure, whether it be sensuality (*L'Immoraliste*), or war (*La Condition humaine* of Malraux) or religious conversion (*Le Voyage du Centurion* of Psichari), is a way of living by direct experience. It is essentially anti-intellectual. It is opposed to a life of convention, even opposed to conventional morality, as in the case of Gide and D. H. Lawrence. This cult of risk and adventure, of which Gide is one of the earliest exponents, will be brilliantly expounded during the twenties by T. E. Lawrence (*Seven Pillars of Wisdom*) and, during the thirties, by Malraux and Antoine de Saint-Exupéry (*Terre des hommes*). In the forties, with a far deeper philosophical emphasis, the cult of adventure will be rebaptized "commitment" (*engagement*) in the writings of the existentialists.

As the fields of knowledge expanded, especially in the positivistic sciences, the hope to encompass this knowledge and assimilate it faded, and a form of pessimism concerning science became apparent, or at least a lack of confidence in the capacity of scientific knowledge to comfort and direct man. As a reaction to the nineteenth century scientific method and doctrines, a strong wave of intellectualism was expressed in the writings of the younger literary figures at the beginning of the century, in the correspondence, for example, between Jacques Rivière and Alain-Fournier. Gide's *Les Nourritures terrestres* of 1897 is a major text in this regard in its emphasis on irrational values such as desire, fervor, instinct. Just prior to *Les*

Nourritures terrestres, Nietzsche's *Thus Spake Zarathustra*
was an even more convincing text in its dithyrambic utterances. And earlier in the century, such isolated texts as
Rimbaud's "Bateau ivre" (1873) and Walt Whitman's
Leaves of Grass (1855) were forerunners of an attitude
which almost took on the strength of a philosophy of life
around 1900.

More in France perhaps than in other countries, young
intellectuals, at the turn of the century and through the
next two decades, felt resentment against the pure life
of the intellect, and tended to disparage such new sciences
as sociology and psychology. The universe again became
incomprehensible. The unity of thought was broken. The
way was prepared for what contemporary critics will call
the Kafkian world where man appears as a lost, bewildered
child unable to understand the forces that oppose him,
unable to will a revolt against them. Rationalism, as a way
of coping with the problems of man and the universe, lost
out. The major supports of man which had provided him
with a sense of security in the world: religion, science, a
coherent psychological life, nationalism—were all being
questioned and invalidated. At one time, it was hoped that
science, as a substitute for religion, would be able to create
a new set of moral values for the conduct of men. By the
turn of the century, this hope had been abandoned. Gide's
protagonist in *L'Immoraliste,* Michel, is an archeologist, a
man of science, whose revolt is as much against science as
a way of life, as it is the embracing of a life of instinct.

In a personal sense, Gide's revolt was against his puri-
tanical background and the rigors of his religious education. But philosophically, in the sensual quest of *Les
Nourritures* and in the *récit* of *L'Immoraliste,* Gide is
attacking the absolutes of philosophy and religion. In his
search for an absolute, to be found in experience itself, his
thought is related to the Nietzschean interpretation of
Dionysos, to certain aspects of Unamuno's *Tragic Sentiment of Life,* and to such a work as Bergson's *L'Évolution
créatrice* of 1907. The writings of Henri Bergson crystal-
lized most of the revolutionary ideas of this moment in

European history, and raised to a philosophical eminence
the wave of anti-intellectualism. By denying the power
and reliability of reason in man's life, Bergson did not
diminish the position of man in the universe. Even possessed of ideas which are chaotic and contradictory, man
will continue his brilliant center in the world, until the
existentialists define man's existence as "absurd."

Guided by a personal crisis in his own life, in 1893 and
1894, Gide became in his early writings a representative
spokesman for a renewed belief in the mysteriousness of
existence and nature, for the vast unknown regions not
only of the physical world, but of an individual's psychic
life. In speaking of life, Gide will constantly oppose to
the word "intellectual" the new word "spontaneous."
Immediate pleasure of the senses will appear in contradistinction to all forms of dogmatism. The attitude of
earlier generations in Europe seemed to be that of judging
life. Gide's new admonition will be that of living one's
life. This belief in the mystery of life and in the value of
sensory experience will pervade the writings of D. H.
Lawrence. But life looked upon as an adventure, as an
immediate daily adventure, will explain aspects of more
resolutely religious writers: Claudel and Péguy, for example, especially in their works of the early twentieth
century. The joy of an immediate sensing of life can be
mystical in an orthodox sense. Nietzsche's famous advice
"to live dangerously," which was first interpreted as meaning to live beyond conventional morality and even in
opposition to conventional morality, can quite easily be
applied to the life of a Christian as described by such
writers as Georges Bernanos in France and Graham
Greene in England. The new goal of man, in Gide's
thought, is the establishing of a relationship between himself and the deep forces which control the world. Bernanos, writing in the thirties, from a Catholic viewpoint,
would not phrase otherwise his conception of man's goal.

The philosophy of Bergson, more perhaps than any
other single force, represented and confirmed the anti-
intellectual vogue to which the early books of Gide con-

tributed more definitively than was believed at the time
of their publication. Such a work as *L'Evolution créatrice*,
in which the value of intuition is placed far above the
value of the intellect, was more eagerly welcomed in
France by the younger writers than studies of Freudian
psychology. In claiming that the intelligence gives an
arbitrary restricted vision of the world, Bergson helped to
define an attitude toward the powers of man, a semi-
mystical approach toward the adventure of man's existence which was to give to early twentieth century
literature its most vital theme.

First, in *Les Nourritures terrestres*, and then, many
years later, in *Les Nouvelles nourritures*, Gide proclaimed
and developed what may be looked upon as his central
message, an attitude which in some form or other, defines
the epithet "Gidian." It seems always to have something
to do with the experience of the immediate moment that
is being lived. To the "instant," to the fragment of time
that is passing, Gide gives an absolute value. The profundity of this kind of experience dominates and controls
all the subsidiary themes associated with the art of Gide:
the restless spirituality of his nature, the sensuality of his
nature, more rich and more poignantly expressed than in
any other French writer, the spontaneity of his nature: a
characteristic he elevates to the eminence of a virtue. No
one of these terms is adequate in describing Gide's point
of view or philosophy. But spontaneity is at all times
endangered by the forces of arbitrariness and habit and
convention. In the famous debate which Gide carried on
in the early part of his career with Maurice Barrès, he
revindicates the virtue of spontaneity. The thesis of
Barrès in *Les Déracinés* emphasizes the belief that man
reaches his highest degree of power by establishing and
maintaining a close relationship with his race, his native
province, his family, with all the familiar scenes and habits
of his childhood. This would be for Gide an impoverishment of his nature, a limitation imposed upon his powers.

Gide was an ardent botanist, and often pointed out
proofs drawn from the cultivation of flowers concerning

the dangers for the beauty and growth of a flower when it is not transplanted. The natural mobility of Gide's spirit accented the distaste he felt for whatever power attaches a man to his past, to the familiar sites of his childhood, to his family. Every attachment compromises all the unknown experiences ahead, all the future realities for which we should remain available (*disponibles*). He would define an attachment as an unwillingness to accept the risks that life offers. Since, in Gide's hierarchy, the experience of desire has primacy, he returns over and over again to his attempts to define such a term.

Desire is that experience which enriches the soul far more than the possession of the object of desire would enrich it. Gide advocates no possession of beings and no possession of things. A man's spirit must remain free and undetermined. The life of the human spirit is the extraordinary range of drastic changes it can undergo, the deep ways in which it may be altered by illness or spiritual crises. This belief would explain Gide's antipathy for Corneille, or for what he considered the *Cornelian* attitude of those who wall themselves up in a belief in the constancy of their spirit, in their unflinching, inalienable character. In one phrase of *Les Nouvelles nourritures terrestres* Gide calls the most precious part of a man's nature that which remains unformulated. (*Le plus précieux de nous-même est ce qui reste informulé.*) The experience of desire will therefore give to life its deepest meaning and its highest value.

Gide's conception of God seems closely related to this emphasis on the present moment, on the necessary freedom of the human spirit to welcome any experience. To reach this state of being present in the world, of being fully aware of the present moment, would seem to be for Gide synonymous with a perceiving of God. A man can neither realize himself, nor the divine in himself or in the world, unless he is free to live the experience of the instant. This is a way of self-knowledge, the Gidian practice of gradually becoming what one is.

2

CHILDHOOD AND
ADOLESCENCE: 1869–1891

On many occasions, and especially in one of his essays in *Prétextes,* Gide has written of the duality of his background, of the contradictions in his nature which this duality may well explain. He doubtless exaggerated the importance of heredity in his effort to explain conflicts in himself which existed and which are important themes in most of his books. He looked upon himself as the product of two races, two provinces, and two religions. In a literal sense this statement is true, but the importance and the gravity of such a condition were far less than Gide believed.

His mother, Juliette Rondeaux, came from a Norman family that had lived in Rouen for five generations. Originally the family was of peasant stock and Catholic, but Juliette's immediate family and her grandparents had been staunchly Protestant. Juliette's father, Édouard Rondeaux, had been prosperous and had purchased the two Normandy estates where Gide lived at various times in his life: one in La Roque-Baignard, a small town in the department of Calvados, and the other in Cuverville, in a region called Caux. He had married a Huguenot woman, extremely pious and austere, who had given him five children. Juliette was their fifth child. The conversion to Catholicism of one of her brothers, Henri, was a major drama for the Protestant family. When Juliette Rondeaux was fifteen, she was given a companion-tutor, Miss Anna Shackleton, a young Scottish Protestant, only nine years older than her pupil. Miss Shackleton introduced into the Rondeaux family a love of literature and art. In addition to her knowledge of French and English, she read Italian and German. Juliette and Anna became inseparable friends.

Gide's father, Paul Gide, came from a southern family in the province of Languedoc. Uzès and Nîmes were the two centers of the family whose origins are not absolutely known but which may go back to a Guido family in Italy. Gide's grandfather, Tancrède Gide, who died before the birth of his grandson, was a judge, a man of great integrity and scrupulosity, who represented the pure Huguenot tradition in the department of the Gard. Paul Gide was born in Uzès and studied at the Collège d'Uzès. A brilliant law student, he became professor of Roman Law at the Faculté de Droit in Paris.

A Protestant minister was instrumental in bringing about the marriage, in 1863, between Paul Gide and Juliette Rondeaux. They lived first in an apartment at 19, rue de Médicis, quite near the Faculté de Droit. Six years went by before their only child, André, was born on November 22, 1869. Paul Gide had more personal charm than his wife. He was more cultivated in a humanistic sense, more tolerant, and had an amiable sense of humor. Mme. Paul Gide was more solemn, more authoritarian, and emphasized, in her relationship with her son, moral problems and moral scruples. Paul Gide died suddenly when his son André was only eleven years old, in 1880. Gide's memory of his father always remained vivid and grateful. He claimed that he owed his love of literature to his father's cultivated mind and interests. He has written of walks with his father in the Luxembourg Gardens, and of the Easter vacations spent in Uzès where his father relaxed and spent a good deal of time with the boy. The elder Gide's library was a source of mystery and attraction for André. There he came upon The Odyssey (in the translation of Leconte de Lisle) and The Arabian Nights, in the translation of Dr. Mardrus. After his father's death, the library was closed to him. His mother preferred that her son read the Bible and religious writings rather than such profane works as *Mille et une Nuits*.

In Dr. Jean Delay's long analysis of the childhood of
André Gide, he proposes the thesis that the boy's moral
conscience was awakened by his mother, and the world of
art was revealed by his father. The thesis would claim that
art remained associated with something masculine for
Gide, and morality remained associated with the feminine.
The severity of temperament in Gide's mother is probably
overemphasized in his autobiography. She seems to have
been a woman of high moral ideals, guided by her reason
and impeccable sense of order. Under the influence of
Anna Shackleton, who came to live in Paris after 1873, on
the rue de Vaugirard, quite close to the Gides' home,
Mme. Paul Gide developed an appreciation for painting
and music and literature. In keeping with Protestant
morality, she emphasized, in the upbringing of her son,
sexual purity and a general condemnation of all sensual
indulgence.

The Protestant background of Uzès was as rigorous as
that of Normandy, but on the Easter vacations when the
boy André visited Uzès, his attention was fixed on the
landscape, on the valley of the Fontaine d'Eure, a stream
which the Roman aqueduct had brought from Nîmes, on
the barren land called *la garrigue,* on the perfume of the
narcissus flower. New Year's vacations were regularly spent
in Rouen and summer vacations also in Normandy, either
in Cuverville or in La Roque-Baignard. There young
André played with his cousins, the three daughters of
Émile and Mathilde Rondeaux. The oldest daughter,
Madeleine, was André's favorite, and destined to become
Mme. André Gide. The discovery of Mathilde Rondeaux's
conjugal infidelity was the cause of a deep grief in Madeleine, and André learned of this drama, when he was
thirteen, from the visible suffering of his cousin. The opening scenes in *La Porte étroite* recall this episode: *tante*
Lucile in the novel is Mathilde Rondeaux; Alissa is, to
some extent at least, Madeleine; and Fongueusemare is
Cuverville.

The Catholic influence in Gide's background was neg-
ligible. Gide vastly exaggerates the facts when he says

he comes from two religions. The two provinces of Languedoc and Normandy are different, but they are both French, and the two families were not exceptionally different. The differences were doubtless more minor than Gide indicated, but he was anxious to prove an aesthetic principle: a work of art is able to reconcile opposites, to fuse them into a triumphant harmony. As a child he felt primarily the influence of the Protestant mentality: marked devotion to the Bible and daily Bible reading, the constant practice of self-analysis and self-examination without recourse to a clergyman, a strict set of rules for moral behavior, and the sense of belonging, in Catholic France, to a religious minority.

Gide's childhood was in many ways a very troubled period. He suffered from nervous tension, from timidity, from a sense of being unattractive, from unnamed fears and nightmares, from an early habit of masturbation which caused him to be sent away from school for a short time, from loneliness, from a feeling of inferiority with schoolmates who made his life so miserable that he invented or developed symptoms of illness sufficient to keep him away from school. The death of his father brought about many changes. His instability at school increased after this event, as well as his feeling of being different from others. Insomnia began to trouble him in his early teens, and this was to plague him throughout his entire life. In October, 1881, Mme. Paul Gide made an effort to have André continue his studies in the *lycée* of Montpellier, and profit from the proximity to the boy's uncle, Charles Gide, a professor of economics at the University of Montpellier. But André was unhappy at Montpellier and bouts of "nerves" kept him away from school. Back in Paris in 1882, he entered the *cinquième classe* at the École Alsacienne in October, but the nervous tension returned and alternated with periods of indifference and apathy. He was thirteen at this time, and was beginning to realize an experience which was to alter his life and affect him very deeply: his love for his cousin Madeleine.

Despite the many advantages of his social position and

wealth, despite the attentiveness and affection of parents
and relatives, Gide had on the whole an unhappy childhood which was also troubled by bad health. It is difficult
to deduce the degree to which his frequent illnesses, his
fits of depression, his attacks of hysteria and insomnia
were brought on by a sense of anxiety and guilt related
to the sexual problem of the boy's onanism which was in
conflict with the moral code of his family. At one point
he was threatened by physical punishment for this habit,
but this did not seem to upset him as much as the fear
of moral punishment, of having disgraced those who were
dear to him. Obsession with carnality and shame over it
are the leading themes of Gide's first book, and they seem
to have dominated not only his childhood but his adolescence as well. There was nothing Oedipal in the relationship between Gide and his mother. His father had always
been aloof from the boy, but gentle and kind to him whenever they were together. Mme. Gide was close to the
tyrannical type of mother for whom the boy felt ambivalent sentiments of love and hate. The various forms of
anxiety he suffered from were later looked upon by him
as forces that shaped his personality and sensibility.
Throughout his life, in all of his personal writings, Gide
was concerned, not so much with the anxiety, which he
was able to consider as beneficial to his artistic temperament, but rather with the causes for this anxiety.

Between the ages of thirteen and seventeen (1882–
1887), André's affection for his cousin Madeleine grew
steadily. They saw each other most frequently during
vacation periods. He was attracted to her on many counts:
the suffering she felt because of her mother's infidelity,
her precarious health, her passion for serious reading, the
communion of thoughts and ideas which was established
very early between the two young people, the moral perfection that Madeleine represented, and the sentiment she
inspired in him which was decidedly mystical in nature.
The awakening of this love coincided with the awakening
of a literary vocation. At the time of their earliest serious
correspondence, about 1885–1886, childhood was over for

both of them, and they were already facing emotional and religious problems, many of which are related in *La Porte étroite* where one of the characters, Alissa, bears unmistakable traits of Madeleine Rondeaux. This first emotional experience in Gide's life was his greatest. It was a love of such purity and idealism that he was never able to associate it with conjugal love in the physical sense. At this very early age, he separated love from desire. His love for Madeleine, which filled a major portion of his life, was at all times incompatible for him with sexual love. Gide looked upon this dichotomy as an essential part of his psychological nature.

During his adolescent years, André Gide was fervently devoted to his cousin Albert Démarest, twenty-one years his senior. Albert lived with his mother, Claire Démarest, sister of Mme Paul Gide, at 78, boulevard Saint-Germain. The two families, which were fatherless, were closely joined. By profession Albert Démarest had been an architect, but soon after the death of his father, in 1879, he returned to his first love, painting. His companionship with Gide was important. They enjoyed music together, they discussed literature, and Albert painted the first portrait of Gide. Albert served as intermediary between André and his aunt, Mme Paul Gide, when, for example, the boy wanted access to his father's library. From a lad just a bit older, Armand Bavretel, son of a Protestant minister, André learned something of the drama of social inequality. Armand suffered painfully from the poverty of his family. Some of his traits are in Armand Vedel of *Les Faux-Monnayeurs*. The boy called "Lionel" in Gide's autobiography was François de Witt. He was a close friend of Gide for approximately four years (1884–1888). Religious discussions were the basis of their friendship.

Before returning to the École Alsacienne, in October, 1887, for the *année de rhétorique,* which was to lead to the first part of the baccalaureat, Gide had become deeply religious. The death of Anna Shackleton, in 1884, had affected him. Many discoveries came about almost simultaneously: the revelation of poetry, his idealistic love for

Madeleine, a renewed religious vigor, a growing sense of
a literary vocation.

At the École Alsacienne, he found a new friend, the
most brilliant student of his class, Pierre Louis (who was
soon to change the form of his name to Louÿs). Not until
Gide surpassed him in the French class, in the second half
of the year, did the two young men become friends. The
basis of their friendship was love for literature and literary
ambition. During the last year of the *lycée,* the *année de
philosophie,* when Gide studied with a private tutor, and
when he read for the first time Schopenhauer's *The World
as Will and Idea* and Bergson's first book, *Essai sur les
données immédiates de la conscience,* he saw Pierre Louÿs
frequently. Through Louÿs, Gide met Marcel Drouin,
destined to become a close friend and, later, his brother-
in-law, when Drouin married Jeanne Rondeaux, Madeleine's sister.

It was at this time that Albert Démarest painted Gide's
portrait and introduced him to the painter Jean-Paul
Laurens, and the painter's son Paul Laurens. This young
man was a passionate student of all the arts: literature,
music and painting. He befriended Gide and accompanied
him on the first trip to Africa. Very much preoccupied by
his physical appearance, Gide, during his nineteenth and
twentieth years, played quite definitely the role of young
artist and dandy.

In October, 1889, he passed the baccalaureat examina-
tions, after having failed them in July. Freed from the
obligations of study, Gide resolved to write his first book
and complete it before the end of his twentieth year. He
chose the Dauphiné as a suitable site for this work, and
traveled alone, first to Grenoble, and then to Menthon
where he lived in a small chalet near the monastery of
La Grande Chartreuse. The book, which would be called
Les Cahiers d'André Walter, is closely associated with
Gide's love for Madeleine, with the problem of marriage,
with the metaphysical problem of action versus inaction.
He allowed nothing to interfere with the schedule of writing. When he was invited by his uncle Charles Gide to

Montpellier, for the six hundredth anniversary of the university, he sent Pierre Louÿs in his place. It was on that visit to Montpellier that Louÿs met Paul Valéry.

Gide did complete *André Walter* by July, 1890. (He turned twenty-one in November.) He paid for the printing of the book which appeared in early 1891 without an author's name and with the subtitle *œuvre posthume*. The narrative of the book is fairly close to the relationship between André Gide and Madeleine Rondeaux, who is called Emmanuèle. André Walter expresses great scorn for a life of action. Quotations from other books abound (*Werther*, for example, and Amiel's *Journal*) and from the Bible. This first book seems to be a condemnation of conjugal love in the normal sense. Woman is so idealized in it that she ceases to be a physical being. The passion of André Walter is never satisfied, or rather, he possesses Emmanuèle in a spiritual sense only after her death.

At one time Gide spoke to Dr. Delay about his admiration for Denis de Rougemont's *L'Amour et l'Occident* in which the Manichean heresy is analyzed in terms of the Tristan story. Tristan's preference for unsatisfied passion over satisfied love is also in *Les Cahiers d'André Walter*. The cleavage between the soul and the body is clearly indicated (and clearly heretical in terms of Christian theology) when the soul is defined as the principle of the good, and the body as the principle of evil. Woman is identified with purity and virtue, and André Walter succumbs, in the section of the book called *Cahier Noir*, to the fantasies of onanism, and an overpowering sense of guilt associated with onanism. The suffering from this kind of guilt is a theme in *Si le grain ne meurt* and is treated in the character of Boris in *Les Faux-Monnayeurs*.

The idea of Gide's second book, *Traité du Narcisse*, may well have been suggested to him during a visit to Montpellier, in December, 1890, when he met Paul Valéry for the first time. The botanical garden in Montpellier was the setting for many of their conversations which initiated a friendship that lasted until Valéry's death in 1945. An allusion to Narcissus is engraved on a tomb in the garden:

Placandis Narcissae manibus, and Gide's short treatise, which will be written and published in 1891, is dedicated to Paul Valéry. After the timidity and endless introspection of André Walter, Narcissus engages upon a sterile quest because the ego, as reflected in the fountain, is fluid or fleeting. *Traité du Narcisse* marks, however, a very definite advance in Gide's power as a writer. The broken-up style of *André Walter,* with its romantic effusions, becomes in *Narcisse* a style of precision and rhythmic beauty. From the young man infatuated with literature, the writer has emerged.

3

FROM MALLARMÉ TO AFRICA : 1891–1895 *(Paludes)*

With the publication of *Les Cahiers d'André Walter* at the beginning of 1891, André Gide, at the age of twenty-two, formally entered the literary world of Paris. Maurice Barrès, one of the most highly respected writers of the day, showed interest in Gide's first book, and at a banquet in honor of Jean Moréas, on February 2, introduced the author of *André Walter* to Mallarmé. For Gide, as for most of the younger men present at this banquet, Mallarmé was aureoled with greater prestige than any other poet. Two days after the banquet, Gide left a copy of his book at Mallarmé's apartment, 89, rue de Rome. In the letter which accompanied the inscribed copy, he wrote: "You have inspired in me shame over my book because you have written all the verses which I might have dreamed of writing. (*Vous m'avez appris la honte de mon livre, car vous avez chanté tous les vers que j'aurais rêvé d'écrire.*)

A few days later Mallarmé invited Gide to attend one of the Tuesday evening gatherings. At various times throughout his career, Gide recalled the joy he felt on reading this invitation. His admiration for Mallarmé the man never abated, and, although at first he welcomed the influence of the symbolist poet, he later rejected what seemed to him the sterile part of symbolism. Many traits of his André Walter seemed reminiscent of the symbolist heroes: a rich meditative inner life and an incapacity to act. The aesthetics of his *Traité du Narcisse* are in perfect accord with Mallarmé's. In the famous apartment on the rue de Rome, Gide met other French writers, still in their

early twenties, some of whom he had already seen: Pierre
Louÿs, Léon-Paul Fargue, Paul Valéry, Paul Claudel.
There he also met several painters: Odilon Redon, Paul
Gauguin, Édouard Vuillard and the American Whistler.

Gide also attended at this time, but less frequently, and
with less interest, Heredia's gathering on the rue Balzac.
The leader of the Parnassian group held a salon that was
more pompously literary and more given over to literary
gossip and throat-cutting than Mallarmé's salon. These
were the leading examples of literary *cénacles* and salons
of 1891. It was the year when Gide met Proust for the
first time, in May. Later he called on Proust several times,
but there was never any real sympathy between the two
men. He met the painter Jacques-Émile Blanche, son of
the doctor who cared for Nerval, and who was to do a
portrait of Gide. At the end of the year, he met Oscar
Wilde for the first time, and was to see him briefly again
in Biskra in 1894. Gide was fascinated by the elaborate
personality of Wilde, by his conversation, by the witty
attacks on Christianity and the accepted immorality.

The entire year of 1891 was overwhelmingly rich for
Gide, but he grew tired of Paris and the social-literary life
he found himself leading. In early 1892 he visited Uzès
for a month to recuperate, and then went to Munich for
three months where he read Goethe, and attended the
theater and the opera. By June he was back in Paris and
engaged in writing *Le Voyage d'Urien*, a short work subtly
charged with sexual fantasies, and obviously inspired by
Mallarmé and symbolism. Gide had become by this time
a close friend of Paul Laurens, son of the painter, who
was one year younger than Gide. He was as shy as Gide
and equally interested in the arts. Gide adopted the
Laurens family where he saw a greater harmony and happiness in family relationships than he found in his own
home. His friendship with Pierre Louÿs had not lasted in
any intimate cordial sense. When Laurens received a
scholarship in painting which would permit him to leave
France for a year, he invited Gide to accompany him, and

Gide, in his journal, interprets this invitation to travel with Laurens as a turning point in his career.

Some of the entries in Gide's *Journal* of September, 1893, show to what degree the Huguenot is becoming the aesthete, to what degree the almost daily reading of Goethe is replacing the Bible, and to what degree a new conception of joy is turning him away from traditional Christianity. Neither Gide nor Laurens had any sexual experiences before leaving for Africa, and they were both determined to look for sexual experiences. In that summer of 1893, Gide completed his third short book, *Tentative amoureuse,* on the vanity of love, which, with *Le Voyage d'Urien,* on the vanity of existence, and *Le Traité du Narcisse,* on solipsism, forms a trilogy on symbolist themes. After the first trip to Africa, he will write, in 1894, *Paludes,* which is a satire on symbolism.

The detailed plans for the voyage involved much more than boat tickets and accommodations. Gide fully believed that he was returning to life and reality, that he would emerge with a new personality, a reincarnation. He was leaving behind him a regimen of morality, and was facing a natural life in which he would make countless efforts toward a knowledge and an acquisition of joy. His continuing love for Madeleine, despite her refusal to marry him, after the publication of *André Walter,* did not seem to run counter to this new amoralistic disposition. Neither did the new life preclude his taking with him a large supply of books. Paul Laurens and André Gide set sail from Marseille on the 18th of October for Tunis.

After an initial outburst of jubilation in Tunis, Gide fell ill with a serious cold. In Sousse, a physician diagnosed his malady as tuberculosis. There, on the edge of the desert, as he relates in *Si le grain ne meurt,* he had his first sexual adventure, with an Arab boy, Athman. In Biskra, where Gide and Laurens took up lodgings, the new experimentation with Africa continued and deepened. A dancing girl, Meriem, became the mistress of both Paul and André, and she was sent away only on the arrival of

Gide's mother, who, worried about the medical reports of her son, came to see for herself what was transpiring.

Gide's convalescence, a theme which he is to analyze with exceptional brilliance in *L'Immoraliste*, began in Biskra. When, after a month and a half, his mother returned to France, André and Paul Laurens set out for Italy, in April. In Rome, where they settled down for a while, Gide consulted a specialist and agreed with the diagnosis that a nervous disorder existed in addition to his physical malady. There in Rome, where he rented a piano in order to continue his practicing, he took walks, wrote quite assiduously—pages that were doubtless incorporated later into *Les Nourritures terrestres* and parts of *Paludes*. On the whole, Rome wearied and bored him. He kept thinking nostalgically of Africa, and made plans to return to Biskra. The huge size and solidity of St. Peter's represented to Gide much of what he thought of Catholicism: the stability of an inflexible institution he had discovered in the sermons of Bossuet and was to rediscover in the writings and the letters of Paul Claudel. The city of Florence delighted him at the beginning of his visit in May. There he met, for the second time, and very briefly, Oscar Wilde, accompanied by Lord Alfred Douglas. But by June, Florence too was beginning to bore Gide. On leaving Italy, Paul Laurens returned to Paris, and André went on to Geneva to consult another specialist about the state of his health which still seemed precarious. Nine months had elapsed since the beginning of the African adventure.

On the advice of the Genevan doctor, Gide spent some time in June at Champel in Switzerland, where he read with admiration and enthusiasm the works of Rimbaud, and especially *Les Illuminations*. In August, he was back at La Roque in Normandy, where he stayed only a few weeks. During this time he was reminded of Biskra by letters from his friend Pierre Louÿs and the poet Hérold who were living in Biskra—with Meriem. It was there that Louÿs wrote his famous *Chansons de Bilitis*, which he was to dedicate to Gide. Gide, in the same month of August,

returned to Paris and began seeing more frequently the
symbolist poet Henri de Régnier for whom he had more
sympathy and more liking than the others in the immediate circle of Mallarmé's admirers.

In Neuchâtel, in September, he made plans for a long
sojourn in the small Swiss village of La Brévine. It was a
moment of self-examination, especially concerning the
religious problem. His *Journal* entries define God in terms
of immanence and pantheism far more than in terms of
Christian theology. The morality he aspires to is that form
which will aid in the fullest possible development of his
talents. He italicizes, like the formula to follow, the need
to assume into himself as much as he can of humanity.
Assumer le plus possible d'humanité. The month spent in
Neuchâtel was a period of quiet happiness, characteristic
of other brief moments throughout his life when Gide the
self-examiner took stock of his feelings and beliefs and
projects, when he carried on with himself a dialogue on
wisdom, on the meaning of God, on the roles he played
or did not play: Ménalque, Lynceus, the moralist, the
immoralist. Toward the end of 1894, a sense of gratitude
filled his heart for the favors he had inherited, the absence
of any economic pressure, which he owed to the frugal
ways and labor of several generations of Rondeaux.

Two months, from the 18th of October to the 14th of
December, he lived at La Brévine (which would be one
of the principal sites in *La Symphonie pastorale*). The
immediate reason for this isolation was the writing of
Paludes. He had planned to stay longer, but the snows of
La Brévine and the austere Calvinistic atmosphere, the
solitude, the lack of human warmth, the nostalgic memory
of Africa with its sun and freedom and primitive charm,
forced him to leave early. He did, however, complete
Paludes, a short work of artfulness and malice, by early
December.

In a letter to Valéry, on November 11, 1894, written
from La Brévine, Gide refers to *Paludes,* and calls it a
troublesome book which he is on the point of finishing:
un insupportable bouquin . . . mais je suis prêt de l'avoir

achevé . . . il s'appelle "Paludes." Later, he was to claim
that *Paludes* had been a literary project forming in his
mind for some time. In his *Journal* of July 3, 1911, Gide
wrote that while he was living *L'Immoraliste,* in Biskra,
with Paul Laurens, he was writing *Paludes.*

On returning to Paris, after his first two trips to Africa,
Gide felt stifled by the atmosphere of the salons and literary circles in which originally he had established stimulating contacts with writers and artists. The writing of
both *Paludes* and *Les Nourritures terrestres* was a means
of self-purgation, of freeing himself from the oppressive-
ness experienced in Paris.

Before the publication of *Paludes,* it was well known in
the Mallarmé circle that Gide was writing the work. When
questioned by his friends, in letters, about what he was
doing, Gide replied: *j'écris Paludes,* and the phrase became a humorous utterance, used in exactly that way in
Paludes itself. Centrally the situation in the book is that
of the man who is writing *Paludes.* It is a masterpiece of
satire and literary skill, and it was immediately recognized
as such by Gide's literary friends in Paris. Claudel, a few
years after its publication, in a letter to Gide, of May 12,
1900, called *Paludes* the most complete picture of the
atmosphere of stagnation, of stifling literariness in Paris
between 1885–1890.

In a comment on his own book, many years after its
publication, Gide, in his *Journal* of March 28, 1935, in the
perspective of many years, opposes the vain activities of
the protagonist in *Paludes* with the dull acceptance, the
submissiveness of most men who never dream of upsetting
the routine and the misery of their existence. In describing
the origins of his book in *Si le grain ne meurt,* Gide analyzes the feeling of estrangement that preoccupied him
on his return to France, his dissatisfaction with the comedy of man, both moral and literary, he encountered. This
sense of strangeness (*un certain sens du saugrenu*) dic-
tated the first sentences of *Paludes.*

Paludes is a book on the absence of human activity, a
satire on the man incapable of using his freedom. It is a

satire on the type of man who, around 1890, was called a "decadent." The author of *Paludes* writes *Paludes* in which nothing takes place. At the end of the narrative, he announces that he is going to write *Polders*. Tityre, the hero of *Paludes,* is a man living in a swamp who does not know what to do with his life. He is the prototype of those people who turn inwardly upon themselves, who fail to grow by contact with and conquest of the outer world. We read that *Paludes* is "the story of a bachelor in a town surrounded by swamps." Tityre turns his back on the beauty and variety of the world either through laziness or through a lack of philosophical conviction. His favorite position is recumbent. We see him as a man lying down. *Tityre recubans.*

The contrast, felt by Gide, between the literary atmosphere in Paris, the sedentary life of the symbolist esthetes, and the African landscapes of his voyages, is doubtless the genesis of *Paludes*. Tityre is a composite figure, too fixed in his traits and psychological habits to be specifically Valéry or Hérold or Pierre Louÿs or Jacques-Émile Blanche. Moreover, Tityre is, in one sense, Gide's own double, Gide's satiric picture of himself. In the book Tityre is not actually described, but it is not difficult to imagine him the pale refined somewhat mannered, somewhat sickly esthete, a bachelor "for the sake of simplicity." Angèle, the one woman in his life, makes countless efforts to involve him in some activity. She points out to him the usefulness of Hubert's life, the civic roles he plays, the business occupations, his interest in hunting.

Tityre's principal characteristics—his need for self-analysis, his incapacity to act, his velleities, his tendency to introspection, his constant references to the past—explain why Klaus Mann, in his judgment of *Paludes,* called it a "satire on Hamlet's complex." Tityre is writing the book *Paludes,* and one realizes that if he were not doing this, there would literally be nothing left in his existence. This literary activity of the protagonist is also a part of *André Walter* and *Les Faux-Monnayeurs.* But *Paludes* has a far greater concentration on the effort to write, and on the drama of the writer's impotency. This creative impotency would seem to be related to the absence of any sexual drive in Tityre.

Tityre's loneliness and his unwillingness to travel would seem to be an expression of Gide's self-criticism, a rebuke to his social life in Paris and to the restlessness of his spirit which led him to Africa. The marsh or swamp where he lives is an obvious symbol of all that is as yet uncultivated in his being, of what is still unknown to him. The swamp could be the new range of experiences and sensations which represent danger and unpredictability. The word *paludes* designates the unknown, the untested, the strange, *le saugrenu*. Tityre, by his way of life, or rather by his absence of any way of life, is the hero of an unrecognizable land. He has to explore what is uncharted and doubtful and even unsavory. The swamp of *Paludes* is related to the desert of *Les Nourritures terrestres*. The discovery of the self is the greatest experience for Gide. To carry out this discovery, the self has to be free. *L'acte libre,* referred to in *Paludes,* is a synonym for what will become famous in Gide's writing as *l'acte gratuit,* that unmotivated act of man.

As Tityre considers all the endless possibilities of his life, and feels unable to realize any one of them, we follow the action of Gide's restlessness. Du Bos called the subject matter of all of Gide's books his *inquiétude* and the need to communicate this *inquiétude* to his readers and thus force them to participate in the same experience. The activity, or the nonactivity of Tityre as a writer, is in one sense a parody of symbolism, but it is also a more philosophical comment in that it is a refusal to be crushed by a hostile world.

When Gide left La Brévine in December, he went to Paris where he saw his mother and Madeleine. On Christmas night, he left for Montpellier, and stayed for a few weeks with his uncle Charles Gide and his aunt. Those first weeks of 1895 marked the beginning of a serious depression in Gide's temperament and behavior. He suf-

fered from a dryness of the spirit, a lack of energy and
willpower. Before embarking from Marseille for a return
visit to Africa, he wrote frantically to his mother and
Madeleine to accompany him, almost as if he were afraid
of traveling by himself, of being solely responsible for his
actions.

On reaching Algiers alone on January 22, 1895, he was
depressed and disappointed by what he saw. Two days
later he went to Blidah, and there also found nothing that
attracted him. He was about to leave for Biskra when he
saw the name of Oscar Wilde among the new arrivals at
the hotel. He put off his departure in order to dine with
the Irish writer. This was Gide's third encounter with
Wilde, and his second encounter with Lord Alfred Douglas. For Gide, Douglas represented a reincarnation of
Beau Brummel or Lord Byron, and Gide observed closely
both Wilde and his traveling companion, and recorded his
observations in *Si le grain ne meurt* as well as in the small
book he wrote on Wilde.

His return to Biskra, where he lived in February, was
not for the purpose of sensual indulgence, but rather for
serious concentrated work. He was happy to have Athman
close to him again, and even made plans to take the young
Arab back with him to France. The project was vigorously
opposed by Mme Gide and Madeleine. They won the controversy, and when Gide left Biskra he left Athman behind. Briefly in Algiers, where he continued to work on
Les Nourritures terrestres in alternate fits of optimism and
depression, he broke off definitively with Pierre Louÿs
whose friendship had never given him deep satisfaction
save in the early months at the École Alsacienne.

The bitter struggle over Athman, carried on in letters
between Gide and his mother, was only one instance,
albeit very acute, of the fundamental antagonism that had
been slowly developing between them. He realized about
this time, and in her own way the mother must have realized it also, that the strict moral education he had received
as a child had broken down and was no longer being
followed. In his New Testament reading, he had turned

away from the writings of Saint Paul, with their emphasis on moral stricture and doctrine, and had chosen the figure of Christ as presented by Saint John, in whom Gide saw the promise of joy as prevailing over all else.

Mme Paul Gide died quite suddenly from a stroke on the last day of May, 1895, at La Roque. Gide was emotionally upset by this death, by the sudden absence in his life of the strong force his mother represented in terms of religion and morality and the traditions of her class. Her death meant the removal of a significant obstacle in the way of the new life he had instituted for himself. But his reaction was far from unified. He felt both hunger for freedom and despair at being alone. His dependence on his mother was to survive her life in a curious way, when it seemed to fuse with his dependence on Madeleine Rondeaux. Seventeen days after Mme Gide's death, André and Madeleine announced their engagement, which, doubtless because of its coincidence with the period of mourning, was not heralded warmly by either the Gides of Montpellier or the Rondeaux of Normandy.

In the small book of confession, *Et nunc manet in te,* which Gide wrote at the end of his life, and which was published posthumously, he speaks of consulting a doctor about his future marriage. He was worried on many counts, but especially over the strong traits of inversion in his nature, and his tendency to justify to himself his sexual practices. His erotic experiences in Africa had deeply influenced him. During his childhood and youth he had had no such experiences. Autoerotism had been a constant practice, save for brief periods when shame and religious scruples had caused an interruption. He knew that he was strongly attracted to a certain type of youth: the vagabond and the prowler, the boy who was outcast from society. He was attracted, in other words, to exactly the opposite type that he had been as a youth: the sedentary and the introspective.

Gide himself was not unaware of the type of woman his mother represented, the strong-willed and almost virile matriarch who by her temperament may threaten the manliness of her son. But others, and notably Dr. Jean Delay, in his exhaustive analysis of Gide's youth, have blamed, and perhaps somewhat unduly, the mother's role in the development of the writer's personality. The very conception which Gide gave to his form of inversion: brief intermittent physical attachments, allowed him to sustain and justify the more important doctrine of his life: his *disponibilité*, that freedom from choice and devotion, freedom from any one prolonged commitment which is the basic doctrine of his art and of his way of life. His heart and his mind were not involved in the usual type of sexual adventure Gide knew before and after his mother's death. But his heart and mind were very much involved with Madeleine. The doctor whom he consulted advised him to marry Madeleine, and claimed there would be no problem, either physiological or psychological. From the questions Gide asked this physician and from the worries he expressed, everything points to his hope that this would be a normal marriage and that there would be children.

The very simple ceremony was performed on the 7th of October, 1895, four months after the death of Mme Paul Gide. The honeymoon started with a visit to the country home of Charles Gide and his wife outside Nîmes. There was a stop at Neuchâtel where Madeleine's health declined, and another stop at Saint-Moritz where she recovered her strength. Literary activity never ceased during the trip. From Neuchâtel, Gide wrote to Francis Jammes, the poet, at Orthez in the Pyrenees, whom he had not yet met; and in Saint-Moritz he completed the *récit de Ménalque* which he sent to *L'Ermitage* for the first issue in January, 1896. The principle of contradiction in Gide is fully apparent in this simple fact: on his marriage trip he completed the writing of this section of *Les Nourritures terrestres* which praises a morality and voluptuousness far different from what he was trying to experience with his bride. Much later in his life, in writing *Et nunc manet in te*, he confessed the humiliation which his impotency in his marriage caused him.

Gide's unconsummated marriage was doubtless the con-

sequence of many problems and theories and habits in his
life, but it was also, to some extent, the consequence of
Madeleine's temperament and health and life. She had
once written that she was not afraid of death, but was
afraid of marriage. During the wedding trip, particularly in Italy and Africa, Madeleine became aware of her
husband's attraction to boys. And yet Gide's love for her
cannot be doubted. It was the deepest spiritual experience
of his life, and he suffered in being the cause of her suffering. Never did they discuss this problem with each other.
The Platonic pattern of their marriage was established at
the beginning, and never changed.

Even during the wedding trip, Gide's literary preoccupations were important. On meeting D'Annunzio, for example, in Florence, he was inspired to emulate the
rigorous work schedule of the Italian writer. D'Annunzio
worked regularly twelve hours a day and already, at an
early age, had published twenty books. By comparison
Gide's output seemed meager: five very small books in the
wake of his first *André Walter.* He was writing *Les Nourritures terrestres* and planning other books: *Prométhée
mal enchaîné* and *La Porte étroite* (which he called for a
long time *La Mort de Mlle Claire*) and possibly *L'Immoraliste.*

The last passage which Gide wrote in 1895, included
in his *Journal,* under *Feuilles de route,* December 31,
speaks of his leaving Madeleine alone in her room in Florence while he participates in the New Year's Eve celebration, and of his worry over this typical separation: *A quoi
pensait Em, toute seule, pendant ce temps?* The whole
passage is strongly reminiscent of *L'Immoraliste,* and could
be juxtaposed with the even more definitive statement in
Et nunc manet in te, when Gide expresses remorse over
distorting the destiny of his wife: *je garde ce remords
d'avoir faussé sa destinée.* The inhibitions in Gide, which
prevented his consummating his marriage, are too complex for any clear analysis today. Unquestionably in his
mind there was some identification between his mother
and Madeleine, although in terms of culture, intelligence

and temperament, the two women were very different. Neither is Madeleine Gide, in any literal sense, the Alissa of *La Porte étroite*. On countless occasions Gide has spoken of the inspiration Madeleine was to him in his writing. In varying degrees, she is in Emmanuèle of *André Walter*, in Marceline of *L'Immoraliste*, in Alissa of *La Porte étroite*, and even in Angèle of *Paludes*. Such persistence of inspiration enabled Gide to claim that all of his works were ways of speaking to Madeleine. She was far more the inspiration or the muse or the fiancée than the wife. The suffering he caused her during her existence seemed at times to have been imposed willfully, and at other times unconsciously. Her profoundly Christian spirit always accepted this suffering, perhaps because she was aware that she possessed the nobler part of Gide's nature and devotion. Both André and Madeleine were humiliated by their marriage, but each derived strength from the love of the other.

As early as the beginning of 1896, the pattern of Gide's art is established, and the ethical considerations which are to develop during the years following are clear in his mind. He has concluded that art deepens as it submits to constraints, and in the same way the artist grows, thanks to the restrictions and prohibitions placed upon him. His life is to be a consecration to art and to the role of writer. He knows that the books he wants to write can be written only by him, and moreover he knows that the writing of these books will be a kind of salvation, a cure albeit momentary, of the ills from which he suffers, both physical and neurological. A sense of confidence and self-realization comes only when he writes. The mystical tendencies of his nature, which might have turned him into another kind of writer, and which Gide felt strongly between the writing of *André Walter* and *Le Traité du Narcisse*, had been subsumed and fused into tendencies of a more purely aesthetic nature.

The most unifying aesthetic influence on Gide throughout his career was already firmly established by 1896. Goethe, whose name is everywhere in his correspondence, was the master liberator for Gide, the writer who had been successful in uniting his life with his art. Gide was never an imitator in his writing, but he used such figures as Goethe and Nietzsche and Dostoevski as masters in whom he found confirmation for his own theories concerning literature and concerning the kind of life a writer should lead. The example of Goethe had taught him, perhaps more than any other single example, that the artist finds in himself the subject matter of his work. Even the great diversity of Gide's writings will never allow him to doubt that they all emanate from his own personality and from the complex problems of his own life. In every voyage he undertook (and for a Frenchman, Gide was an assiduous traveler), he sought a cultural climate that would be propitious for his thoughts and his projects of that particular moment. He sought always to establish a favorable relationship between the inner experience which his writing was analyzing and the setting, the climate, the *milieu* which he had chosen for the moment.

In accordance with the basic hypothesis of his art and his way of life, Gide, as a writer, never stayed for long with one of his characters, or with one side of his nature. No one experience was ever worthy of engaging his total commitment, and likewise no possible experience was to be avoided. The strong contrasts that existed in his life in 1895 and the antagonism that must have existed between his wedding trip and the writing of the *récit de Ménalque* are evidences of a nature both volatile and serious, both eager for absorption and determined to reject. Already, in his writing, the difference between the character of André Walter and that of Ménalque is indicative of the law by which Gide will allow opposites to grow within himself, not only successively but simultaneously. The existence of opposites is as fervently cultivated in Gide as the very desire and need to write. The creation of a literary work is a catharsis and a liberation for him. It is both a self-revelation, and the preparation for a new project which will be the projection of a new self. Happiness is not the goal for Gide in his life or in his writing.

Rather it would be defined as the cultivation of self, or the cultivation of the many possible selves of a man. And for this cultivation, all will be used: theories and experience of the Huguenot ascetic as well as the indulgent sensuality of the hedonist.

4

THE EARLIEST QUEST:

Les Nourritures terrestres (1897)

The award of the Nobel Prize to André Gide coincided with the fiftieth anniversary of his first important book, *Les Nourritures terrestres,* which was published in 1897, when Gide was twenty-eight years old. It was composed, however, in 1895. This fact is stated in Gide's preface to the German translation. The story of the book's initial lack of success is well known. It took exactly ten years to sell the five hundred copies of the first edition.

It is the kind of book that could hardly be written to-day, and yet it remains curiously unmarked by time. The final page of the *Envoi,* in which Gide tells his imaginary character and reader Nathanaël to throw away his book and free himself from it, is still startling. The phrase: *jette mon livre,* has the opposite effect even on new readers today. "Leave me" (*Quitte-moi*), Gide says to them on this final page, but he himself has been unseizable and unapproachable throughout the entire book. And this for the simple reason that Gide had been undiscoverable to himself. *Les Nourritures terrestres,* like every other work of Gide, represented an effort to know himself. But this self was constantly changing. Each book is a quest, and *Les Nourritures* stands at the beginning of Gide's career as a guidebook to the pattern of self-inquest. From Gide's viewpoint, it was ironical for Claudel to advise his friend to turn to the Catholic confessional, because *Les Nourritures terrestres* is the first version of a *Journal* and a career in letters that are essentially a public confession.

In the preface written for the 1927 edition, Gide calls his book a manual of escape, the book of a sick man or of

34

one who has just recovered from a long illness and who feverishly longs to live again and know all the excesses of living. But Gide reproves those who see in his book only a glorification of desire and instinct. He himself sees it as an apology for asceticism or renunciation, and he describes three stages the reader should pass through. The reading of the book, the first stage, should turn the reader back to himself, to a new interest in himself. After this intermediary stage of self-interest, the reader should reach the third stage of engrossment in everything else in the world, everything that is *not* the book and *not* himself.

There is perhaps no adequate term for the literary genre which *Les Nourritures terrestres* illustrates. It has some affinity with the prose poem, as developed by Aloysius Bertrand in *Gaspard de la Nuit*, by Baudelaire in *Spleen de Paris*, and especially by Rimbaud in *Les Illuminations*. And yet Gide's book has none of the narrative quality of Baudelaire's prose poems, and none of the condensed powerful imagery of *Les Illuminations*.

Neither can it be called a journal in any strict sense, although passages in it are extremely reminiscent of the *feuilles de route* and the *feuillets détachés* which Gide includes in his *Journal*. It appears to be a journal, but it lacks the usual journal notations. It appears also to be a kind of *récit* or tale, annunciatory of the more formal tales such as *L'Immoraliste* and *La Porte étroite*. But it would be a *récit* without the most important element of a *récit*, namely, events and episodes. *Les Nourritures terrestres* has only commentaries on events and episodes. It is a life recalled by commentaries from which the story is deliberately concealed. The commentaries that make up this spiritual autobiography follow no logical plan or coherence.

Maurice Blanchot once likened the form of the work to the *Essays* of Montaigne, but there is no story behind the *Essays*, and there is a story behind *Les Nourritures terrestres*. The book might be defined as the absence of its story, the comments on a story that is willfully effaced or which is never allowed to form. The term "novel" would, of course, be even less appropriate than *récit*, because of the lack of characters engaged in anything that resembles action. In addition to the narrator, the "I" of the book, two characters are named, Nathanaël and Ménalque, but their existence is denied by the author-narrator. The narrator even refuses to define himself in any recognizable way. He is invisible. He refuses to *be*. There is no term for the kind of fiction where the hero is always dissolving. Only the vaguest outline of the narrator is given, because he is continually changing and is very much in love with this mobility, with his multiplying and changing sensations.

If it is true that *Les Nourritures terrestres* is far from being a novel in the usual sense, it is also true that many novels, since 1900, contain passages that resemble it. The formal influence of *Les Nourritures* has been marked in those novels—and they seem to be the prevalent kind during the past half-century—in which the hero engages in long bouts of confiding in the reader, of talking minutely about his sensations and much else that is extraneous to the literal action of the novel.

If in *Le Traité du Narcisse*, the influence of Mallarmé is obvious, in *Les Nourritures terrestres* Gide seems to have been trying to liberate himself from Mallarmé's influence, to write about his direct contact with the real world without recourse to symbol and metaphor. The new style of writing was opposed to the current literature of its day, which was highly artificial and airless. The possible influence of *Le Livre de Monelle* published by Marcel Schwob in 1894, has been denied by Gide, although he states that both books, his own and Schwob's, testify to a similar need for freshness and spontaneity. But another more important influence has been acknowledged, that of Rimbaud, whose *Illuminations* Gide had begun to read about 1891. In letters to Valéry and Paterne Berrichon, he has described the intoxication it induced. Other possible influences would be *Un Homme libre* of Barrès, Oscar Wilde's *The Picture of Dorian Gray* which Gide read in 1895, and, possibly, Rousseau. The essential problem of influence remains that of Nietzsche.

What the book expresses is a personal experience, or a

series of personal experiences, that have no logical or se-
quential relationship with one another. It is the account
of a soul in the presence of many things—landscapes, gardens, deserts. The soul is one, unified and continuous, but
it absorbs, in its peregrinations, a profound lesson on the
instability of things and states of feeling. The ideas and
emotions of the book are always expressed in the present.
We never see their genesis nor their ending. It is a book
of travel, but no progress is described because there is no
goal to be reached. The various scenes are unrelated. They
serve to generate and exalt different emotions, but they
do not advance toward any point. With each scene, the
book begins all over again. The soul of the narrator is
always impatient to have new scenes presented to it, and
eager to obey new impulses. The unity of the work is
almost indefinable. It is the soul of Gide, multiple and
exacting, welling up in constantly new thoughts. The soul
is also the stage of a drama where sensations are minutely
described, provoked and liberated. In this one soul, the
entire universe, inexhaustible and multifaceted, has to be
reflected and apprehended. Ideas and emotions are equally
gratuitous, all spontaneously generated. Whenever an
event is about to come into focus, it is quickly abandoned
so that the author can concentrate on the hundreds of
movements and impulses which an event would create.

In the midst of such wealth of sensory indulgence, Gide
is unable to choose. His book is about his incapacity to
choose. His passion is impartiality. The words which recur
the most frequently in his text seem to be *fervor, waiting,
moments (ferveur, attentes, instants)*, and especially *disponibilité* or the freedom to welcome every new sensa-
tion, every new experience. This central attitude of *Les
Nourritures terrestres* is not unrelated to the Gide of the
earliest book, *André Walter*, who feared any contact with
the world and who believed that life was most deeply felt
in the waiting for life. Precociously Gide was the ascetic,
the chaste adolescent who deliberately avoided adventure
and experience. There are passages in *Paludes* which
parody any realized life. As soon as life makes a choice

and takes on a form, it dies. To make a choice by performing any act, the very ambiguity of our most intimate nature is destroyed. Much of *Les Nourritures* explores a doctrine whereby all action and all attachment is considered evil and debilitating because it will turn us away from ourselves. All that is necessary is the knowledge that we are. At the beginning of the third section, Gide speaks tenderly of the word *volupté,* and describes it as synonymous with *being.* Fervor can survive only if it remains constant in an inconstant world or in a perpetual flux. Such themes as these continue throughout the work of Gide. Even Alissa, of *La Porte étroite,* in her act of total renunciation, bears a relationship to Ménalque, whose fasting produces a delirious intoxication. What is dangerous is a bookish culture which will alienate man from direct contact with the real elements of nature. The song of desire in *Les Nourritures terrestres* is not so much the celebration of what is desired as the proclamation of the need for a constantly renewed state of desire.

An overfacile definition of *Les Nourritures terrestres* has tried to pass it off as poetry. But Gide is not a poet, not even in this, his most poetically written book, of which the beauty is essentially a beauty of syntax. The text, when examined closely, proves to be without metaphor. What counts most is the literal transcription of the sentiment aroused in the presence of the object. Gide is not a poet in *Les Nourritures;* he is infinitely closer to being what he is in his other books, part-novelist, part-moralist.

Yet he disguises to some degree his real literary function by his poetic style, in which adjectives often precede their nouns, pronouns are widely separated from their antecedents and their verb, and sentences tend to be unusually long and undulating. The words seem to obey the length and the rhythm of the sentence. And the sentences unfold slowly and uncertainly as if the gestures and the desires they describe are only tentative. This is because the story of *Les Nourritures terrestres* is not one of action, in the usual sense, but one of a soul which is unknowing of its movement until it has created it. The book narrates a personal experience, which turns out to be less a personal experience than a means for metamorphosis. The soul remains one, but it is constantly undergoing changes of form and desire. It is a soul of velleities, and the kind of sentence that Gide has elaborated in the book is that best suited to the expression of spiritual metamorphosis.

Notwithstanding this unusual verbal form of expression, *Les Nourritures terrestres* inaugurated Gide's principal vocation of moralist. The book is a combined essay on things and an essay on the author. It completed the first period of his career. The second period begins with *L'Immoraliste,* and the main difference between them is one of style. In the style of *Les Nourritures* the reader becomes aware of a sensual delight in the flow and articulation of the sentences. Their form, a voluptuary form, holds the attention of the reader. The style of the *récits,* beginning with *L'Immoraliste,* and continuing with the one novel, *Les Faux-Monnayeurs,* is more bare and severe, more devoid of ornamentation. The actual subject matter of *Les Nourritures* and *L'Immoraliste* is much the same, but Gide's style of writing has so changed that the two books appear very different from each other. The final sentence of *Les Nourritures* is a good example of the troubled searching rhythms of the book; it also contains the subject matter of *L'Immoraliste,* the principal preoccupation of its protagonist Michel. This is nothing less than a proposal for the quest of total individuality, for the development of that part of us that is different from every other man. *Ne t'attache en toi qu'à ce que tu sens qui n'est nulle part ailleurs qu'en toi-même, et crée de toi, impatiemment ou patiemment, ah! le plus irremplaçable des êtres.*

What might·be called the stylistic composition of *Les Nourritures* is carried over in the subsequent books in the spiritual makeup of their heroes. It is expressed not stylistically but psychologically in the awakening and the resurrection of Michel in *L'Immoraliste,* and in the self-effacement and renunciation of Alissa in *La Porte étroite*. Before analyzing the souls of Michel and Alissa, Gide had analyzed his own soul in *Les Nourritures* by means of half-moralistic, half-lyric meditations and imagined adventures.

A study of *Les Nourritures terrestres* in relation to the work of Arthur Rimbaud would demonstrate the formal similarity and at the same time the fundamental difference between Rimbaud the poet and Gide the nonpoet.

Literature may well be the art which transforms its creator the most profoundly. Each book that Gide published transformed him. The poetry of Rimbaud, following the original function of primitive poetry, tried to modify the universe in a magical way as well as transform the poet. It shows no interest in any possible reader. The poet is less directly concerned with communication than he is with an exploration of his own inner chaos. He pays little heed to his reader in the absolute compactness and detachment of his poems. But Gide's work is in prose, and does not neglect the reader. It takes the reader into its confidence, and explains to him the landscapes of the book and the effect of the landscapes. Rimbaud as a poet is a reciter of spectacles, but he makes no effort to attune the spectacles to the sensibility of the reader. Gide, on the contrary, is eager to train the sensibility of his reader, to indoctrinate him, even if it is for an ultimate liberation from all doctrine.

Despite this fundamental difference of approach, which indicates the difference between a poet's use of language and that of a prose writer, *Les Illuminations* and *Les Nourritures terrestres* are both the notebooks of travelers in the *terra incognita* of psychic phenomena. There is a relationship between the *Je* of *Mauvais Sang* and Ménalque. Combined they foreshadow the portraits of the later heroes of Gide, Michel, especially, defying convention with an excessive sensuality. They are prototypes of the modern hero who is the most opposed to the mythical hero, the antithesis of Odysseus who returns home, who reaches an end in his quest. They are the ancestors of the homeless heroes, found in such different novelists, for example, as Alain-Fournier, Graham Greene and Samuel Beckett.

The language of both *Les Illuminations* and *Les Nourritures terrestres* appears to unfold according to some magical accident. It never betrays any premeditated intention. The author knows that he is speaking, but he does not always know what he is saying; or rather, he is lost in some kind of ignorance concerning the matter of which he is speaking. If he learns anything about his subject matter, he learns it at the moment he is uttering it. Rimbaud especially noted this presence at the creation of his own thought. He provoked it and watched it grow. He remains therefore at its center. The traveler's notebook, in the cases both of Rimbaud and Gide, is composed of unpredictable and spontaneous revelations. They are writers who question their subject matter. They do not possess it.

This definition of *Les Nourritures* as a work of dictation rather than of deliberate creation may explain the effect it has had on its readers of a liberating force. This effect has often been acknowledged, especially by younger readers. Both the experience and the form have an absoluteness which liberated the author and which liberates the reader. The very unpossessiveness of the narrator, his *disponibilité* and freedom to welcome all experience and states of feeling, promotes in the reader a habit of suppleness identical with the experiences described in the book itself. Gide tested himself on those experiences, and the reader tests himself on the exercises of the book. What is constant is the doctrine of inconstancy, which means sincerity or the hatreds of lying, vitality or the love of life in all its manifestations, liberty or freedom from dogmas and influences. The composition of the book is so delicate and pliable precisely because it has espoused its subject matter. The form has so become the experience, that the reader is led to a self-liberation. Of all Gide's books, *Les*

Nourritures terrestres would seem best to exemplify the
power of literature to create of itself an absolute existence,
which in turn is able to liberate the reader from himself.

The book is the first record of Gide's lifelong fight
against falsehood. The superficial reader has often accused
him of inconstancy and even betrayal, because he has
seemed to flirt with Nietzscheism, with Christianity, with
Communism, and then repudiate them. In *Les Nourritures*
he sings of immediate pleasures and sensations, and of
the necessary freedom he must possess in order to welcome
them. And yet at the same time one senses a fear of the
very freedom he is seeking. The dithyramb on freedom
was necessary for Gide to be able to limit it, to compromise and reduce it. The exercise on individualism
taught him the limitations of individualism, the need of
being oneself by others and for others. One of Gide's
leading traits is sympathy, a great sensibility to injustice
and an aptitude for admiration. These are all stages of
self-purgation initiated by *Les Nourritures terrestres.* In it
he learned how repulsive happiness was to him because
of its static quality. In his resolution to speak the truth
about his feelings at any given moment, a spiritual exercise which *Les Nourritures* illustrates, he prepared himself
for the writing of his *Journal,* a work, as far as one can
tell, exempt from all studied preparation and artifice. It
was a preparation, too, for the particular kind of literary
criticism that Gide has written, second, it might be
claimed, in its penetration and honesty only to that of
Baudelaire. At the head of his works, *Les Nourritures
terrestres* stands as the record of a wanderer, a vigilant
self-tester, a kind of literature therefore which is the opposite of Claudel's, Gide's friend and foe, who found the
Absolute at the beginning of his career and never left it.

The most exalted of Gide's books in its style and its
individualism, *Les Nourritures* marks the point from which
the subsequent books descend in a progressive simplification of style and personal exaltation. Education is freedom
for Gide. He wrote this in his *Journal* of 1917. (*Éducation,
c'est délivrance,* 1ᵉʳ novembre.) But he had already writ-

ten it in other words in *Les Nourritures terrestres* of 1897, when he said that he has esteem for himself only in what he may be able to do. *Je ne m'estime jamais que dans ce que je pourrais faire.*

If the narrator denies himself the conventional kind of happiness, his state of *disponibilité* maintains him in a perpetual state of "joy." As soon as a state of exaltation threatens to disintegrate, he moves to another. The formal composition of the book follows this high pitch of joy. The utterances are essentially dithyrambic. Even when the form is reduced to bare simple words which are unrelated to what precedes and follows them, it testifies to a perpetually sustained inner rhapsody. A double refusal pervades the work: the narrator refuses to be a person in any recognizable way, and the form of the writing refuses to be a "genre" according to any recognizable definition. *Les Nourritures terrestres* is both a form by itself, and an exercise or essay out of which *L'Immoraliste* and *La Porte étroite* will be created.

It continues to be for the new readers of each generation one of the most upsetting of books. It is of such subtle ambiguity that it answers two needs, one for those readers who have a sense of order and will profit from a salutary upsetting of order, and another for those readers lost in a sense of disorder who can find in it a new order. It has the quality that prophetic books possess, of supplying whatever remedy is sought. On the one hand, it sings of energy and plenitude of character, of self-realization and self-fulfilment; and on the other hand, it sings of a submission to the inevitable in life. The two themes of fervor and poverty are somehow reconciled. Gide makes both words, *ferveur* and *dénuement*, equally luminous and seductive.

Of all the concepts in *Les Nourritures,* that of *dénuement* seems to have been the most precious to Gide and the one he always referred to in speaking of his work. It was his word for asceticism and renunciation, the willful giving up of all things that hold man, so that he may move on to the unknown, to the desert and the next oasis in the desert. The fourth book of *Les Nourritures terrestres*

contains the story of Ménalque. It represents the one
defect in the otherwise unified tone of the work. Gide
himself acknowledged this, and stated that he did not like
the *récit de Ménalque*, because it clashed with the more
dominant apology for asceticism or *dénuement*. And yet
he always included it in the various editions of the work
as if he were thereby obeying a secret need to add further
mystery to this mysterious and profound autobiography.

The opening sentence of the book is addressed to
Nathanaël, a word of counsel claiming that God is to be
found everywhere. *Ne souhaite pas, Nathanaël, trouver
Dieu ailleurs que partout.* Instinctively one thinks of the
guileless young man of the New Testament: "Jesus saw
Nathanael coming to him, and saith of him, Behold an
Israelite indeed, in whom there is no guile!" (John 1: 47).
Nathanaël is the young man, the reader possibly, who is
to be indoctrinated. A few pages after the opening, the
name of Ménalque appears for the first time, as the character who teaches not wisdom but love. *Tu ne m'as pas
enseigné la sagesse, Ménalque. Pas la sagesse, mais l'amour.*
The resonance of this name, more Greek than Christian,
will pervade the work. Ménalque is dangerous because his
role is that of indoctrination. And yet, Gide tells us in the
foreword that neither Nathanaël nor Ménalque ever
existed.

Ménalque, who is to reappear in *L'Immoraliste*, is the
most mythic figure in Gide, a kind of prodigal son who
returns home, as in the parable, but who leaves again. He
represents the myth of the road, the nomad, the sensualist
and adventurer, whom André Gide never became as literally as he sets forth in Book IV of *Les Nourritures terrestres*. He is the forerunner of the existentialist hero, who
lives in the present and who projects himself into the
future.

The availability (*disponibilité*) which Ménalque revindicates, is a freedom of inspiration, a revolt against
both an intellectual approach to life and traditional morality. To a certain degree, it is Dionysian, but the Dionysian
element is far more flagrant, far more decisive in *Les*

Illuminations of Rimbaud and in *Thus Spake Zarathustra* of Nietzsche. Gide's Ménalque is somewhat closer to what the twentieth century will look upon as the artist, who by temperament expresses his individualism by living outside the law and duties of convention. There is basically a difference between the character Ménalque and the personality of André Gide, even the personality of Gide at the age of twenty-five (1894) when momentous events occurred in his life: his first sexual experiences, his mother's death, his marriage with Madeleïne Rondeaux. In his career of a writer, the creation of Ménalque, with episodes in Book IV of *Les Nourritures,* somewhat reminiscent of Lautréamont's Maldoror, is equally momentous. Ménalque is one extreme of Gide's character, the Dionysian, as opposed to the Christian part of his nature. Such an antagonism, such a sheltering of contradictions, will have to be resolved. Gide's work is the experiencing of contradictions. Perplexity, and not torment, however, is the result of this cohabitation of extremes.

5

L'IMMORALISTE (1902)
AND THE PROBLEM
OF FREEDOM

It has been pointed out many times that *L'Immoraliste* is a story version of *Les Nourritures terrestres*. Taken together, these two books seem to be the most pagan of all of Gide's writings. And taken separately, they are different in tone and style, and in the effect on the reader. *Les Nourritures* is a dithyramb. *L'Immoraliste* has the coolness of an exercise, an astringent exercise, but one that has also considerable delicacy.

The general lines of this carefully constructed story are easy to describe. Michel, a young, wealthy archeologist is nursed back to health from a serious illness, by his young wife Marceline. During his convalescence in Biskra, Michel becomes aware of a part of his nature which is urgent in its demands and which, by comparison with his character as he has known it heretofore, is disreputable. Wherever he goes, from this time on, in search of health, and in family life and professional activity, in Italy, Normandy and Paris, he will feel a growing insistence from this new self, an insistence so acute that he acknowledges it to be the sincere part of himself. On his estate in Normandy, in order to steal from his own steward, he conspires with a young poacher. Even to himself he confesses that he is drawn to some dark power he only half comprehends. Marceline falls ill with what had been her husband's malady, and before she dies, she comments on the new doctrine that has taken hold of Michel. The doctrine cannot take into consideration the weak of the earth.

The entire narrative of *L'Immoraliste* is told by Michel

to a group of friends, and at the end he acknowledges that no happiness has come to him from this experimentation with freedom. Something of the paganism of Nietzsche is in Michel's doctrine, although it is cast in a more aesthetic form. The goal of Michel's experimentation is freedom. He feels that if this freedom is reached, an energy which he has never known will be released in him. But first, he will have to cut himself off from those bonds which have blinded him to the existence of such an energy in him. The bonds are, quite simply, his possessions and inheritances, the usual prejudices of his class, and all personal ties of devotion and loyalty. In keeping with the Manichean heresy, this energy, which is an exaltation of the self, is looked upon as divine. Courage is needed, a godlike courage, to know this energy and to expend it.

At the head of the book, as an epigraph, Gide placed a verse from the Psalms: "I will praise thee; for I am fearfully and wonderfully made." The full irony of this passage is felt at the end of the narrative when Michel pauses for a moment, before giving the final sentences, and the three friends who are listening find it difficult to distinguish, or separate one from the other, the traits of his character which seem to manifest themselves at that moment: pride in the experimentation which has just been narrated, the forcefulness of will which has made the experiment possible, the dryness of spirit which now depresses him, and finally the modesty of his natural instincts which has possibly been violated. These four words in the French text: *orgueil, force, sécheresse, pudeur,* designate the rich complexity of Michel's nature. This is the man who is still young (Michel himself deliberately makes this point at the end), who has made a great effort to understand his humanity by creating for himself an existence beyond the bounds of his normal existence.

In his life story, which runs parallel to the narrative of *L'Immoraliste,* André Gide had felt very deeply the problem involved in the experiment. It was the problem of reconciling what he believed to be true freedom with the

suffering he caused in the heart of the woman he loved.
Gide knew, and his protagonist Michel knew, that man
is not alone in the world. If a man takes it upon himself
to devote all his energy to the full realization of himself
and to his own pleasure, he will inevitably destroy someone else. As Michel struggles to free himself from the
chains of his past and from the social nature which he
feels to be false, as he learns to accept the ethics of the
present moment, and to worship the fullness of the passing
moment, he slowly brings about Marceline's death. Gide
compared the writing of *L'Immoraliste* to a recovery from
an illness. (*J'ai fait ce livre comme on fait une maladie.*)

Somewhat past the midway point of the narrative, when
Marceline and Michel are in Switzerland, and Marceline's
health seems to be improving under the attentions of her
husband, Michel, who has been enjoying sled rides in the
snow and has given up all thoughts of resuming his
archeological studies, asks the important question: "What
is man still able to do?" (*Qu'est-ce que l'homme peut
encore?*) The answer to this question is what Michel felt
he had to learn. The search is always described as being
something underneath, something hidden and dark (*ma
fortune ténébreuse*). Each day he felt closer to a great
fortune, to a treasure that had never been tapped by him
and which was still hidden under layers of civilization and
conventional living and morality.

L'Immoraliste is one (one of the earliest) of many
modern books on the theme of man's revolt against his
world. In Gide, the revolt is quite specifically against the
sources of the morality that controls today's world. The
criticism of this morality will be carried out by many
writers of differing persuasions and philosophies: by Huxley, D. H. Lawrence and Graham Greene in England, by
Pirandello and Moravia in Italy, by Henry Miller in
America, by Bernanos, Julien Green, Camus and Sartre
in France. The criticism is leveled not so much against
Christian morality as the form which bourgeois society has
given to Christian morality.

The tone of *L'Immoraliste* is completely modern. The

situation, the language, the ruminations of Michel belong to this age. And yet, the revolt itself is ancient. The theme of the rebellious hero and the explorer (even if it is an exploration of the self) go far back in history to mythology. There is something of Daedalus in the mathematical devices of Michel, and there is something of Lucifer in the plunge he makes into dark recesses of his own nature and of the world. At times he takes on the traits of the one sacrificed for others, of the scapegoat, of the man punished for his courage because he is the visionary, the unaccepted, the misunderstood leader. Michel's wedding trip is indeed the voyage of a grave apostasy. It set out to be a voyage to the sun, to Africa, as bold as the scheme of Daedalus. It ended by a fall from great heights, a Luciferian fall into the blackness of a prosaic familiar world in a French province. In the immediate narrative of the story, Michel learns that nothing discourages his power to think as much as the persistent blue of the sky and the ever-present sun. And yet Africa was necessary for the awakening of his senses.

In Michel, as well as in the reader who tries to follow his revolt, there is a series of vacillations concerning the meaning of the revolt, or as to the basic impulse guiding the revolt. Does it come from some diabolic source, or is it a courageous quest for one man's personal value? Is the hero amoral or immoral? Is he guided by an ideal of purity or by a diabolic possession? Gide never clarifies the tone of equivocation. Ambiguity is the atmosphere in which he is most at ease. Michel fails in his quest if we accept as definitive the discouragement narrated on the last few pages. His self-styled liberation ended in tragedy, or, at least, defeat, because he was unable to rid himself completely of his love for Marceline. By his turning away from her, by renouncing any active sense of responsibility for her, Michel causes her suffering, and, ultimately, her death. And yet, it is because of Marceline, because of his attachment to her, which is never completely eradicated, that the immoralist fails in his experiment in human conduct.

Manicheism is the major heresy of Christianity, and its
role in literature at times seems to be more widespread
than manifestations of orthodox theology. In the sense that
L'Immoraliste accentuates the reality of evil, its positive
value in the moral life of an individual, one may claim that
the leading philosophical idea of the work is Manichean.
Michel is convinced that if he is able to join the dark
forces of his own nature with those of the world, he will
succeed in reversing the values of good and evil, and discover the real destiny of his being. When he realizes that
the conventional morality of his world no longer seems
reasonable or viable for him, he seeks another source for
his personal morality, and finds it in his subconscious, in
the innermost forgotten part of his being. But the rules
of this personal morality are not stable and enduring and
codified. They change with the change of days and seasons, and with the fluctuations of desire. In Michel's new
life, each day demands a renewal, a complete renovation
of belief and moral behavior. For the man who cannot
accept passively the moral code, each day will lead him
to a problem of human conduct which he himself will
have to solve alone.

Prior to his marriage, Michel believed himself a man
completely absorbed in the serious problems of his profession, in his archeological research and his teaching. Moreover he felt himself adjusted or subjugated to the way
of life of his class. During his wedding trip, as he recovers
from his illness, he discovers another self, or rather a
multiplicity of possible selves. This discovery is an intoxication, a delirious sense of freedom. He believes himself
able to become a nonconformist. The social-Christian
morality in accordance with which he had heretofore lived,
must have obscured the sense of freedom which now fills
his being. His wife Marceline is of course associated with
his former life, and he will tend to abandon her or turn
aside from her, whenever he is tempted to experiment with
his newly acquired sense of release. Their marriage was
not a marriage of love, but a feeling of love grows in
Michel, and quite soon after the wedding. He will feel it

intermittently, and, when it diminishes, he replaces the attentiveness of love by gallantry, by the cliché expressions and sentiments of gallantry.

The illness of Michel, diagnosed as tuberculosis, may well have been subconsciously induced as the means of separating himself from Marceline, of relinquishing his responsibility of husband, of preparing the way to a more egotistical life. Whatever the obscure reason for this illness may have been, with his convalescence and recovery, he emerges as a new man eager to experience life and nature that he would never have dreamed of formerly. Michel leaves his past as a man leaves his prison. In Italy, he discovers, for example, the very simple sensual pleasure of sunbathing. As he takes off his clothes, he seems to be performing a rite, and offers his body (which he is surprised to find is almost beautiful) to the fire of the sun.

The sun, first in Italy, and then in Africa, is both the reality and the symbol of Michel's resurrection. Gide's close friend, the Catholic critic Charles Du Bos, has called L'Immoraliste "the masterpiece of high noon." Michel is going to assimilate not only the sensuous warmth of the sun, but its cruelty as well. As he grows in self-knowledge, he grows also in his ability to inflict pain. As he opens himself to all the forces of nature, it is impossible for him to distinguish between the good and the evil forces.

There is so little precise moral preoccupation as such in Michel that his drama would seem to be less one of moral disapproval than one of a more positive nature, of a duty to be performed for himself, of a program of sincerity which will enable him to direct his inner life in accord with its outer manifestations. He is the spirit of unrest and search, whereas Marceline, whose actual words in the novel are very few, and whose participation in actual scenes is very slight, is the opposite spirit of waiting and endurance and immobility. If Michel portrays the classical male principle of change and quest, Marceline reenacts the female principle of duration and conservatism. Every element of change brings with it some degree of destruction, and Michel's drama may in one way be looked upon as heroic, as the heroic sacrifice of what is secure and established in his life. Like Heathcliff in *Wuthering Heights,* he does not fully realize to what degree his involvement with nature has made him into an earth spirit.

With the example of Michel, Gide is emphasizing the theory that each day a man has to invent a new moral system that will be true for that day and then must be discarded for the next day. Forty years later, in the history of French thought, Jean-Paul Sartre in his system of existentialist philosophy, will express a similar conviction. Throughout most of French literature, but especially since Rousseau, the major writer has tended to denounce the corrupting forces of society as they reveal themselves in an individual man. Christian morality, based upon a series of sins which, if they are perpetrated, will offend God, gradually, in Europe, turned into a middle-class morality, where interdictions exist, not in terms of a divine order, but in terms of society itself, in terms of punishment for offending our neighbors. Such philosophers as Rousseau and Nietzsche, and such artists as Stendhal and André Gide, see man caught between these two systems, one divine and one strongly adulterated, and, rather than accepting the adulteration, finding in himself his own divinity, his own divinely inherited status, and setting himself up as the one not to be offended by his own deeds and his own thoughts. In this sense, Gide is the immediate forerunner of Sartrian existentialism.

In all the books which preceded *L'Immoraliste,* Gide the writer, under the various pseudonyms of André Walter, Narcisse and Ménalque, had appeared as a solitary figure. The introversion of the symbolist hero characterizes the earliest contrafactions of Gide, and Ménalque and the "I" of *Les Nourritures terrestres* are alone in their experimentations with the natural fruits of the earth. A momentous change occurs in *L'Immoraliste* where, for the first time, there is a second character, who is decidedly not Gide, an antagonist, the young wife Marceline. The ardent conscience of Michel is enriched by the existence beside him of a second conscience, which appears more reserved and more silent, but which in reality is equally ardent. One of the initial themes of the story is Michel's discovery of his wife's totally separate and real existence. It is almost a surprise because he had married Marceline without having fallen in love with her. When, during his convalescence, Michel turns his full attention to himself and his physical needs, he at first instinctively turns away from Marceline, and then, as the new life of the senses begins for him, he conceals from her the various stages of his development. But this act of concealment indicates how fully conscious he is of her presence. She is never absent from the story, although she rarely counts as a character in the full sense. Marceline is more a warning than a woman, more an effulgence than a personage.

At that point in the narrative, when Michel, in love, possesses his wife physically, he has a distinct premonition of what is going to happen. Happiness, like success, is difficult to repeat, because of the memory of happiness. Michel feels that this memory will always hinder a repetition of happiness. *Rien n'empêche le bonheur comme le souvenir du bonheur*. It is one of Gide's most despairing statements about human love, but it is coherent in terms of his basic assumption and central theory of *disponibilité*. Before trying to love again, Michel announces his future impotency. Marceline is at his side, and the action of the book becomes Michel's effort to thwart this presence, to rid himself of Marceline's lucidity which, although rarely expressed, is fully felt by the reader, and devastatingly felt by Michel. Unlike the protagonist in Benjamin Constant's *Adolphe,* Michel is never able to cease caring for Marceline. And intermittently he feels a sentiment for her which can only be called love. His initiation to the new life is so overwhelming that he is incapable of thinking for any length of time of anyone else's existence. Marceline is therefore silent throughout most of the narrative, and yet the reader has no difficulty in imagining her thoughts. The spotlight is fully focused on Michel, but his drama would not be the same if Marceline were not near him in the shadows. Her almost invisible tragedy is more and more deeply felt by the reader, as Michel's more and more histrionic exaltation is watched in the full African sunlight. Michel's triumphant movement of ascent is in direct contrast with Marceline's slow descent into anonymity and death.

This study in contrast, which represents one of the principal qualities of the book, is admirably balanced in the deft, clear precision of Michel's character as it develops swiftly like some biological phenomenon which has been accelerated, and in the subtle restrained effulgence of Marceline whom we do not see in the same way, but who bears the terrifying weight of Michel's rise and is finally crushed by it and sacrificed to it. The autobiographical elements are altered and surpassed in *L'Immoraliste* which Gide first called a *roman* and then a *récit*. He moves far beyond factual evidence in his impulse of a novelist to deepen and understand for himself the moral significance of situations and problems which a man only partially understands as he lives through them. The geographical distinction, for example, between the north and the south, which Gide has often referred to in his autobiographical writing, takes on a fuller, more objective meaning in *L'Immoraliste*. The serenity of the *Midi,* its denser sensuality, the classical traits of its landscape, revealed in the sunlight, form an integral part of Michel's drama, where the province of Languedoc leads to Italy and to North Africa, where a geographical climate is raised to the intensity of a dramatic force. The southern latitude is a pagan philosophical reality in *L'Immoraliste*. And likewise, the scenes in Normandy where Michel plays the perverse role of poacher on his own estate, are related to the Christian background of Gide, to the northern climate propitious for religious meditation and austerity. Normandy, which has almost no importance in *Les Nourritures terrestres,* plays in *L'Immoraliste* a more significant role, although far less dominant than the sun lands of the south, and plays the leading role in *La Porte étroite*.

Gide completed *L'Immoraliste* in October, 1901. In his journal entry of July 12, 1914, he states that the idea of the book had been on his mind for a little less than fifteen years before he wrote it, and that he had carried concurrently in his thoughts the ideas for three books that were to be written at different times and that were to seem, at least on casual reading, very different one from the other: *L'Immoraliste, La Porte étroite* and *Les Caves du Vatican*. Gide had been· disturbed by the almost total lack of commercial success of *Les Nourritures terrestres* and *Paludes*. He hoped that a more fervent reception would be given to his *L'Immoraliste*. Yet he asked for a first edition of three hundred copies and confesses in his journal of January 8, 1902, that if there were a lack of sales, the disappointment would be lessened by the very limited printing. Gide's fears were justified. *L'Immoraliste* had no success whatsoever—for at least ten years. He was so deeply affected by this lack of recognition that he had little inclination to work on his writing for five or six years. *Le Retour de l'enfant prodigue* of 1907 interrupted this long period of silence.

In letters to Paul Valéry of July and September, 1901, Gide speaks of writing *L'Immoraliste* and of his feeling that the book should have been written earlier, that he was already mentally engaged with other works, and that *L'Immoraliste* corresponded to his past, to experiences that were over. In *Si le grain ne meurt*, he lists several clues or sources of various sites in the novel. The apartment at Biskra, for example, is a fairly accurate description of one he had occupied with Madeleine. La Morinière, where the episode in Normandy takes place, was the château de la Roque-Baignard, in the department of Calvados, an estate belonging to the Gide family and one which stood for many childhood memories. The harshest letters of attack on *L'Immoraliste* came from one of Gide's best friends, the Pyrenees poet he greatly admired, Francis Jammes. Jammes denounced the theme of the book and its lack of morality.

It has been claimed, but without much justification, that Ménalque bears traits of Oscar Wilde. Marceline faintly resembles at times Madeleine, and Michel, just as faintly, resembles Gide. But in a letter to Scheffer, Gide explicitly stated that because he was not Michel, he was able to tell his story. (*Ce n'est que parce que je ne suis pas Michel que j'ai pu raconter son histoire.*) He redefines a basic law of fiction—that if René is in Chateaubriand, all of Chateaubriand is not in René, and adds two other examples: the character Adolphe in the novel of Benjamin Constant, and Werther in Goethe.

Always sensitive to and hurt by negative criticism, Gide learned early to profit from it. It forced him to more intense self-examination and to a clear analysis of motives and motifs in his own writings. No book of Gide existed alone for him. *L'Immoraliste* and the book he called its twin, *La Porte étroite,* grew in him concurrently, the one offsetting the other, as if the writer did not dare allow one side of his nature to develop at the expense of any other. Biographical explicitness is always difficult to determine in any work of a creative nature. Several years after writing four of the earlier books, Gide acknowledged in his journal (June 16, 1931) the dominant forces which account for them. He names his early Christian training and Madeleine as the influences which formed his religious temperament and without which he would not have written: *André Walter, L'Immoraliste, La Porte étroite* and *La Symphonie pastorale.*

In all the books which preceded *L'Immoraliste,* there are faint indications of the moral struggle, the moral investigation that will characterize all the future writings of André Gide, and which, first, in *L'Immoraliste* is the central preoccupation. The problem is perhaps the gravest which each man has to solve for himself. He has to decide whether he is answerable morally to himself or to the rules of society. Although Michel's experience ends in bitter unhappiness, there is no explicit indictment of him. Neither is there any explicit defense. The novel remains faintly a parable which the reader will interpret in the absence of the author's interpretation. The next book that Gide will complete is his interpretation of a New Testament parable.

6

THE PRODIGAL AND THE SAINT: *Le Retour de l'enfant prodigue* (1907) AND *La Porte étroite* (1909)

During the years that immediately followed the publication of *L'Immoraliste*, Gide lived through a period of dryness and unproductiveness. He was working, but in a desultory fashion, on *La Porte étroite*. The lack of attention paid to *L'Immoraliste* had deeply affected him, and he speaks in his journal of a sluggishness of spirit (*engourdissement*), of his vegetative existence. He worked in his garden, made a short trip to Germany, corresponded with and visited his Catholic friends Henri Ghéon, Jacques Copeau and Paul Claudel. Then abruptly, in early 1907, he wrote in a brief space of time and without difficulty the short work *Le Retour de l'enfant prodigue*.

He interrupted work on *La Porte étroite* in order to begin the writing of *Le Retour* on February 1. On the 16th of March, he records having completed *Le Retour* a few days earlier, and his surprise at the swiftness with which the writing was done after the idea was conceived. It was published first in *Vers et prose*, in 1907, and almost instantly brought forth strong opposition. The reaction of Claudel was more restrained than that of Francis Jammes who, in a letter of June, 1907, denounced his friend's distortion of the New Testament parable. More than any other single work of Gide, with the exception of *Corydon*, *Le Retour de l'enfant prodigue* scandalized the Catholic world in France and contributed to having the totality of his work prohibited by Rome. This brief text, which has been adapted for the stage and performed several times in Paris, presents a prodigal son who returns home, not through repentance, but because of hunger and poverty and despair.

Once again, the resemblances between Gide the man and his protagonist the prodigal son, are striking. Each left his Father's House because it had become painful for him to live in it. Gide at the age of twenty-five and the prodigal son left their home in order to go to a distant country. Gide at least had pondered deeply over the right he had, or did not have, to leave the austere atmosphere of his early life in order to find his real life and the way of his life.

The opening dialogue in *Le Retour de l'enfant prodigue* centers upon the problem of the Father's House. In his conversation with his father, the prodigal insists that men have different vocations, that some remain at home as guardians of tradition, and that others are called upon to leave. However, despite the multiplicity of vocations, all belong to the Father, all find their role in life in terms of their relationship with the Father. From the very beginning of the dialogue to the end, Gide maintains a tone of religious belief. The "return" would not have taken place unless the prodigal had felt some degree of nostalgia for the love and the security represented by the Father, but the returning son insists that the House is not the Father (*La Maison, ce n'est pas Vous, mon Père.*) Gide emphasizes in the opening scene the distinction between the Law, the set of rules establishing the authority of the Father, and the Love of the Father, which embraces those who follow the Law and those who move outside it, in their search for what they call the freedom of Love. Gide is persistently asking the question whether the Law is suitable for all men.

Le Retour de l'enfant prodigue, which is half treatise and half dialogue, reflects not only the personal preoccupations of Gide the moralist, but also the idealistic confusions of an era, of the decade and a half that preceded the First World War, when the problem of conformity to established moral order was raised by artists and by an important segment of the public. Had the moral code, adhered to by the nineteenth century, lost some of its efficaciousness? Gide neither opposes nor defends in any absolute sense. He poses the problem, and offers the mirage of solutions. In a letter to Francis Jammes, written in May, 1906, at a moment when the Pyrenees poet had been urging Gide to consider a conversion to Catholicism, he says that he has not decided who he is himself, that his ideas and doctrines are still in a state of flux. When, a few months later, at the age of thirty-eight, Gide wrote *Le Retour,* he uses the famous parable taken from the Gospel according to Saint Luke in order to reveal, not the precision of a new doctrine, but the state of ambiguity which has come to be known as Gidian.

If the prodigal son had been successful in his flight from home, he would not have taken the tone he does in the second dialogue, with his older brother. He has come back to the House in a state of fatigue and disenchantment. He accepts the strong admonitions of the older brother with a surprising degree of docility. He speaks of his physical weariness, and dispels any impulse to quarrel or revolt. In his mother's presence, he is humbled and one feels that the return has been consummated in fact as well as in spirit. After the exaltation and love felt in the presence of the Father, after the fatigue and submission felt in the presence of the older brother, after the resignation he expresses to his mother, the prodigal is, in the final dialogue, alone with his younger brother.

Here the art of Gide reaches its dramatic climax and the lesson of *Le Retour* reaches its fullest degree of ambiguity. On the literal level, each brother, in this dialogue, discovers the other. The younger brother forces the prodigal to describe his experience of discovery in the distant land and in the desert, and his experience of disenchantment. And the prodigal gradually forces his younger brother to reveal his plans to escape and his dreams. By the end of the dialogue, when the prodigal helps the younger boy to leave and bids him farewell, we realize that the two brothers are one symbolically, that the return has become the departure. The hero in Gide is the divided self: the prodigal who returns and the younger son who must leave; Michel who detaches himself from all responsibility and Marceline who is the very symbol of faith and loyalty; Bernard in *Les Faux-Monnayeurs* who refuses to attach himself to fervor, and Olivier who is the very symbol of fervor. The dual action in Gide's adaptation of the parable, of the returning brother and the departing brother, is in both *L'Immoraliste,* where Michel is the prodigal in the distant country, and *La Porte étroite* where Alissa illustrates the fervor of renunciation and submission to a life of obscurity.

There is balance in this short work, an almost musical form of counterpoint where the two themes of departure and return are closely associated. The prelude to the story speaks of a triptych, and one can easily see this pattern in the departure of the prodigal, which antedates the text, and the House where the scene of the dialogue takes place, and the new departure of the *alter ego.* No voice is heard alone. Of the five voices we hear in this work, that of the Prodigal is of course the most constant, but each is clear and each is characterized by a tone of opposition. *Le Retour* is marked by a dramatic antagonism that was absent from the fervent search of *Les Nourritures terrestres.* The quest of the prodigal is behind him. The experience of discovery is over, and even the disenchantment is over. The reasons for his return are enumerated with simplicity and frankness. Impoverishment is the immediate reason, but the underlying and more noble reason is fidelity to his love of the Father.

The antagonism of voices and thoughts is paralleled by the dualism of the religious and the profane. The parable of the prodigal son is a brief bare story in Saint Luke. Gide reproduces this bareness and adds to it a dramatic form and a closely knit series of psychological motifs. The figure of the Father remains perfectly ambiguous because He is at every point the Divine Father whose love pardons the sinner, and the human father who rejoices at seeing his son again. His love is serene and enduring whereas his son's love, despite its profundity, is tortured and fitful.

The older brother is both the heir, the responsible member of the family who must maintain its fortune and dignity, and at the same time he is the body of dogma in the Church, the representative and interpreter of the law whose role is to punish or reward. He is the spokesman for order on both the human and divine levels.

The figure of the mother is one of the many additions or liberties Gide takes with the Scriptural text. She is maternal, possibly a symbol of Mother Church in her love, in her understanding and solicitude. The worry she expresses over her youngest son is human in its awareness of weakness, and divine in its desire to include all men within the Mystical Body.

The power of the Gidian parable is in the constant presence of the prodigal who provokes each dialogue and concludes each dialogue by his submission. In each scene the tenseness of his nature, the unresolved quest and the failure represented in his return give to the work its quality of restlessness and contradiction. When he meets himself, as the younger brother, the tension reaches its peak. In this scene he is simultaneously the return and the departure, the love of the Father in its endless freedom and the Law of the Church in its demands and in its strictures. The exuberance he had once known has passed into his younger brother. He has succumbed, however unwillingly, however hesitatingly, to the idea of permanence and stability illustrated in the older brother. *Le Retour de l'enfant prodigue* is a delicately orchestrated work on the purity of devotion and on the revolutionary boldness of flight.

It has the classical clarity, the precision of most of Gide's works, and it has at the same time his tantalizing ambiguity of thought, the tension between submission and revolt, between austerity and a hedonistic view of life, between the familiar in style and the archliterary.

When in 1909, two years after *Le Retour,* Gide published *La Porte étroite,* the first readers felt more deeply than they were to thereafter the shocking disparity between any two books of this writer. The drama in *La Porte étroite* seemed to them in total contradistinction to the drama of *L'Immoraliste* that did bear a relationship in ideas with *Les Nourritures terrestres* before it, and *Le Retour de l'enfant prodigue* after it. With *La Porte étroite*, Gide firmly established his reputation of unpredictability. Henceforth he was the French writer unwilling to allow his work to be easily categorized, to be allocated to one philosophical system. Mobility of thought and mobility of attitude will characterize him. Taken singly, each work, such as *Les Nourritures terrestres* does seem to announce a theoretical aspect that tempts the critic and the reader to identify with Gide. With *La Porte étroite* it began to be clear that theory for Gide is not an idea but a confession. Truth is difficult to compress and contain. As soon as Gide defines an aspect of truth in one of his books, and with the disarming simplicity that so often characterizes his theoretical passages, it dissolves or is transformed. Truth for Gide is that power of man's mind which will not allow itself to be constrained. The subject matter of his books is not the world of ideas, even if this world is always present in his work. Rather it is the world of sentiments that cannot be conceptually realized, the moments of lucid consciousness that are usually not the result of thinking or logical argumentation. Whenever a thought in Gide approaches a completed form, it is diverted into something else as if it had to obey not the reasonableness of conceptual thinking, but the variations and the impatience of man's sentimental and sensuous life.

The bare drama in *L'Immoraliste* and in *La Porte étroite* is in many ways identical. But the drama in Gide is never the book. As an artist he is preoccupied with the incidents that provoke the drama, that call it into life and torment it. The incidents in these two *récits* are very different, and the ways in which they stimulate the drama are very different. From chapter to chapter in *L'Immoraliste* every detail serves, directly or indirectly, Michel's resurrection to a new life. It is a terrifying egotistical resurrection, but Gide relates it with such power that he makes it seem inevitable and necessary. In the same way, from chapter to chapter in *La Porte étroite* every incident serves to deepen the heroic and appalling renunciation of Alissa. We are literally forced, in Gide's art, to give up one attachment after another to life, and accept the vocation of sacrifice. Michel and Alissa are Gide in only the most restricted sense. They are primarily two protagonists of novels, two invented characters who testify to the creativity of Gide's mind.

All of the autobiographical elements of *La Porte étroite* have been fully discussed by Gide himself in *Si le grain ne meurt*, in letters, in the *Journal* and in *Et nunc manet in te*. Every reference he has recorded indicates that these elements were merely the starting point for the novel or *récit* which had been on his mind for several years, and which took him a long time to write. The death of his mother's close friend, Anna Shackleton, in 1884, in a cold hospital room, in total solitude, had deeply affected Gide, and the early titles he used when writing the book reveal the part played by Miss Shackleton in the formation of the character of Alissa: *L'Essai de bien mourir*, a Montaigne-like title used in 1891, and *La Mort de Mademoiselle Claire*, a title used in 1894, that gives primary importance to the death scene of the heroine. This work occupied Gide's mind at the very beginning of his literary career. In a letter to André Beaunier, of July, 1914, he said that he would not have been able to write *L'Immoraliste* if he had not known that he would also write one day *La Porte étroite*. *Je n'aurais pu écrire "L'Immoraliste," si je n'avais su que j'écrirais aussi "La Porte étroite."* (quoted in the Pléiade edition, p. 1546.) When he speaks of inventing the name Alissa for his heroine, he disclaims any motive of preciosity. The choice was made in order to indicate the divergence of spirit and drama in Madeleine Gide and Alissa. The virtue of his wife never appeared forced or excessive to Gide (cf. *Et nunc*), whereas the heroism of Alissa's renunciation is almost gratuitous.

Despite these and other important comments Gide himself made concerning *La Porte étroite*, the fundamental subject is a conflict that tormented his adolescence and early manhood, and that, in some degree, remained as an unsolved problem throughout his marriage. It is the conflict arising out of the demands of virtue, when virtue is believed in and admired, and the demands of the natural man, all those demands of the physical nature of man and of the role he plays in society. Paul Claudel, in his very penetrating comments on *La Porte étroite*, analyzes the character of Alissa in the light of what he believed a Protestant heresy, namely, the will to love the good quite independently of any hope for reward for this good. Anything that represents a recompense for loving God and leading a virtuous life seems almost repulsive to the orthodox Protestant spirit. That is why Claudel characterizes Alissa's aspiration to holiness as a heretical aspiration to angelism, to a state of spiritual purity that man as man cannot hope to reach. In the rough draft of an introduction Gide had once planned to write for *La Porte étroite*, and which is reproduced in the *Oeuvres complètes* (*Feuillets*, February, 1918), he explains how he bore simultaneously within him Michel and Alissa, and how the hedonistic excess of Michel permitted him to portray the saintly excess of Alissa.

Gide was approaching the age of forty when he completed *La Porte étroite*—on October 15, 1909. On the following day, he notes in his *Journal* (October 18, 1909), that he shaved off his moustache, as if he had been freed of a weight of responsibility and was eager to begin a new life. The writing of the book had been for him a painful demanding rehearsal of a part of his adolescence when a religious exaltation had governed his life. Later in his career, but not very much later, these religious problems would reappear in the short tract, *Numquid et tu,* and in the short fictional work, *La Symphonie pastorale.*

Simultaneously with his first comments on *La Porte étroite,* when the book is completed, Gide expressed the hope that his books would be judged solely from an aesthetic viewpoint. The only possible solution to moral contradictions is in the artistic triumph of a book. The first readers of *La Porte étroite* undoubtedly exaggerated the importance of the personal experiences which they sensed there. This was the first of Gide's books to reach a wide public, and this was surprising to the writer and his friends because it appeared at a time when religious and moral issues were not of primary importance to the reading public. Although Gide claimed that he had been able to put the best of himself into this book, he noted extensively certain dissatisfactions he felt with the writing. The dialogue scenes, the letters and the journal of Alissa, seemed to him more successful than the other parts of the book, the more transitional passages where he felt an overuse of a "precious" style. Excessively self-critical of his writing, Gide acknowledged a lack of control in the writing of *La Porte étroite*. Certain aspects of the book were so close to him that his initial intention of writing a satire on Alissa's self-sacrifice was diverted, almost without his realizing it. The book seemed to demand of Gide its own purity, and the self-effacement of Jérôme became more and more apparent as the tragedy of Alissa grew more intense.

The one form of happiness which Jérôme and Alissa experienced was their powerlessness to reach any form of human happiness. Their love was of such a nature, or rather their religious temperaments were of such a nature, that, when together, they were uncomfortable, ill at ease, guilty in such a way that they could not explain their guilt. When Alissa says that they were not born for happiness (*Nous ne sommes pas nés pour le bonheur*), she was possessed by the ecstasy of self-privation. Her action throughout the book is the gradual giving up of all manifestations of love, of all indulgences of the mind and the spirit and the body. She fasts for the joy of fasting, as Michel in the desert fasted in order to feel his desires more acutely. The early theme of "waiting" which was sung of in *Les Nourritures terrestres* as an exercise in sensuality (*je te parlerai des attentes*), is recast in *La Porte étroite* as an austere exercise in spiritual progress and perfection.

The "strait gate" of the title, taken from Saint Luke: "Strive to enter in at the strait gate," symbolizes the life of austerity and privation. Jérôme, the less strong, the less

independent of the two central figures, is compelled by
Alissa to enter upon this way, and convinced by her that
it is his way too. As a child, Alissa had seen her mother
in the arms of a man, and this spectacle she had come
upon unwillingly had signified for her the ugliness of the
world and the degradation of love. As love grew between
Alissa and Jérôme, the fear grew in them that any physical
consummation of love would bring with it a disillusionment. As children, they had listened together to a sermon
by their pastor on the Gospel text of the "strait gate," and
Jérôme at the end of the church service was convinced
that he would deserve the love of Alissa all the more if
he ceased seeing her.

The early experience of Alissa, when she suffered in
feeling her mother had degraded herself, and her serious
religious training, caused her to turn away from what is
usually called reality, and to pattern her life on a concept
of purity which contradicts and even invalidates the forces
of reality around her. Alissa's belief in purity and her
quest for purity are the subject matter of *La Porte étroite*.
Although theoretically Gide condemned this seeming use-
lessness or gratuitousness of Alissa's way of life, and had
planned to stress the irony of her goal and her tragedy,
the treatment of the subject exerted its own power over
the writer. Alissa's idealism triumphed over Gide's ironic
intention, and *La Porte étroite*, despite the final solitude
and despair of Alissa, stands as one of the most successful
novels in the twentieth century on the subject of spirituality. Alissa has already been accepted by two or three
generations of readers, not as a demented, tortured,
psychiatric case, but as a courageous heroine whose love
for a man demanded the sacrifice of that love. Gide's
triumph as a writer is here apparent in the sense that
those readers who would look upon Alissa's sacrifice as
useless and almost reprehensible have been moved by the
strength of her character and by the human loneliness she
chose for herself.

Even in those moments of deepest spirituality, when
Alissa's love reaches a degree of sublimity, her experience

is never without a physical component. She is drawn sensuously to Jérôme as well as spiritually. Her strong reactions to his presence close by her in several scenes give ample proof of this. *L'Immoraliste* and *La Porte étroite* are so obviously antipodal books, that they are also, in accordance with the strange law of the attraction of opposites, the same book, or two books that testify to the same quest for happiness. Michel's quest is for the unknown in the terrestrial sense, for the secret undiscovered life of the senses, for the dark and possibly demonic powers of the earth and the body. At moments when he seems to have established a relationship with mysterious physical powers, he resembles Heathcliff in *Wuthering Heights*. Alissa's quest is for the unknown in the superterrestrial sense, for the ethereal, distant goal far above her. Michel's desire to know the secrets of the body is as intense as Alissa's to move beyond the body. Both are restless, volatile, dissatisfied spirits. And each is accompanied by a partner who is silent and passive and self-effacing. Marceline for Michel, and Jérôme for Alissa, exist in order to throw into greater relief the flight from the normal world of convention. Michel and Alissa are equal in their courage, in the immoderateness of their desires, in the excessiveness of their social defiance. The demon and the angel both represent a temptation for man to move beyond his human condition, to know more than he is allowed to know in his existence as a man. As soon as Gide advocated, in *Les Nourritures terrestres,* man's necessary liberation from conventionality and his new *disponibilité,* he then set about, in *L'Immoraliste* and *La Porte étroite* to demonstrate the ironic danger of this freedom. A pure life of the senses and a pure life of the spirit are both destined to frustration and failure. The defiant courage of Michel is equal to the mystical exaltation of Alissa, and both characters are defeated in terms of their quest. Michel did not reach the serenity of self-realization and satisfaction, and Alissa did not experience the reward of sacrifice and its exaltation. But both were free and both chose the way of freedom.

7

THE GRATUITOUS ACT:
Les Caves du Vatican (1914)

From Gide's *Journal,* we learn that he completed the writing of *Les Caves du Vatican* on June 24, 1913. He noted at that time that he would probably make changes in the manuscript after he had read it to his friend Jacques Copeau. The book is dedicated to Copeau, in its publication in the summer of 1914, after it had appeared in four installments in *La Nouvelle Revue Française* (January, February, March, April, 1914). In the dedicatory letter Gide mentions the long time he had been carrying the idea of the book in his head, and the period of time, with its many interruptions and moments of discouragement, during which he had composed the book. *Les Caves* was indeed a very old project, and goes back to the time when Gide was writing *Paludes,* about 1893. He worked quite intensively on the book especially during 1912. During a sojourn in Italy that year, Valery Larbaud visited him and the two friends discussed the book. In May, Gide served as juror at the Cour d'Assises in Rouen, and then spent some time in Cuverville where he found it difficult to work on *Les Caves.* A good deal of time was spent that year on studying English.

Many questions have been raised about the sources of *Les Caves du Vatican.* Gide was practically accused of plagiarizing a book by Jean de Pauly, published in 1895, on an elaborate swindle connected with the imprisonment of the true pope in Rome and the extortion of money from pious Catholics in order to restore the true pope and expel the false pope who occupied the papal throne. Gide claimed never to have seen the book of de Pauly, but he did know, by newspaper clippings, of the alleged swindle of 1892 when it was believed that Leo XIII was imprisoned.

Although *Les Caves* has some traits in common with *Paludes* and *Prométhée mal enchaîné,* it is unique in the literary career of Gide. Its strong comic vein, its tone of an irreverent hoax, places it in a very special lineage with Rabelais, Boccaccio, Defoe and Voltaire. It stands apart from the central tradition of European fiction, which from Prévost to Stendhal, from Tolstoi to Proust, is characterized by extreme seriousness. Gide takes great care not to call his book a novel. In the letter to Copeau he explains that he calls it a *sotie* and his three preceding books *récits,* in order to make it clear that they are not novels.

In the fourteenth and fifteenth centuries, a *sotie* was a parody or satirical play put on by law students and clerks of the Paris law courts. One of the themes was the election of a Pope of fools. In *Les Caves du Vatican,* Gide will mock the Roman clergy and pious believers as vigorously as he will mock the materialists among the freethinkers and freemasons. A newspaper article became the pretext for one of Gide's most skillfull and elaborately devised compositions. Even in the authentic *soties* of the Middle Ages, there was the attempt to demonstrate the madness of the real world by showing it capsized and led by fools. In *Les Caves,* likewise, several serious problems are grafted on the complicated plot: the freethinker Anthime and his ludicrous conversion, for example, and especially the problem of the gratuitous act and human freedom as exemplified in Protos the chief fool and bandit, and his pupil Lafcadio.

Disguised as a priest, Protos, the principal philosopher-crook, convinces the Countess de Saint-Prix that the pope has been abducted and is kept confined in the Vatican cellars, while an impostor is on the papal throne. The check she makes out to found a crusade that will rescue the pope is given to a friend whose husband is Amédée Fleurissoire. This gentleman has a series of hilarious misadventures, especially in a Roman brothel. In an express train, between Rome and Naples, he is occupying the same compartment with young Lafcadio. This is the famous scene of the gratuitous act when Lafcadio, without any evident motivation, pushes Amédée out of the fast-moving train, and thereby kills him.

By the early critics of the book, Gide was again accused of plagiarism, of stealing the episode from *Crime and Punishment,* where Raskolnikov murders an old woman. There are too many differences to call this plagiarism. Raskolnikov commits the murder as the result of an intellectual obsession, to prove that he is an exceptional being. Much of Dostoevski's novel is given over to the suffering of remorse and the effort to do penance for the crime. By definition, an *acte gratuit* is a disinterested act, pure of any motivation. Lafcadio does what he does in the train because he feels like doing it.

Who is this hero, this new kind of jester and criminal? From his mother, Lafcadio inherited his fine looks and his lack of scruples, his total lack of inhibitions. From his father, the old Count of Baraglioul, he inherited his elegance of manners and speech and dress. He has the charm and seductiveness of an adventurer who is only nineteen. He speaks several languages, has lived in many places and is rootless. Lafcadio explains himself by saying that he is without logic: *je suis un être d'inconséquence.* His vigor is matched by his sensuality. And yet he has also the self-control of a young aristocrat who is detached from the usual systems of living. Whenever he does something in contradiction to his nature, an act which might endanger his freedom of choice, he stabs his thigh with a knife. The familiar Gidian pattern of alternating moods: of wild impulse (reminiscent of Michel) and of self-control (reminiscent of Alissa) is in Lafcadio. He has traits of the earliest Gidian hero, Narcisse, in his eagerness for self-knowledge.

One of the guiding characteristics of Lafcadio's life, which will be especially applauded by the surrealists, is the flamboyant way in which chance (*le hasard*) governs his conduct. In the train scene, he decides that if he can count to twelve before a light appears on the landscape, then he will assassinate Fleurissoire. In a far more blatant and humorous and seductive way, he incarnates the *disponibilité* of Gide's heroes, the antilogical point of view that protects individualism. Despite the fact that Gide claimed Lafcadio as an imaginary character, Jean Cocteau claimed that he was inspired by the surrealist hero Arthur Cravan, the gigantic boxer who became a lengendary figure for the early surrealists, and who published his own paper called *Maintenant* as early as 1913. In the July, 1918, issue, Cravan published a violent attack on Gide.

A brief notation in his *Journal* of December 3, 1909, in which Gide refers to the story of Lafcadio, announces the striking thesis that there is no essential difference between a gentleman and a knave. (Gide uses the terms *honnête homme* and *gredin.*) For Gide, it is an undeniable truth that a gentleman can become a knave. Protos is the master knave of the book, the leading rascal who indoctrinates Lafcadio. If, in a histrionic sense, Lafcadio recalls Voltaire's Candide, he is far closer, in a psychological sense, to Stendhal's Julien Sorel. When, in the final scene, he announces to his half-brother Julius de Baraglioul that he has just murdered the brother-in-law of Julius, he then seduces the daughter of Julius and departs. The reader finds it difficult to blame Lafcadio. His very impishness has its charm.

The harshest act of Lafcadio is his gratuitous act, perpetrated in the train between Rome and Naples, when he pushes Amédée Fleurissoire out the door to his death. It is a surprising act, not in the least premeditated until a few moments before it is carried out, during which Lafcadio observes Amédée sitting opposite him in the train compartment. The act is consummated almost haphazardly. It illustrates more dramatically than any other episode in *Les Caves* the temperament of Lafcadio, freed from the conventional laws of behavior. Whether the act was totally gratuitous is impossible to ascertain. Gide himself said in a letter of 1929, many years after the publication of the book, that a purely gratuitous act is impossible to imagine. He claims that there must be some motivation in everything. What he meant by "gratuitous act," in the case of his hero Lafcadio, is one whose motivation is not apparent, one which seems disinterested, but one in which the real self of the perpetrator is revealed (*un acte dans lequel ce que l'individu a de plus particulier se révèle, se trahit* (Pléiade, p. 1571).

If therefore the so-called gratuitous act will always seem equivocal, it is a daring effort on the part of Gide the moralist to resolve the eternal conflict between man's basic freedom and determinism, all those forces outside of him which form and determine his behavior and his character. This kind of act would be sufficient unto itself. It would have the minimum of relationship with the past or with the future. It is known that Gide had wanted at one time to write a play on the subject of a pimp who was totally disinterested, who practiced his profession without wishing any lucrative gain. The gratuitous act is discussed in some detail in the conversation between Julius and Lafcadio, which follows the train scene. It is a brilliant dialogue in which the two men create an imaginary criminal, and the *brio* of the scene is in the fact that Julius does not realize he has before him, in Lafcadio, the man who has actually carried out the crime he is building up in his imagination. "Think of it," Julius says, "a crime not motivated by either passion or need." (*Songez donc: un crime que ni la passion, ni le besoin ne motive.*)

In his analysis of the Dostoevski characters, Gide emphasizes the contradictory sentiments that inhabit them. Freud might call this the ambivalence of sentiments. Gide was fully aware at all times of the belief that a scientifically trained person would doubtless articulate: there is no such thing as a gratuitous free act, one without consequences and one that is purely unmotivated. *Les Caves du Vatican* is not so much the novel of the gratuitous act as it is a parody of the novel of adventure, a caricature of the novels of Eugène Sue, and a work reminiscent of the famous Fantômas stories of the first decade of the twentieth century, that were adopted as models by the surrealists. The example of Lafcadio will continue to be felt in the works of the surrealists and in novelists as different as Jean Cocteau and Jules Romains.

Lafcadio is portrayed as being the only free character in *Les Caves*. The others, in their comic traits, are all shut off from the rest of humanity because of their personal manias. They are partly parrots or puppets. In this combined social satire and mechanization of character, Gide follows in the steps of Molière, applies theories of Bergson and announces comic characterizations in the plays of Anouilh and Ionesco. The background of the book is both historical: the papacy under Leo XIII and the organization of the Mafia; and the sociological-psychological study of the manias, the narrow viewpoint and the limitations of most men.

In his satire, Gide does not limit himself to one world. There is first, Anthime Armand-Dubois, a freemason, a freethinker, a scientist carrying out experiments on rats and who has a pious wife Veronica. The French call him a *libre-penseur* or an anticlerical. Then there is his cousin Julius de Baraglioul, a fashionable novelist, a believer who has announced his candidacy more than once for the Académie Française. The French would call him a *bien-pensant*. These are the two outstanding types of characters who live in accord with a very definite system. But for Gide they are close to the *sots* of a *sotie* in whom the real self has been dispossessed by manias.

Protos and Lafcadio belong to the other world of freedom. They had met in school, where Protos had excelled as a student. Protos is the indoctrinator, the leader of the criminal organization of Mille-Pattes, the creator of the false pope. We see him in Pau, disguised as a priest and taking from the Countess de Saint-Prix a large sum of money for the purpose of restoring the true pope to his throne. He is able to disappear with the ingenuousness of the master crook, and thus emulates the sea-god Proteus, on whom his name is based, and who was able to take at will any form he wished.

Lafcadio is the supremely free, disengaged being who has learned about the ways of life and the manners of freedom from his "uncles," the long succession of his mother's lovers, each of whom taught the youth something concerning the method of remaining intact. Lafcadio has chosen to live freely rather than to be right, rather than to choose a side that claims it represents what is right. He believes that men belong to one of two categories: the first, *les crustacés* (the crustacea or shellfish) over whom conventions and prejudices form a hell, men like Julius, who tries to become the ideal candidate for the Académie Française; and second, *les subtils,* those who are subtle and who appear eternally different according to the circumstances and the company, whose face is a series of masks adopted for some inner preservation of purity.

If Lafcadio is the incarnation of an attitude toward life and the resilient life force that Gide admires, Amédée Fleurissoire, in the *sotie* as such, comes closer to being the real hero. (This point is made and brilliantly sustained by Mlle Germaine Brée in her book: *André Gide, l'insaisissable Protée.*) Although he is a comic figure, he has the integrity of the hero, the ideals and the sublime goal. He undergoes trials and adventures, all of which are burlesque, but which relate him to the lineage of heroes: his fight with bedbugs (*punaises*), with fleas (*puces*), with mosquitoes (*moustiques*), and the culminating scene in the brothel, which he thinks to be a hotel, and where he is seduced by Carola. Amédée recalls Don Quixote and, at times, Candide, although he has none of the personal charm of Candide. In the train compartment, before plunging him to his death, Lafcadio looks upon Amédée as ludicrous and grotesque. A tapir, he calls him. But then, later, when it is gradually revealed to Lafcadio, in his conversation with Julius, who Amédée Fleurissoire is: the half-brother of Julius, and the man to whom Carola gave the cuff links (which he had once given to her), he states that the old man he killed was a crossroads (*ce vieillard est un carrefour*). Chance encounters, an adventure in life that was particularly significant to the surrealists, form in reality a new structure of the world. The jewel that Lafcadio gave to his mistress Carola, before leaving her, she gave to Amédée after seducing him. She also warns him against the evil machinations of Protos who has succeeded in subjugating her. Like an elaborate detective story, like a parody on a fantastic adventure story, *Les Caves du Vatican* unfolds in an atmosphere where chance seems to dominate, and yet where chance seems to be devised by the mastermind of the novelist.

Little wonder that there have been several projects to adapt *Les Caves du Vatican* into a film. At one point, a Russian company was very serious about this project, but when Gide learned that they intended changing the band of crooks (*les Mille-Pattes*) into real priests of the Catholic Church, he refused permission, probably because he was weary of quarrels with his Catholic friends and enemies, and felt this would be the last straw. Gide himself made an adaptation for the stage that was first performed in Lausanne in 1933. Not long before his death, this version, somewhat revised, was performed at the Comédie Française, in December, 1950.

The book is skillfully composed to show the humor of situations that are only half-understood and half-known. Amédée Fleurissoire fervently believes in the pope, and undertakes what for him is a prodigious adventure to help liberate the man he believes is the captive pope. He meets his death by a chance encounter with Lafcadio who has no interest in the pope and who hardly knows there is a pope. Between these two characters, the one ridiculously heroic who will be tormented in several half-comic half-trite ways before being annihilated by pure chance, and the other, joyously free and Protean in his ability to disengage himself from all tenacious snares, the other characters move back and forth in efforts to pierce the mystery of human action. Fleurissoire and Lafcadio both represent extreme traits of character in Gide himself. Fleurissoire's seriousness of mission is not without its parallel in Alissa's drama in *La Porte étroite*. And Lafcadio's freedom of spirit and rootlessness are part of Michel's adventure in *L'Immoraliste*. Gide's character contains simultaneously a bedrock seriousness of purpose and a scathing mockery of seriousness when it imprisons the human spirit.

8

THE ART OF THE
RÉCIT : *La Symphonie pastorale* (1919)

The five years between the publication of *Les Caves du Vatican* and *La Symphonie pastorale* were dominated in an exterior sense by the trials and anxieties of the war, but in a more personal sense they were characterized by an almost feverish literary activity in Gide's life and by a growing sense of the importance he was being accorded in the world of literature. During the latter part of this period, and especially during the first years of work on *Les Faux-Monnayeurs*, Gide reached what can be called a marked degree of public fame. And since fame is always accompanied by hostility, *Les Caves du Vatican* was vigorously attacked by Claudel, and especially Henri Massis, who was to remain one of Gide's most persistent adversaries.

The *Journal* during these years records work done on a large number of projects. But this was already Gide's pattern of literary activity. He rarely worked on one book at a time. One is especially struck by the variety of these projects, and Gide's apparent ability to move from one to the other without losing his powers of concentration and enthusiasm. The two extremes would be, first, the religious tract he is going to call *Numquid et tu,* which is an examination of his religious beliefs and the meaning of various religious problems in his life, and second, *Corydon,* a defense of inversion which he wrote with considerable anguish and circumspection and which he will refrain from publishing in an available edition for some time. There are references to a novel, which is undoubtedly *Les Faux-Monnayeurs*, and to Tagore and Whitman. The major work he completed and published at the end of this period is *La Symphonie pastorale* in which some of the ideas discussed in *Numquid et tu* are used.

It is evident, again from entries in the *Journal,* that Gide's literary associations and activities were becoming increasingly rich and complex. He prodded himself toward more and more writing, telling himself that his most important books were still to be written and that it was high time that he write them: *me répéter chaque matin que le plus important reste à dire, et qu'il est grand temps.* His relationship with his Catholic friends, especially with Claudel and Jammes, was fairly intense at this time. He resisted them, and somewhat gloried in this resistance. They appeared to Gide too comfortable in their faith and in the practice of their religion. The Protestant in him was still very strong in the abhorrence he felt for the moral and religious *comfort* he ascribes to Catholicism. Laconically and humorously he noted, in January, 1916, the conversion of his old friend, the playwright Henri Ghéon. Gide's vacillation on religious matters, which is concentrated in *Numquid et tu,* is referred to spasmodically throughout these years. On the one hand, he wants to believe, and on the other hand, he finds it impossible to believe. His thoughts on religion were constantly being interrupted or put off by more worldly occupations, by meetings, for example, with famous foreign writers: Edith Wharton, Henry James and Arnold Bennett. Moreover, an important sentimental episode had started, his love for Marc Allégret, which had added a lyrical form of happiness to his life.

The solicitude and the infinite care that Gide took in the training of this young man, in his education, in the development of his mind and sensitivity, form one of the important themes in *La Symphonie pastorale,* where the love of *le Pasteur* for young Gertrude is transmuted into the slow laborious education of a blind girl and into the daily efforts to reveal to her the beauty of the world and the love of God. It is a curious work, of great delicacy and purity of composition, with surprising gaucheries and melodramatic effects, especially at the end.

La Symphonie pastorale is a subtle and critical work on the subject of love, of love which is blind and which therefore brings with it a series of disasters. The critical value and intention of this *récit* are far more evident than in *La Porte étroite*. It is divided into two parts which are the two notebooks (*cahiers*) of the pastor. The first narrates the finding of Gertrude, wretched, neglected, vermin-ridden, and her installation in the minister's home, as if she were the lost sheep. She begins to participate in the life of the family, and the pastor devotes to her training far more time than he devotes to his own children. He is quite literally Pygmalion as he forms the mind of Gertrude, educates her and changes the darkness of her inner life into a radiant spiritual love for life and for the family that has adopted her.

The painful conversation between the pastor and his son Jacques, who has fallen in love with Gertrude and wants to marry her, is the turning point in the narrative, the bridge between the two *cahiers*, the moment when the pastor has to articulate the false reasons for not wanting Jacques to marry Gertrude. He himself has fallen in love with the blind girl, and offers a series of specious arguments to disguise to himself and to others his real feelings. He opposes the religious law, as defined by Saint Paul in his epistles, to the gospel of love in the words of Christ. The entire second *cahier* develops the subtle opposition between the lucidity of Gertrude, who recovers from her blindness only to see the tragedy she has caused in the home of the pastor: the sadness of Amélie, the pastor's wife, the alienation of Jacques, and the tormented spirit of the pastor—and the ever-growing blindness of the pastor in his words and actions. He is the victim of sophistry, the man who has learned to interpret words of Scripture for his own benefit, for the excuse of his love which is bringing about a series of disasters. Gertrude's entrance into the world of light is literally her vision of the world of evil. She sees on the face of Amélie the husband's sin. She realizes, too late, that she loves Jacques and not the pastor. The melodramatic ending is precipitated: Jacques's conversion to Catholicism, his entrance into the priesthood, and Gertrude's suicide.

No work of Gide is more delicately organized in terms of themes. He celebrates almost naturalistically, with the change of seasons in the Swiss décor, the theme of blindness, illustrated by the one who sees with his eyes, and the theme of lucidity, illustrated by the one who is physically blind. The idealization of every event, in the unctuous words of the pastor's journal is constantly offset by the grim reality of the same events which he refuses to recognize. Passages from the New Testament are everywhere in the notebooks, and they are almost always related to the harassing problem of Christ versus Paul, to the words on freedom and love as opposed to those related to dogma and law. The warmness of Gertrude's heart and the youthful sincerity of Jacques's love are constantly being opposed by the stagnation of the pastor, by the ever-corroding lie of his thoughts and deeds.

The parable of the lost sheep is referred to at the very beginning of the story. The pastor uses it wisely and reverently as his justification for rescuing Gertrude from her impoverishment and abandonment. The tone of the parable remains throughout the work, and emphasizes the bitterness of the irony as it deepens. Since the book is the journal kept by the pastor, he is the central figure. The morality of his religion forces him to play the role of hypocrite, not only in an overt sense, in the midst of his family, but also in his own inner spiritual life. He listens not to his conscience as much as to the ruses and the specious arguments devised by his conscience. As he continues to speak of his love for Gertrude as his charitable duty, he becomes more and more hypnotized. He finds in certain statements of Christ a justification for his love, and refuses to accept the strictures of Saint Paul. He reads the Gospels as a sophist, and devises for the passages which seem related to his personal dilemmas, meanings which placate not his conscience but the ruses of his conscience. The parable of the lost sheep is quite swiftly converted into the myth of Pygmalion, the man who falls in love with an object of beauty he has created, and which comes to life in a world characterized by beauty as well as by the defects of man's sinful nature. In *La Symphonie pastorale*, the tone of the Christian parable is maintained even after the distortion has taken place, and the first purity of the pastor's intention has been contaminated by the secrecy of his desires. His sophistry presents Christ's teaching on love as having nothing to do with moral obligations.

La Symphonie pastorale is the third and last of the major *récits* of Gide. It will be followed by the novel *Les Faux-Monnayeurs,* and by *Thésée,* representing an intermediary genre between the *récit* and the novel, a legend more philosophical than fictional, a synthesis of belief and moral candor. Taken together, the three *récits: L'Immoraliste, La Porte étroite* and *La Symphonie pastorale,* represent an important contribution to the short novel in the French tradition of Chateaubriand's *René* and Mérimée's *Carmen.* A relationship exists among the three works, in their form and intention, and moreover, they transcribe very closely moments in the development of Gide's thought and in his powers as a writer.

L'Immoraliste is a thesis, but so skillfully fused with narrative and character analysis that the thesis appears as an adventure of the human spirit, as Michel's adoption of some dark, ill-defined, earthly power. Michel exalts a perversion of his mind and his senses in his will to live through the adventure of his body and thereby renounce the life he had previously known as a member of society and as an intellectual. *La Porte étroite* is another thesis, and, moreover, the antithesis of the first, where perversity wears another name, of idealization or of sublimity. Alissa's adventure is as extreme as Michel's. It has the same characteristics of solitude and of ultimate tragedy. The African desert where Michel feels the full rays of the sun, becomes, in *La Porte étroite,* the Normandy garden where no element of natural beauty and no natural instinct can be accepted by Alissa without an overpowering doubt. The pastor, in *La Symphonie pastorale,* is the third Gidian protagonist who sets out, in an exceptional setting of solitude, for an adventure of the mind, for a drama that will lead him into the heart of a dilemma he himself defines and fashions.

In the temptation to group together these three *récits*, because of their resemblance in form and theme, one should not neglect to point out that *La Symphonie pastorale* is distinctive in its more blatant critical tone. The irony is deeper in it. The author's impatience is more apparent in his portrait of the Swiss pastor who keeps separated in himself the two warring voices of his conscience and his instinct. Throughout the second half of the book, Gide's antipathy toward his pastor grows because he seems to understand him more fully than he had understood or wanted to understand Michel of *L'Immoraliste* and Alissa of *La Porte étroite*. Marceline incarnates the suffering part of Michel, the part she sacrifices for the life she believes exists beyond happiness. But the blindness of the pastor, the obduracy of his will in not recognizing the lie he is living, affects everyone: his wife Amélie, his son Jacques and his ward Gertrude. The protagonist in each of the *récits* is ruthlessly active and determined and strong: Michel, Alissa and the pastor. And this very vitality of the protagonist throws into greater relief the ineffectual passivity of the antagonist: Marceline, Jérôme and Gertrude. The egotism of Michel, the sacrifice of Alissa, and the blindness of the pastor are all separate dramas, and Gide's convictions concerning the moral problems they illustrate are not necessarily his full convictions. He cannot be limited to any one of these dramas. Neither can he be limited to all three. But each book contains the theme of the next. Each one answers and announces at the same time. Each one of the books ends in a death, and yet it would be an oversimplification to call them tragedies. Is the action of Michel criminal or is it a courageous expression of freedom? Is the sacrifice of Alissa useless or is it the expression of a religious vocation? Is the pastor to be judged as a criminal or are the inhibitions created by his way of life so strong that he himself is victimized? Each

of these major human sentiments is presented as universal
and at the same time as perverse.

In the broadest philosophical sense, each of these *récits*
is a tract on human destiny, on the destiny of someone
who has made a choice, and who has therefore limited and
falsified his life. The power of each is in the picture it
gives of a willed destiny, of a fate created by choice, in
an effort on the part of the protagonist to be sincerely
himself. They represent three different choices: the first
is, in a general sense, sensuality; the second, mysticism;
and the third, love. They represent therefore: the life of
the senses, the life of the spirit, and the life that combines
the senses and the spirit. The story of each can easily be
called a story of Gide's life, but the ironic form, the semi-
tragedy into which he has cast them, detached Gide from
their meaning and implication. Gide's inevitable answer
to the theory that he is one of his characters states that he
does not know who he is, that he is always in the state
of becoming someone else. (*Je ne suis jamais, je deviens.*)
Within the stories themselves there is a constant vacillation
between moments of affectionate warmth (Michel-Marce-
line; Alissa-Jérôme; Le pasteur-Gertrude) and moments
of detachment and cruelty. The *récits* are constructed on
the opposing theme of sentiment and intelligence. The
sentimental theme is the romantic quest for passion, for
the absolute of passion. And the intellectual component
is both the criticism of this passion and the will to construct clearly the composition of the book which itself will
be a liberation from all passionate entanglements and all
deliberate choices.

It would be more accurate to look upon the *récits* of
Gide, not as easily identifiable transcriptions of his own
life, but as exercises in self-rehabilitation. The writing of
each book represented for him a cure, a means of moving
beyond a personal problem or dilemma. The form of the
writing is sparse because Gide, unlike a Balzac, does not
amplify. He retraces the story succinctly, and almost
always, at the end, feels and makes the reader feel, impatience to bring to an end what he is considering. But

if there is a personal need in the writer which motivates the writing, Gide comes to the task of writing, as an artist, as a man for whom an aesthetic triumph is more important than the analysis of a moral problem, and for whom the intrinsic beauty of the literary work is in itself the solution of a moral problem. Even within a given *récit*, as in *La Symphonie pastorale*, one story offsets the other, as a theme in a musical composition enriches another theme. As Gertrude recovers her sight, her early happiness turns into a form of despair, and at the same time the expansive exaltation of the pastor in his teaching of the blind girl turns into bitter introspection and disillusionment when his pupil can finally see the real world. For each character, and especially for the major characters: Michel as fervent seeker, Alissa as secretive mystic, the pastor as the leader of a flock for whom he must remain the model, Gide discovers exactly the right tone by which the personal problem will be conveyed and transcended.

In writing the three *récits*, Gide discovered and created the literary style that was the most appropriate for his temperament and his ideals. It is a form that combines an experience of *malaise*, of troubled uncertainty and search in the characters, with a serene formal lucidity in the literary expression. Gide's art combines a clarity of writing with an obscurity in the human motivations of all the characters. The content of the work, therefore—Gide is interested only in situations that are complex, ill-defined, tortuous—is in distinct contrast with an elegance and simplicity in the expression and with the modest proportions of the whole. Gertrude, in *La Symphonie pastorale*, takes her life at the end when she realizes she is the cause of sin, and this momentous decision is reached after a minimum of details in the narrative which at times retains the simplicity of a parable.

To explore oneself assiduously and relentlessly as Gide does in his three short novels, and in his *Journal*, demands a certain kind of courage that his readers have not always granted him. The quest of Michel, the ideal of Alissa and the blindness of the pastor are all treated by Gide as dangerous. A self-revelation may turn out to be disastrous in terms of the coherence and the unity which our social self tries to establish. The very form of the *Journal* that plays so important a part in the entire career of the writer (it even has an important part in *La Porte étroite* and *La Symphonie*), forces Gide to an almost daily investigation of what is pose in his character and in his actions, and what is sincere. When he writes about himself, Gide shows very little self-indulgence. The theme of dissatisfaction, as well as the theme of desire, is equally important in the three *récits* and in the *Journal*. Contradictions abound in these books because Gide finds human destiny complex and contradictory. To detach oneself from the imposed patterns of life demands courage, but to know how to remain detached, to live continuously outside the formulated strictures of daily living, is more difficult than any single act of liberation. The dialogue that Gide carries on with himself in the *Journal* and with his characters in the *récits* concerns first the acquisition of freedom, and then the disheartening difficulty of maintaining that freedom. The desires of men are as multiple as the roles they play. Fervor, that favorite word of Gide, that designates an experience forever moving and changing, makes it impossible to find Gide completely in any one of his books, or in any one of his characters.

9

THE ART OF THE
NOVEL: *Les Faux-Monnayeurs* (1925)

More brilliantly than in any of his other books, with richer complexity and with greater skill in re-creating a world, André Gide composed in *Les Faux-Monnayeurs,* one of the major novels of the century. The principal reservation expressed by critics concerning the value and the power of this work has been what they usually call Gide's excessive interest in the techniques of the novel itself as it was being written, in his almost continuous comments on the problems of the novelist in the novel as he attempts to convert into a book the events of his life, the encounters he makes and the sentimental and moral problems that arise from them.

In answer to this objection we would hold that the aesthetic problems of a novelist form as legitimate a theme for a novel as any other, and that this preoccupation is reflected in so many contemporary works of literature that it seems to have usurped, not only for Gide, but for countless other writers, a position of predilection, an almost necessary theme for an age when art is being submitted to a metaphysical as well as a moral investigation. The meaning of poetry is the subject matter of such key poems as *Prose pour des Esseintes* of Mallarmé, of *Ode sur les Muses* of Claudel, of *Le Cimetière marin* of Valéry. Proust called his novel the history of a literary vocation. In the Hamlet section of *Ulysses,* James Joyce examines the process of literary creation, and announces the theme in the very title of his earlier book: *A Portrait of the Artist as a Young Man.* Thomas Mann's novella, *Death in Venice,* is, among other things, a meditation on the rela-

5

tionship between art and life. Henry James treats the
problem in *The Beast in the Jungle*. It is a constant theme
in all the writings of Henry Miller. The writer is protagonist in *Les Faux-Monnayeurs*. He has grown to the stature
of hero who struggles in his own way and with his own
weapons, to conquer. Édouard, in *Les Faux-Monnayeurs*,
is a hero of his age, and he takes his place beside Aschen-
bach in *Death in Venice* and Marcel in *À la Recherche
du temps perdu* and Stephen Dedalus in *Portrait of the
Artist*.

But not only in this choice of hero does Gide align himself with his eminent contemporaries. In his choice of
a moral theme, indicated in the title of his book, he places
himself centrally within a tradition of French moralist
writers who have raised, each in his own way, and in
accord with his own age, the problem of counterfeit sentiment, of falseness in human behavior induced by the social
forces that surround man and lead him into the role of
hypocrite. Montaigne in the Renaissance, La Rochefoucauld a century later, Rousseau just prior to the French
Revolution, Stendhal in *Le Rouge et le noir* of 1830, are
representative of this persistent moral problem throughout
the history of French letters. How can man maintain his
naturalness? How can he resist the temptation of so many
different forms which plague his role of social being:
affectation, conformity, deceit, hypocrisy. Almost every
influence seems to be an effort to deform his natural self,
to constrict it and to turn him into someone different from
himself.

Les Faux-Monnayeurs is precisely a novel on this problem of authenticity that involves so many other problems
of human conduct and human happiness. Gide is asking
whether, in a society made up of so many conventions, it
is possible for a man to maintain his naturalness. In addition to the role of novelist as hero and the problem of
authenticity in social behavior, Gide's novel contains within
itself a satire of the novel. There are three related problems on the novelist who tries to understand his motives
of action as well as the process by which he converts life

into art, and the traditional form of psychology that
novelists tend to use in order to depict coherent logical
characters. In accepting the falseness of social convention,
the novelist has depicted a travesty of men in their rela-
tions one with another. Deliberately Gide wished to startle
his readers with the lack of coherence in the structure of
his novel, with the unpredictable behavior of some of his
characters, with the multiplicity of plots that begin and
are never resolved. In an effort to attach the novel more
closely to life, Gide does not force subordinate plots to fit
into one common plot. During the writing of *Les Faux-
Monnayeurs*, Gide kept a special diary in which he noted
the problems he faced and tried to solve, and theories concerning the art of the novel. He explains how life presents
the beginning of countless dramas (*la vie présente quan-
tité d'amorces de drames*) that are never resolved or that
merge into other dramas. Only a fortuitous connection
joins them.

It is incumbent on the novelist to allow these associations to continue for a while and then disappear or change,
as they do in life. He advises himself in his *Journal des
Faux-Monnayeurs* never to profit from a new impulse, a
new intrigue, and by this he seems to mean never to force
the construction of a new plot. The scheme of such a
novel is almost impossible to outline, but essentially we
can see in it three principal motifs: the efforts of a young
man, Bernard Profitendieu, to plunge into life, to enter
the mainstream of human existence; the observations of a
novelist, Édouard, who keeps a record of his experiences
and reactions as part of the novel he is writing; and finally
the actions of a band of counterfeiters who exploit and
corrupt some schoolboys.

Of all the characters in *Les Faux-Monnayeurs*, Édouard
is associated, either as observer or participant, with the
largest number of families or groups in the narrative. He
is the half-brother of Mme Molinier, mother of three boys,
all of whom figure in important episodes: Georges, Olivier
and Vincent. Bernard, the illegitimate son in the Profitendieu family, and a close friend of Olivier, will interest

Édouard in his will to live and profit from all experience
without submitting himself to any ideas or people. The
third major family is that of Pasteur Vedel, who runs a
private-school pension. This is a strongly Protestant milieu
and is represented by Laura, who has been made pregnant
by Vincent Molinier, and who is loved by Bernard, and
who loves Édouard. Her brother Armand is secretly one
of the most desperate of all the characters we meet, but
he wears the mask of dilettante and joker. There is, in
addition to these family groups, the avant-garde literary
world of Robert de Passavant and Lady Griffith, the world
of the piano teacher La Pérouse, and the Swiss sanatarium
world where we see La Pérouse's grandson Boris and his
doctor Mme Sophroniska. On the margin of the bourgeois
centers are the criminal groups of Ghéridanisol and Strou-
vilhou engaged in prostitution and counterfeit money.

Three newspaper clippings that Gide kept for a long
time before using them have no relationship one with
another, but they form, in a documentary sense, the
sources of the novel. Gide listed in the *Journal des Faux-
Monnayeurs* the three clippings of 1906, 1907 and 1909.
The first two articles (or *faits divers*) are related to the
machinations of a counterfeit gang that had involved
young sons of some of the outstanding bourgeois families.
Le Journal de Rouen and *Le Figaro* had referred to this
group as *La bande du Luxembourg*. The third article related the suicide of a young pupil in the lycée Blaise
Pascal of Clermont-Ferrand. There are scenes in the novel
reminiscent of Gide's Protestant background in Uzès and
Normandy, especially in some of the discussions between
Édouard and the piano teacher La Pérouse, and in the
atmosphere of moral stricture that characterizes the pension Vedel. However, the work is not a *roman à clef* where
under false names Gide describes characters he had
known. As Édouard the novelist meets the various characters—Bernard, whose personality is still unformed, but who
will remain the freest throughout the novel; Vincent and
Olivier, brothers who are less strong than Bernard, more
volatile and more easily influenced—Édouard tells us—and

we can easily hear the thoughts of Gide in such declarations—that the novelist must enter upon a connivance with them and follow them in their actions rather than control them. The novelist must have no illusions about his characters, but he must adhere to them through the great law of man's curiosity about the behavior of human beings.

With every episode *Les Faux-Monnayeurs* seems to begin all over again, and no theme is ever concluded. Gide skillfully prepared the ending of his novel, which is no ending. Édouard, as he watches the youngest son of the Profitendieu family, Caloub, expresses a desire to know him: *je serais bien curieux de connaître Caloub*. A subtle provocative last sentence for a novel that has not come to a conclusion. During the six years when Gide kept his *Journal des Faux-Monnayeurs* (June 17, 1919 — June 9, 1925), he wrote *Les Faux-Monnayeurs* and worked on other writings as well, notably *Si le grain ne meurt, Corydon* and *Dostoievsky*. In his personal life he began a long intimate relationship with Marc Allégret, and became in 1923 the father of Catherine Gide, daughter of Elizabeth van Rysselberghe, the daughter of one of his oldest friends, a lady he refers to as Mme Théo. But the novel was the principal occupation during these years. He worked with the same zeal, the same industriousness as other hard-working novelists, as a Balzac or a Flaubert, but he claimed that they knew what they were doing much more clearly than he did.

At one time during the composition of *Les Faux-Monnayeurs,* Gide's intention was to put all of life into his novel, to make of it a *summa*. But this proved impossible, and the final sentence of *Les Faux-Monnayeurs,* like the last speech of the prodigal in *Le Retour de l'enfant prodigue,* testifies to the incompleteness of both works. But Gide did revise the traditional view of the novel. He changed its scope and intentions by making of it a center for human and aesthetic problems, a meeting place where a frank discussion on the endlessness of man's strivings replaces the well-constructed and artificially imposed plot. Every kind of theme therefore has to be welcomed, even elements of evil, forces of evil, which in their influences may reveal values and turn out to be factors of progress. A faint trace of Manicheism pervades *Les Faux-Monnayeurs* because Gide as a novelist is interested in following (rather than creating) the destiny of his characters, and in observing what life does to these characters. The positive values of human character are in very few of the personnages of Gide's drama. They are visible in Laura, who is capable of deep affection and loyalty, and in Bernard, the youth who refuses to compromise himself, who refuses to follow for long one leader or set of principles. But the book is much more a study of false values, of those negative forces which impair the naturalness and the authenticity of a human being. Passavant and Lady Griffith are blatantly motivated by evil, but Édouard often realizes that his own exterior kindness and thoughtfulness are secretly false and at times can be explained by an unavowed desire to corrupt. Olivier's facility of speech is at times the result of extreme nervousness or the desire to attract attention.

The absence of any real center in *Les Faux-Monnayeurs* permits Gide the author (and Édouard the novelist) to move easily back and forth between an event or an episode and Édouard's effort to make something out of the event or the exterior datum. The first and third sections of the novel take place in Paris, and the second part in Switzerland, at Saas-Fée. At Saas-Fée, where Édouard discusses the novel he is writing, with Bernard and Laura and Mme Sophroniska (Chapter 3), one realizes that the principal motif of the book is Édouard's effort to create a novel out of the real life he is living and observing. The scene is one of high comedy and high seriousness. The dialogue is rich in witty remarks where each of the four characters is distinct,· and at the same time, Édouard, by answering the questions directed to him by the others, defines what is almost a manifesto on the art of the novel. He calls for a new regime of lawlessness for the novel, of freedom in creation which will not be bound by an announced subject, and declares that his own interest lies far more in the gestation of the work, in the origins and beginnings of the novel, than in the completed work that may never be accomplished. Gide's interest in the Dadaists and early Surrealists is apparent here. They would approve of this freedom in the composition of the work, of the absence of any one protagonist, of the latitude of each character to develop as he will and a disappearance in the author of arbitrariness and authoritarianism.

In *Le Journal des Faux-Monnayeurs*, Gide quotes a significant passage from the critic Albert Thibaudet that seems to have influenced him considerably. The theory claims that the authentic novelist creates his character out of the innumerable directions his own life might have taken (*le romancier authentique crée ses personnages avec les directions infinies de sa vie possible*). The work therefore is not based upon the real life of the novelist, but upon the many lives he might have led or which he did lead imaginatively. It is Laura who calls Édouard, at one point, Proteus, the God-figure, who is perpetually changing his form. He is literally unseizable because as soon as he appears in one guise, or represents one value, he will alter the guise and the value in order to take on another role or espouse another value. This trait of ceaseless mobility in Édouard accounts for the constantly new relationships he is forever establishing with those around him. He is many diverse characters, and in fact this trait is studied in others as well as in Édouard because Gide's belief about the creation of a character is opposed to Balzac's who defined, once for all, gestures and clothes and lodgings and speech in order to fix the definitive portrait of an individual.

As Proust had already done in *À la Recherche du temps perdu*, Gide was attempting, in *Les Faux-Monnayeurs*, to purge the novel of all traits of realism. It goes without saying that every great novel is forced to incorporate some elements of realism, because a novel has to re-create a world. But more than the evocation of a society, Gide wanted to trace the story of a mind, and, in fact, the story of more than one mind. When Bernard says to Édouard, when they are discussing the writing of Édouard's novel: "I see that reality does not interest you" (*Je vois, hélas, que la réalité ne vous intéresse pas*) the novelist confesses that it does, but that it is cumbersome for him. (*Si, mais elle me gêne.*) What does interest Édouard is the adventure of the critic in him, of the technician who is learning how to move from the blunt facts of life to their polished form in a work of art. The making of the book is for the novelist far more exciting than the finished book. No novel in our Western tradition analyzes more profoundly or even more humorously than *Les Faux-Monnayeurs* this theme of the creation of a book and of the effect of this creation on the writer. On several occasions, Édouard in *Les Faux-Monnayeurs*, and Gide in *Le Journal des Faux-Monnayeurs,* discusses, as the significant subject in question, the rivalry existing between what we call the real world and the picture that each of us has in his mind of the real world. This very personal picture of the world of appearances is the force that directs our conduct in society and forms the role we play there.

Because of its scope and because of the aesthetic and moral problems it raises, Gide called *Les Faux-Monnayeurs,* first published in 1926, when he was fifty-seven years old, his only novel. It is a novel of many themes and dramas, written so as to resemble the art of the fugue. Each character is involved in several actions at one time, and for each action he has a different rôle. Vincent, for example, is a son, a brother, a lover, a criminal. Édouard, who is writing *Les Faux-Monnayeurs*, is the most ubiquitous of all. Midway in age between the young and the old characters, he listens to both sides and comments on the dramas of the youngsters and the adults. An expert in introspection, in analysis of himself and others, Édouard is somewhat ineffectual in external practical matters. He tends to abandon them as soon as they become arduous or complex. Before the opening of the story, he had loved Laura, but had feared that he would, in love, lose all sincerity and would compromise his feelings. *C'est Protée. Il prend la forme de ce qu'il aime.* With such comments as these, one realizes the closeness between Gide and Édouard. Édouard is not Gide but a portrait of what Gide would like to have been and what he was potentially. When Édouard says that his morning self will not recognize his evening self (*mon être du matin ne reconnaîtrait pas celui du soir*), we can easily believe that Gide the man never equaled the Gidian heroes.

Gide's triumph as a writer in *Les Faux-Monnayeurs* is the subtlety, and at times the profundity, with which he utilizes introspection. Especially in the person of Édouard, and to some degree in most of the other characters, introspection manifests both the objectivity and curiosity that Gide used to manifest in his botanical studies. He isolates a phenomenon and treats it in terms of its rare and exceptional characteristics. The most telling psychological passages in the book are those concerning Édouard the older man who is approaching middle-age, and Bernard and Olivier who are just entering young manhood. Gide establishes a network of relationships: Bernard and Olivier as two close student friends; Édouard and Bernard in a very complex and ill-defined relationship; Édouard and Olivier in a love relationship. Each of these relationships comes from or leads into relationships with other characters.

In the mythological sense, Bernard is the real hero of the novel. He is by far the most likable of the male characters in the book. He is more manly than Olivier, more virile, more deliberate in his actions. Like the mythological hero, he runs away from home, in a spirit of revolt. He is the prototype of the prodigal son who passes through a series of adventures, and then returns home at the end. Bernard dissimulates far less than others in the book. Living becomes for him a way of self-discovery and a means of self-realization.

The character of Olivier is drawn with far more vagueness and far more subtlety than that of Bernard. There is almost no detail about his physical appearance, but one senses from him, whenever he appears in a scene, a youthful radiation. His background has been utterly traditional and utterly without human warmth. He has learned to mask the impulses of affection and enthusiasm in his character with a facile kind of indifference. He is fearful of showing his heart and his feelings. He has limitless admiration for Bernard whom he would like to emulate but cannot. Olivier is primarily mystified by his own desires. He would like to know what they are, and he tries tentatively to test them on this character and that one. He is incapable of the simplicity of spirit he would like to manifest, and Bernard also is incapable of simplicity. But Olivier is far more tremulous than Bernard in his approach to human beings.

When Olivier feels he has lost Édouard's affection, he turns to Passavant. With Passavant he plays a part, as a kind of revenge. He accepts flattery, and offers a devotion he does not really feel. He allows himself to lead a life of idleness and luxury as a form of self-destruction, as a prelude to his attempt at suicide. The banquet scene is in reality his confession of love to Édouard, and after it, when he experiences a sensual ecstasy, he believes that that kind of emotion can never be recaptured, and prefers to take his life rather than continue to live in a way contrary to his heart. Olivier's main problem throughout the book is how to liberate his real self. He fears being the counterfeiter more than most in *Les Faux-Monnayeurs*.

In the midst of Olivier's drama, Édouard seeks to curb his inclinations. This is not too difficult for him, because his principal love is, when all is said, his work. He is the protagonist, not in the heroic-mythological sense, but in the sense that he unites all the disparate themes and motifs and characters in the book. He functions first as the prime mover, the one who instigates the episode, and then he continues to function as the commentator, almost as the demiurge who observes with curiosity his creatures as they flounder about in their assumed roles. Édouard is Proteus in the center of his ocean, or the writer copying in his notebook the details of a scene he initiated and watched. Édouard's commitment to Olivier, in a sentimental sense, has hardly begun when he states that he must break off the attachment. His rule of life demands this, his horror for any complacency with whatever promises a stable kind of happiness. He fears that the unity of his being will be compromised by such an action. This is one of the most persistent themes in Gidian morality, clearly articulated in *Les Nourritures terrestres,* and studied in varying ways in Michel and Alissa and the prodigal son. When the same belief is reiterated in *Les Faux-Monnayeurs,* in the case of Édouard, the justification is more purely egotistical, more purely the result of the novelist's vocation that demands detachment.

Everything in the book: characters, situations, themes, is transposed from Gide's life. But the transposition is re-creation and therefore a novel. Gide as novelist feels no need to describe in detail and to explain motivations and events. This is what he means by a "pure" novel, by a non-Balzacian novel. During the composition of the book, Gide was struck by a process taking place that is comparable (although he does not make this equation) to the hieratic power of poetry and the lines that come to a poet without his willing them. This would be the strange autonomous life of characters in a novel that begins as soon as they have been born. Almost as soon as they are first referred to, they begin to exist by themselves. Seemingly of their own will, they begin to submit to their own plans and consider their own acts. This problem becomes, for such a novelist as Gide, a mysterious lesson on freedom and fantasy. The real novelist, according to Gide, learns how to surrender to his characters their independence. He knows profoundly that anything might happen to them in the course of the composition. Life is constantly presenting us with the beginnings of dramatic situations. But they rarely continue and complete themselves in anything we could call a form. They rarely come to an end as the situation in a novel does. The novel deals with life as it might have been or as it might become. A fictional character lives and grows in a novel thanks to this limitless possibility of becoming more or less than his or her creator originally planned, of inducing in an unknown future some significant formal pattern and resolution.

In the journal he kept during the writing of the novel, Gide would serve as a brilliant spokesman for this problem of the novelist and his subject matter. The novel, between 1919 and 1925, grew for him into a unique book. He wanted to put everything into it, the full richness of his thought and understanding of human nature, the best writing he was capable of, all of his preferred themes. While he was writing it, he wanted to consider it his last book, the one that would represent the most fully his art and thought.

The book evolved for Gide as a very curious novel with two centers. On the one hand was the event or the series of events, the exterior plot of the novel, and on the other hand, Édouard, who was concerned with an effort to make a book out of what he was observing. *Le Journal des Faux-Monnayeurs* is still another work, completely outside the novel, which is the record of Gide the author watching the problems of his character Édouard, the novelist in *Les Faux-Monnayeurs*. Both Édouard the novelist and Gide the author are not so much concerned with the structure or the architecture of the novel as they are with the characters living close to them or being created by them. Gide felt their weight on him. He felt them living at his expense. He wished they could be isolated creatures in the world, without ties, or only children or bachelors. This would make his task lighter. Of all the characters, he confessed that the one who was closest to him, Édouard, was the most difficult to handle. He had an easier time with the characters who were more purely invented. He believed they were responsible for the best parts of the book.

In the journal comments of Gide and Édouard are several remarks on the relationship between the author and his characters, almost all of which seem to substantiate this essential freedom of fictional characters. What they lack is perhaps the good sense that keeps the writer from going as far as they do. But by going as far as they do, in their actions and gestures that are often more absolute than those of the more conventionalized living author, they change a situation into itself. Gide's principal advice to the author engaged in this process of conversion is not to force it. It is better, he would say, to let the situation compose itself and find its own order through the limitless freedom of the characters. Even when one of them coherently follows his own nature, and yields to it rather than opposing it, he is practicing his own freedom. A character is just as free in his life of fiction as the author is free in his life as a man. The total freedom of both of them is somehow related to their incapacity to communicate in any total way their thoughts and their feelings. Gide acknowledges this final mystery when he writes that he can listen to his characters and hear what they say, but that he cannot hear what they are thinking or feeling.

In the history of the French novel, Gide fulfilled, with *Les Faux-Monnayeurs,* a function similar in some respects to the action of James Joyce in the English novel. It was the attempt to renovate and even upset the usual logical presentation of material, and to diminish the importance of traditional psychological analysis. These tendencies would be somewhat sympathetic to surrealistic aesthetics, and they are not without some bond with the aesthetics of the "new" French novel of the fifties. The many disparate elements—the various families, a novelist, an old piano teacher, an intelligent young woman, a minister, two or three young men who are trying to escape from parental guidance—do not form a plot in the usual sense, but resemble the outline of an Ionesco surrealist fantasy. As in Aldous Huxley's *Point Counterpoint*, characters meet by chance, separate, form relationships or do not form relationships. For Gide, his novel is something that would be like the art of the fugue. *Les Faux-Monnayeurs* teaches that the novel can be as inconclusive, as incongruous and as surprising as life itself.

10

1925–1945

The publication of *Les Faux-Monnayeurs* marked a culminating point in Gide's literary career. Between that date and his death, only one other book, *Thésée*, of 1946, will give the impression of greatness. But everything in the life story and the written testimonial of such a figure as Gide has its importance. The twenty years between *Les Faux-Monnayeurs* and *Thésée* were far from being sterile. But a somewhat new pattern of thought is apparent in these years which will explain the writing of such a last testament work as *Thésée*, and the maturing of philosophical and moralistic inquiry that characterizes the *Journal* and many of the shorter works written during the last part of Gide's life.

Between the young man of 1890—deeply influenced by symbolism, by the example of Mallarmé and the doctrine of total consecration to art—and the mature writer of 1925, who in his "one" novel gave a work typical of its age and whose importance has extended far beyond its age, André Gide grew into the kind of writer and thinker destined to become in the following twenty years a figure of international prestige. Certain of his traits, certain of his convictions, do not change but deepen. Quite early, Gide became once for all the kind of writer known for his emotional attitudes of attentiveness and sensitivity, combined with an indomitable will to achieve architectonic clarity in his writing. His readers have always been surprised by the daring, profound questions he asks in his books, and relieved when they follow the graceful clear formulations he composed as the solution to the problems.

Gide's aesthetic discipline was exemplary in an age famous for such a discipline: Proust, Mann, Joyce, Henry

James, Eliot. And at the heart of each book, as in the works of these other contemporary writers, are the major conflicts of life which reappear from age to age as the permanent shibboleths of the artist. Between *Les Nourritures terrestres* of 1897 and *Les Faux-Monnayeurs* of 1925, Gide's writings and his life had emphasized his search for individualism. He had been essentially the iconoclast, in his fervor to break with such forces as the family, and in his protests against taboos. Throughout those years, he had given many evidences of interest in the underworld of crime and criminals, and especially in the motivations of crime. Even in *L'Immoraliste,* in the episode where Michel watches the Arab boy Moktir steal a pair of scissors, one senses, through his protagonist, Gide's attentiveness to such an aberration. In *Les Caves du Vatican* and *Les Faux-Monnayeurs* this interest becomes predominant, and the novelist appears almost as an expert in underworld tactics. *Souvenirs de la cour d'assises,* written in 1912, and published in 1914, is Gide's account of his experiences as juror in the law courts of Rouen. He was surprised at the lack of interest by the other jurors in the cases being tried, and especially at the lack of understanding on the part of the judges who seemed to pay no attention to the causes of the crimes, and who had little awareness of their responsibility in their condemnations.

It has been asked, and with some degree of justification, whether Gide was not biased in his favoring of the criminals. His entire nature would incline him to taking the side of the outlaw, and this inclination was unquestionably the basis for his social consciousness that did manifest itself in several ways during the ten years after *Les Faux-Monnayeurs.* Gide defended Dreyfus and the criminals of Rouen and Oscar Wilde as exceptional figures in the minority. His travels in the Congo in 1925 were recast in book form in 1927 as *Voyage au Congo,* and in this work Gide attacked the excesses, the injustices and the criminal aspects of French imperialism. This book, more than any of his earlier works, marks an awakening of what his critics have called a political and a social conscience. This kind

of conscience was certainly felt by Gide as a young man
during his first trips to Africa, but other problems at that
time overshadowed the social injustices he observed. His
pages on the brutal treatment of Negroes are explicit,
clearly stated accusations against those in power, but they
are pages of reporting and not sentimental outpourings.
Behind the book, which has many pages on rituals and
botanical observations, one realizes that Gide is protesting
against the. cruelty of man's treatment of his fellowman.
It is significant that he dedicated the book to the memory
of Joseph Conrad.

Written in flatter style, without luster, the three short
novels: *L'École des femmes* and *Robert* of 1930, and
Geneviève of 1936, which are often referred to as a
trilogy, do not seem today as important as his play *Oedipe*
of 1931, or even the short occasional pieces Gide wrote
during the decade preceding his visit to Russia. His essay
on Montaigne, of 1929, and his preface to *Vol de nuit*, in
which he introduced a new French writer, Antoine de
Saint-Exupéry, are texts that reveal Gide's position of
major importance in world literature. It was during the
thirties that every small detail connected with Gide's life
and his role in European thought and politics and literature were discussed everywhere with the same degree of
eagerness and avidity accorded to the comparable positions of Proust and Joyce. His correspondence grew to
vast proportions during the thirties. He answered letters
from known and unknown correspondents with far more
zeal and curiosity than Joyce, for example.

An entry in his *Journal* of May 13, 1931, relates Gide's
first encounter with Thomas Mann and the cordiality he
felt in this meeting. Here he speaks in no veiled terms of
his deep interest in the Russian plan, and expresses his
hope to see this plan succeed. Never before had he felt
such impassioned curiosity concerning the future of the
world. (*Jamais je ne me suis penché sur l'avenir avec une
curiosité plus passionnée.*) He berates the Catholics for
their indifference to the Russian experiment, and accuses

them of not being able to accept any practical system that differs from their own mysticism.

Julien Green notes in his own *Journal* the following year, March 15, 1932, that Gide had confided to him that he could think of nothing else save the program of Communism, that the writing of books no longer seemed important to him. Green asked Gide if this was disturbing to him, and the answer was: "No, it exalts me." (*Non, je trouve ça exaltant!*) Gide's conversion to Communism took place between 1932 and 1935. He was welcomed as a new convert by *L'Humanité,* and his *Voyage au Congo* was singled out for particular praise. At this time the most important left-wing literary figures were André Malraux and Louis Aragon, and both expressed satisfaction and jubilation over Gide's adherence to the party.

The Catholic group called *Union pour la vérité* held an important public meeting where Gide's Communism was carefully and respectfully examined by such men as Jacques Maritain, Gabriel Marcel and François Mauriac. Henri Massis was the most hostile speaker, but his attack was offset by the far more understanding liberalism of Jean Guéhenno and Ramon Fernandez. In January, 1935, the statements of all the speakers were published in book form by Gallimard: *André Gide et notre temps.* In all his recent public pronouncements, Gide had been almost scathing in his attacks on the Catholic Church which, he claimed, had deflected and deformed the teachings of Christ. Notwithstanding this, the examination of his thoughts and his position by *L'Union pour la vérité* placed him, with Claudel, as the most significant figure in modern French literature. It would seem to be, in the perspective of subsequent history, the moment when Gide represented, especially for his youthful audience, a vital force in aesthetics and moral philosophy, a force as strongly felt as the force emanating from Maurice Barrès a decade or two earlier, and from the example of Ernest Renan a generation earlier.

As it turned out, the basic distrust that Gide felt for

all orthodoxies survived his impermanent flirtation with
Communism. While some of the Catholic thinkers in
France were trying to understand Gide's conversion, he
went to Russia, in June, 1936, on the invitation of the
Soviet Union. He was accompanied by several friends:
Jacques Schiffrin, a member of the Gallimard publishing
house, who was soon to be put in charge of the Pléiade
editions; Pierre Herbart, a young writer who had been an
intimate friend of Gide for some time, and who recently
published a book on Gide; Eugène Dabit, a young novelist
and protégé, author of *L'Hôtel du nord*, whose death from
scarlet fever, in August, in Sebastopol, greatly saddened
Gide at the end of the trip; Jef Last, a Dutch novelist and
a member of the Communist Party, a man of prodigious
vitality who had once been a sailor. During the course of
the visit, Gide gave several speeches, in particular at the
state funeral of Maxim Gorki. The visit was a distinct
disappointment. Its narration became the small book,
Retour de l'U.R.S.S., published in the fall of 1936.

Despite some panegyric passages on the happiness of
the Russian people as he observed them, the book was
interpreted immediately as an attack on the Soviet Union,
and Gide was denounced as an impostor and a traitor. In
order to answer the insults he received, he wrote a sequel
to the first: *Retouches à mon Retour de l'U.R.S.S.*, in
1937, but it was impossible to repair the harm or to justify
his position. He had suddenly become the enemy of Communism, and despite the fact that his name was everywhere in the biggest newspapers and weeklies, he was
alone once again, completely outside any party or church.
Ironically his first best-seller, *Retour de l'U.R.S.S.*, was a
book in which the writing was far below his usual level.
It was attacked by such men as Romain Rolland and Ilya
Ehrenburg, but Gide, almost seventy years old, suffered
the attacks rather than attempting any compromise with
his convictions.

As in so many previous cases, the book that Gide published in 1935, before and during his attempt to accept
Communism, had occupied him intermittently for several

years. *Les Nouvelles nourritures,* by its title and form a sequel to *Les Nourritures terrestres,* was begun as early as 1917, and completed at the time when he was seriously involved in the cause of Communism. The book has more elements that go counter to Communism than elements which might be interpreted as harmonious with the new faith. The author of *Les Nouvelles nourritures* looks upon himself as a new Adam, in love with all of nature, and born for happiness. He is speaking directly to someone he loves and also to some adolescent in the future who will read his book and find in it an answer to his questions.

Perhaps the deepest personal experience Gide ever had was his love for Marc Allégret, which was very intense during 1917–1918, and which is doubtless the happiness he refers to on the opening pages of *Les Nouvelles nourritures.* He uses the name "Marc" in the first of the sections called *Rencontres,* and dedicates the last section of Book I, also called *Rencontre,* to Marc's older brother Jean-Paul Allégret. In his hymn to the beauty of life, Gide disparages all such matters as logic and remorse and introspection. This disparagement is the major theme of Book II, after establishing in Book I a deep attentiveness to joy and to an awareness of the presence of God in the world. Some of these early passages were published in the first issue of *Littérature* (March, 1919), the surrealist magazine directed principally by Philippe Soupault.

There are inevitably many themes, and even conflicting themes, in a book written over so long a period of time. The paean to personal happiness, that was luminously clear in *Les Nourritures terrestres,* is, in *Les Nouvelles nourritures,* more rational and more argumentative. There is a deeper tone of serenity, especially toward the end of the book, a serenity that seems to come from a willingness to accept obligations and duties. This theme of acceptation, of resignation, is scarcely discernible in *Les Nourritures terrestres.* It is, in the new book, quite in keeping with the major thought expressed by Gide in his preface to Saint-Exupéry's *Vol de Nuit:* "man's happiness is not in his freedom but in the accepting of a duty." (*Le bonheur*

*de l'homme n'est pas dans la liberté, mais dans l'accepta-
tion d'un devoir.*) The new joy sung of by the new Gide of
1935 was that arising from the possibility of a better
world. The man approaching his seventieth birthday is far
more the world citizen than he was on his first visit to
Africa.

The death of Madeleine Gide in 1938 was a momentous
event in the personal life of the writer. Gide's relationship
with his wife had been the most concealed drama of his
life. The sudden freedom that Madeleine's death gave him
was a terrifying experience. In his first book, *André Walter*, Gide had written of death, as a young man often does,
as if it were a literary theme. But in the subsequent books,
death was never a theme. It was an event: Marceline's
death in *L'Immoraliste*, Amédée Fleurissoire's assassination
in *Les Caves du Vatican,* the Ophelia-like death by drown-
ing of Gertrude in *La ·Symphonie pastorale*. It was an
event dramatically and often quite swiftly used in the
narrative. The suicide of the young pupil Boris in *Les
Faux-Monnayeurs* is typical of death as a dramatic culmi-
nation to a series of events.

Gide's sense of personal loss in the fall of 1938 combined with the distress he felt over the massacres in Spain
and the general tension throughout all of Europe. The
threat to world peace was coming from the broadcasts of
Hitler, and Gide had for a long time looked upon himself
as something of a Germanophile. When he left for a brief
trip outside of France in January, 1939, he took with him
five books, of which three were German: a volume of
Goethe (*Dichtung und Wahrheit*), one of Thomas Mann
(*Joseph in Egypt*) and Nietzsche's *Birth of Tragedy*.
Throughout his life, Gide had loved the more classical
type of German music, that of Bach and Mozart, as
opposed to the romanticism of Wagner and Strauss. He
knew the richness of German culture and the need to have
Germany in Europe, even if he feared its domination.

One of the signal traits of Gide's work was the interpretation he made to France of so much of the culture of
Europe, and even of America in his praise of Walt Whit-

man. He never tired of praising Goethe. He was one of
the first Frenchmen to speak of Blake and Conrad, of
Kierkegaard and Pushkin. In summers at Pontigny he met
several foreign writers and philosophers, and was stimulated by discussions with them, held in the old monastery.
Gide used to attend these meetings, directed by Desjardins,
one of the administrators of the Ecole Normale Supérieure,
in company with such friends as Charles Du Bos and
Jacques Rivière and Roger Martin du Gard.

Gide was seventy years old when war was declared, in
September, 1939. He went to the south of France, first
briefly to Vichy, and then to the home of friends in the
small town of Cabris-sur-Grasse, near Nice. During the
next two years, he talked with many refugees who came
to the Côte d'Azur, and he kept an account of his thoughts
and worries in his *Journal*. Several other French writers,
of his age and slightly younger, were also living in the
unoccupied zone: Valéry, Mauriac, Malraux. His enemies
used the event of the war to heap insults upon him, to
threaten him and to blame him for all disasters. When his
name was announced for a lecture in Nice, he received
anonymous letters threatening him with death if he appeared on the platform. He had the courage to appear
unaccompanied, at the hour announced, and read one of
the letters. Gide was one of several writers, among whom
were Proust and Valéry, who were denounced by members
of the Vichy government as being responsible for the
weakness of France. The writer was an easy scapegoat,
and Gide was used more than most as being instrumental
in bringing about the capitulation of France and the shame
of 1939–1940. The sensual exuberance of *Les Nourritures
terrestres* and Lafcadio's crime in *Les Caves du Vatican*
were pointed out as examples of flagrant immorality that
had devitalized France.

During the last twenty-five years of his life, between
Les Faux-Monnayeurs of 1925 and his death, Gide traveled extensively. Even during the war years he moved
about a good deal. In one sense, his work was over and
he was facing the multiple problems of old age. As the

need to express himself in fictional works diminished, the *Journal* grew into Gide's principal work. In the *Journal* he records during the final years the degrees of serenity he reached. Up until the very end, however, Gide does not shut himself in one attitude or one system of belief. He willingly takes a position, but only for the moment, as in the early thirties when he abandoned a moralistic view in favor of Marxism. Even during the war itself, when the daily events seemed cataclysmic and momentous to him, he refused to trust himself to the forces of history. The very diversity of his nature was its unity.

THE HEROIC MYTH:

Oedipe (1931) AND *Thésée* (1946)

In *Oedipe*, the play of 1931, and in *Thésée*, the narrative of 1946, Gide wrote two further treatises on his famous doctrine of individualism. These two works, under Greek masks, proclaim the mystical fervor that had been apparent in earlier incarnations. The span of fifteen years between these two works was filled with many voyages, with a world war, and with a literary output on the part of Gide that included a faithfully kept *Journal*, prefaces, essays, translations, books on his travels, and studies of legal case histories.

The most permanent theme in all the writings of Gide and in his personal life is opposition to doctrines. At first his friends would argue with him, and then, weary of his endless evasions, surprised and irritated by the Proteus character in Gide, they would leave him. This was the case of both Paul Claudel and Francis Jammes, who, more fervently than most of his friends, pleaded with him to systematize his thought. Such a suggestion and such an effort were always repulsive to him. Morality as such was not the enemy for Gide, but morality led to hypocritical behavior and a false method of systematizing. These were the perils of morality that Gide never tired of denouncing.

Oedipe is the first important work after *Les Faux-Monnayeurs*, and *Thésée* is the last. One is a dramatic version of a Greek myth and the other is a narrative version of a second Greek myth. They are both, clearly, important additions to the repertory of works expounding Gide's opposition to doctrine. Oedipe is presented as an

anticonformist and the priest Tirésias is the conformist.
The center of interest for Gide throughout the action of
the play seems to be the eternal dialogue between the
priest and the king. Tirésias reproaches Oedipe for not
possessing a sense of submissiveness and for having an
overabundant confidence in himself. Tirésias of course is
right because the pride of Oedipe is destined to bring
about his fall. The myth unfolds inexorably as Oedipe
discovers that he killed his father and married his mother.
But Oedipe, for Gide, is supremely the man who was
willing to live in the midst of great peril, who accepted
all the risks as he himself made the decisive choices in
his life. It is not so important that he is a criminal and
has to be punished. It is far more important that he
turned his life into an adventure and acted with vigor
and brilliance.

Tirésias, in Gide's play, is obviously the type of man
who does not approve of an Oedipe, of any man whose
life is a search for truth, and who is capable of inventing
situations by which he may accede to truth. Tirésias is
presented as the man who will do his utmost to keep
those in his care from understanding their personal problems. The kind of peacefulness Tirésias wishes to maintain
is repulsive to Oedipe-Gide, because it is a forced peacefulness, unreal and insidious in the way it covers up
constrictions and limitations. For Tirésias, Oedipe is too
happy, too optimistic, too confident in his own power.
Tirésias, representing the church, wants to instill in the
king a worry, a disquiet that will make him dependent
on the wisdom of the priest. Since so much of *Oedipe* is
couched in modern idiom and related to modern preoccupations, it is not impossible that Gide was describing
in his Tirésias the Catholic critic Henri Massis, who had
been most articulate in his attacks on Gide.

Each of the characters corresponds to a theme or a
situation associated with Gide's ideology. Créon, for example, like Tirésias, is opposed to man's freedom. He is
the conservative, the defender of a society of hypocrites,

the prudent man opposing Oedipe's belief in progress, the opportunist. The sons of Oedipe, Étéocle and Polynice, demonstrate the standard reactions of young Frenchmen of 1930: they speak of *notre inquiétude,* and of Freudian doctrines of repression. Their incestuous interest in their sister Ismène is doubtless meant by Gide to be a contemporary comment. Jocaste is the woman who implicitly trusts the priest, and Antigone is the pure young girl, the mystic who attends her father at the end.

The Pitoëff production of *Oedipe* in 1932 seems not to have been satisfactory, but Jean Vilar's production in recent years at *Le Théâtre National Populaire,* in which he himself played Oedipe, brought out the wit, the dryness and the Gidian commentary. From the opening monologue to the end, Vilar played Oedipe as the king bent upon reaching a full sense of freedom and full knowledge of himself. Vilar understood the simplicity of all that Gide's Oedipe had to say, and the deflation of pomp and tragedy to which Gide submits the ancient Sophoclean text. In this modern treatment of an ancient tragedy, Gide wants above all to fix the limitations and the measure of his powers. It is predominantly an intellectual play, but there is wit in the contemporary reflections on recurring problems: on the birthplace of man, for example, and on the sense of universal guilt. Ideas, both Gidian and non-Gidian, invade all the characters. There is a certain degree of dryness in much of the dialogue, but a sense of liveliness arises out of the juxtaposition of the Greek myth and the Gidian preoccupations.

One of the most cogent themes is related to the blindness of Tirésias and the gesture by which Oedipus blinds himself. This theme has occurred before in the writings of Gide. The truly blind in his works are those who see: the pastor in *La Symphonie pastorale,* Pastor Vedel in *Les Faux-Monayeurs,* and Oedipe before he pierces his eyes. The theme of false blindness is related to the false happiness of Oedipe at the beginning of the play. His happiness is based on ignorance. Despite the real blindness of Tirésias, he sees better than most the sins of men. The successive errors of Oedipe are committed because of his ability to see: first, Laïus, and then Jocaste, and finally the Sphinx. He will see only when he has lost his sight. His blindness is his atonement. In his false happiness, in the power that came to him from lies, he gave no heed to anyone else. The greatness of his fall is not measured by Gide as it was by Sophocles, but the Gidian Oedipe accepts his fate with a curious combination of humility and joy. When finally he leans on his daughter Antigone, *Viens ma fille, je ne me laisserai plus guider que par toi* (she alone will guide his steps henceforth), we realize how far Oedipe has moved from the early picture he gave us of himself as the natural son, the bastard, who felt exalted by his freedom, and the need to create everything from the beginning, because he had no country and no ancestors. For a moment he resembled Lafcadio in *Les Caves du Vatican*, because the bastard, who does not reflect a family, is related to the gratuitous act, the act without a past and without a future. At the beginning of the play, Oedipe moved across the stage with the feeling of having reached the summit of happiness: *Je suis Oedipe. J'atteins au sommet du bonheur.* And at the end of the play, he again moves across the stage in a state of sacrifice, of renunciation. He has given up his kingdom and his glory: *Je ne suis plus un roi; plus rien qu'un voyageur qui renonce à sa gloire, à soi-même.*

Contemporary critics and historians of French literature have pointed out on several occasions the absence of national myths in the literature of France. There is no myth comparable to Prometheus or Oedipus or Theseus. There is no French mythic figure as important as Faust in Germany or even Moby Dick in America. Gargantua was a comic distortion of a myth, but it has not served in France since the time of Rabelais. Roland and Jeanne d'Arc, who might easily have become national mythic figures, have barely survived as literary characters. Racine, in the seventeenth century, preferred not the historical figures of France, but the Greek characters with the long traditions and traits attached to each one: Andromache, Hermione, Orestes, Phaedra, Theseus, Hippolytus.

The hero of a myth, in the traditional sense, is usually characterized by his sense of a community or of a nation. At the beginning of the story he usually leaves the community or the city as a gesture of defiance and opposition, but at the end he returns to the city and strengthens it by his renewed participation within it. Gide, throughout much of his writing, is against the integration of the individual within the collective power of society. He would speak against the collective, when it is static and stultifying. During the thirties, he demonstrated, momentarily, in his interest in the Russian experiment, a belief in the collective. His *Thésée* is the last in a series of works in which he showed deep interest in the Greek myths, and great skill in adapting them in his own beliefs and for his own use: *Le Traité du Narcisse, Philoctète, Le Prométhée mal enchaîné, Oedipe, Perséphone.*

His preoccupation with the type of bastard hero, of the emancipated man, with the gratuitous act which by definition is detached and free, with his doctrine of *disponibilité* —all of these are associated with the Greek heroes and those other heroes closer to him in time and in self-identification. Gide was always more concerned with the second phase of the mythic pattern, with individual dissidence and opposition to conformity. The integrated hero appears at the beginning and at the end of the myth when he acknowledges his position in the collective, but the hero of Gidian temper is the explorer, both self-explorer and world explorer who recalls the admonition in *Les Nourritures terrestres: ne demeure jamais, Nathanaël.*

Thésée is the book of a life summary, a book of prodigious affirmation in the realm of adventure and self-knowledge, and also a book relating the final integration within the collective, the book of communal ethics. A tone of high comedy, and, at times, of licentiousness, dominates the book, but the episodes of the life of Theseus are joined in an almost mystical unity. Ariadne's thread is used literally in only one episode, but symbolically it relates all beginnings with all endings. The rebel at the beginning, always conscious and calculating as a rebel, ends by becoming the founder of a city.

A persistent parallel between Gide's life and thought, and the adventures of Theseus, imposes itself on every careful reader of *Thésée*. The serenity of a life's example is matched by the mastery of a literary style. There is serenity reached at the end of a tumultuous egotistical life, and the narration of this wisdom is a triumph of balance, of interweaving themes, of limpid elucidations. The writing of *Thésée* was completed in May, 1944, and Gide speaks in his *Journal* of the intense excitement this composition provoked in him. It recalled for him two earlier very fertile moments in his career when he wrote steadily and in a fever of excitement: the moment of his *Prométhée* and the year 1913–1914 when he was completing *Les Caves du Vatican*. Like most of Gide's literary projects, *Thésée* has a long history, a slow maturing in his mind that goes back as far as 1931. The first idea seems to have been a dialogue between Oedipus and Theseus, a meeting between the two heroes, each one of whom would be explained and illuminated by the other. This opposition and this juxtaposition will quite literally become important in the final version of the work. The project viewed from so many different moments, and therefore from so many varying perspectives, grew into one of the richest, and possibly the richest work of his career by the skill with which myth is fused with autobiography, and comedy offset by seriousness, and pure narrative relieved by license. It is a work of retrospect in which the satisfaction comes from the adventures of an extraordinary life and a literary expression which Gide the writer created at the age of seventy-five.

For this ultimate *récit*, Gide found a brilliant interpretation for the labyrinth and for the thread, the two principal symbols of the leading adventure in the life of Theseus. The labyrinth is that place where the hero is tested, where he undergoes an ordeal and an initiation. The new danger in the Gidian labyrinth is represented by the vapors that affect the will and strip the victim of any desire to escape. These vapors would seem to be the complexities of a man's mind, the torment of his very strength which he turns into a weakness, into a factor of debilitation. The seductiveness of the mind's power acts as an ally of the devil, as the disguise for a demonic possession. The second symbol is that of Ariadne's thread, which is used by Gide not as a mere means of escape, but as salvation itself. He interprets it as a symbol of duty. Theseus must go back to Ariadne, he must renew contact with the past, he must return step by step to tradition. The Minotaur is far less important in Gide's *récit* than in the myth. First, the Gidian Minotaur is beautiful, and whatever struggle goes on between Theseus and the monster is quite vague. The physical power of the monster is not at all stressed, but rather his attractiveness.

Even in this early episode of Theseus' encounter with the Minotaur, the heroic physical prowess is lessened in order to make way for the humanist—not the thinker, exactly, but the man who will end as a statesman and who will show his devotion to all the humanistic triumphs on this earth. One of the principal themes of the work is Gide's interest in pointing out the triumph of Theseus, in the worldly sense, and the defeat of Oedipus which brings with it an elevation of the spiritual and a renunciation of worldly values.

There would seem to be very little taken from Plutarch's *Life of Theseus*, which Gide probably knew in the translation of Amyot. There is doubtless more, although taken obliquely, from Racine's *Phèdre*. Theseus is the character who illustrates many of the familiar themes in the writings of Gide, but incarnates them in a more moderate way, without the usual tone of provocativeness. In accordance with his custom, Gide alters several details in the traditional story, or adds to them. The failure, for example, on the part of Theseus, to change the black sails to white, was deliberate in Gide's version, because of the son's need to do away with his father, to succeed his father and begin his life's mission. This is in keeping with Gide's belief concerning the pernicious effect of family influence. Murder, carried out in an almost demonic way, is therefore introduced at the beginning of Theseus' life story. To some extent every detail is re-created and refashioned with the feelings of a twentieth century writer: the appearance of the Minotaur, the seductiveness of the labyrinth, the strong designation of Icarus as the symbol of human restlessness and poetic effort, the principle of redemption in Oedipus brought about through suffering.

The subject matter itself of *Thésée* and the moment in Gide's career when he wrote the definitive version of his *récit* allowed him to combine the richness of contradictions which always fascinated him, and the new gravity, the new wisdom of his advanced age. Greece and Christianity are both represented in *Thésée*: the polytheism of Greek mythology and the seriousness of the Gospels. Theseus as a character so combines virtues and moral defects that Gide could easily discover in him affinities with himself. The restlessness and the unappeased yearnings of the youthful Gide, as narrated in *Les Nourritures terrestres*, are not in the least contradicted by the note of satisfaction that marks the ending of *Thésée*. Such a satisfaction, such a pride with self would not have been attained without the earlier dissatisfaction. The final serenity of Theseus is all the more credible because of the ruthlessness of his career. The last two words, *J'ai vécu*, express a pagan satisfaction, a pagan apology for a life that is looked upon as reaching completion on this earth. At every point in the career of Theseus, his critical spirit dominated, and turned the hero year after year into a figure of universal power and universal appeal. Like Lafcadio of *Les Caves* and Bernard of *Les Faux-Monnayeurs*, Theseus is the essentially free spirit, charmingly casual in appearance, and deliberately calculating in his inner life. Less intelligent than Lafcadio or Bernard, Theseus makes up for this by his physical strength and the supernatural endowments of a mythic hero.

Every phase of his existence, every human contact,

every test of strength and shrewdness served Theseus as
training and education. He was always the adventurer
in the full Gidian sense, unwilling to remain satisfied with
a single exploit, unwilling to remain attached to any one
form of life, eager to move ahead to the new and the
unknown. Theseus' enthusiasm for whatever was new and
untried was always followed by an ability to detach himself from the enthusiasm. No conquest ever became a
prison or a way of life or an end in itself. Truth was
multiple for Theseus. Had he learned to live by one
form of truth, it would have been comparable to remaining inside the labyrinth. The labyrinth of Dedalus was
only one of the many dangers that would have arrested
his development and held him within one doctrine, one
mode of life, one view of life. Truth must not be looked
upon as a definitive value but rather as the exciting
challenge and risk of the future in its unpredictability
and variability.

Gide's long distrust of dogmatism is lucidly exposed
and developed in his version of *Thésée*. Every adventure
is to be wished for, first, and then it must be left behind.
The critical spirit which Gide advocates is equivalent to
the spirit of detachment and freedom. An act in itself is
temporal. Its meaning or its universality can be understood only in terms of other acts, of varied successive
acts in time by which a man is able to renew himself. All
of life is therefore a way of discovery, not only of the
world but of the self also. Each act must be carried out
with the conviction that it possesses a unique value, but
one detachable from all other values. Theseus, through
the number of his acts, makes amends for his limited
intelligence. He has kept himself from falling into what
Gide would define as the most serious moral defect: that
of his spirit's immobilization.

As always in his use of Greek myths, Gide stresses, in
Thésée, the humanistic value of his hero's existence. The
Greek elements of the supernatural are forgotten or
avoided or diminished to an almost imperceptible point.
The presence of the gods is not felt in Gide's *Oedipe* and

Thésée. The man in the hero interests him first, and then
the hero in his relationship to the community. Theseus
does not conceal the egoism of his sexual adventures. His
treatment of Ariadne is despicable, but Gide emphasizes
in his portrayal of Ariadne her petulance and coyness and
insistent demands. Throughout the narrative the licentiousness of Theseus' character and his infidelity are made
clear. But his fine sense of tolerance on political and
social issues offsets the egoism of his amorous conquests.
Between Oedipus and Theseus, Gide establishes a set of
resemblances and differences that form one of the richest
themes in the work. These two sons of kings, who become
kings in their turn, represent two manipulators of destiny,
and two victims of destiny. Analogies and divergences are
many, and Gide exploits them all. Oedipus, for example,
marries his mother, but was unaware of their relationship.
And Theseus is responsible for the death of his son,
through an excessive sentimentality. Oedipus interests
Gide on many counts, but he demonstrates his preference
for Theseus, for the Lafcadio qualities in his Theseus.

There is directness of naïveté in the voice of Theseus
as he narrates his life. But he is not easily duped by the
world. Shrewdness and even duplicity mingle with his
expressions of frankness. He is an earth creature, and he
fights with the weapons at hand, with weapons devised
by man. He has the strength of Hercules and the wiliness
of Ulysses. It is never exclusively Gide who speaks in the
voice of Theseus, but Gide is more present in Theseus
than Giraudoux in his Hector or Anouilh in his Antigone.
The narrative was to have been made for the son Hippolytus, but the son is dead, and Gide's young readers
have replaced the son of Theseus. Oedipus also undertook the instruction of his sons. The Sphinx had to be
overcome by Oedipus, and the Minotaur by Theseus. But
before the enigma and the monster, there was the father,
and each prince, in his own way, slew his father in order
to mount the throne.

Twelve brief chapters compose *Thésée,* and each one is

dominated by Theseus in his relationship with another character.

1. Theseus is the sensualist adolescent, the carefree boy who understands and encourages the expression of all his appetites. The seducer of women is clearly visible in the adolescent who does not yet know women. His father Aegeus tells him to look for weapons under rocks, and he develops his muscles and trains his willpower in this activity.

2. When Theseus confesses that he was responsible for his father's death by not changing the black sails on his return voyage from Crete, Gide imposes an important innovation on the myth. Laconically and ruthlessly, Theseus merely says that Aegeus was in his way (*Égée m'empêchait*). The swiftly told narrative lists the brigands and monsters Theseus overcame in his brilliant series of combats. In Gidian terms these could easily be the conventions the hero had to pass through in his initiation to life, in his *rite de passage*. His many seductions of women parallel his physical feats. One in particular is named: Antiope, the Amazon, because she is the mother of Hippolytus, destined to be Theseus' favorite son.

3. This is the beginning of the most elaborate episode in the life of Theseus: the Cretan adventure undertaken in order to liberate Greece from the Minotaur and the annual sacrifice of youths and maidens. Theseus travels as a hostage with his friends and especially his close friend Pirithous. At a festival in Crete he observes Pasiphae, mother of the monster, and the two daughters of Pasiphae and Minos, Ariadne and the young sister Phaedra. Bulls are foremost in the festival and foremost in the strange erotic background of Pasiphae and Minos.

4. Theseus is tested by Minos who has him dive into the sea. Hidden under Ariadne's scarf, that is twined around his thighs, he has in a bag some precious stones which he lies about, claiming Poseidon gave them to him for Pasiphae and Ariadne.

5. Drunk on the dinner wine, after he has passed the

test, Theseus is fondled by Pasiphae who pleads with him not to kill her son the Minotaur. She explains her family's obsession with bulls.

6. A love scene with Ariadne is prolonged by her to the discomfort and boredom of Theseus. She explains the labyrinth to him, and he heeds this useful information, although he is irritated by the terms of endearment she uses. During the latter part of the scene, Theseus has only one thought in mind, that of leaving Ariadne as soon as possible.

7. More useful information concerning the labyrinth is offered to Theseus by Dedalus, the man of science, who enjoys the exuberance of the young hero. He instructs him about the dangerous vapors that come from fires in the labyrinth and create a strange intoxication that weakens the will. Ariadne's thread is interpreted by Dedalus as Theseus' attachment to his past. The labyrinth is the attraction to the unknown. The danger it represents is a total severance from the past.

8. One of the richest and one of the most original episodes in its presentation is the apparition of Icarus. He died as a victim of the labyrinth, and his case history is explained by his father Dedalus to Theseus. When he appears, half naked, his father describes him as the image of human restlessness, as a youth characterized by a mystical predisposition. This is the temperament of the artist who converts the accomplishments of heroes into continuing symbols for humanity. Fate models each man. The labyrinth represents the danger of avoiding one's fate. It is easy to enter the labyrinth. There is nothing harder than finding one's way out of it.

9. Then comes the scene of action and Theseus' confrontation with the Minotaur. The thread the hero holds cannot be cut by a sword, and he is provided with a protective mask against the enervating vapors of the labyrinth. The Minotaur is described as beautiful and reclining in a garden when Theseus comes upon him. The struggle itself is not evoked, but the carrying out of the slaughter provides Theseus with a sensuous pleasure. His thirteen

companions, including Pirithous, had preceded him into the labyrinth and had been affected by the vapors. Theseus has to use force to get them to leave.

10. With the aid of Pirithous, an elaborate plot is devised and carried out by which Phaedra, dressed as her young brother Glaucos, is abducted by Theseus, and Ariadne is abandoned on an island. In accordance with Cretan sexual customs, Minos hopes that his son Glaucos will attract a man, such as Theseus, and willingly aids in the strange plot of abduction. But Theseus had already clearly stated to the reader his preference for women.

11. Theseus' marriage with Phaedra is concurrent with his founding of Athens. His fidelity to his wife and to his city appears as one fidelity. He is now preoccupied with the public good, and argues with Pirithous over the problem of human equality. He insists that all men be welcomed to Athens, and especially Oedipus, the fallen king, the figure of tragedy, who appears noble and profound in his plight. This stage marks the hero's return to his origins. The cycle is completed. The wisdom of Theseus, as he surveys his life, is first expressed in his acknowledgment that there is a time for conquest, a time for adventure and for purging the earth of monsters, and that there is finally a time for the founding of a city and the cultivation of the land.

12. The ultimate passage shows at its beginning the influence of Racine's *Phèdre*, and at its end the clearest statement of Gidian philosophy. The portrait of Hippolytus, especially, is both Sophoclean and Racinian. Phaedra's infatuation with her stepson, induced by her scorn of Aphrodite, is the classical myth. At Colonnus, where Theseus meets Oedipus, one has the impression of watching two destinies join hands. This encounter would seem to be the one consolation, in the human sense, which Theseus experiences after the death of his son. The blindness of Oedipus has given him insight into himself. *O obscurité, ma lumière*, he says, and one remembers that Tirésias had once said that to see God, a man has to blot out the world: *Il faut cesser de voir le monde, pour voir*

Dieu. The deep contentment expressed by Theseus at the end is joined with a belief in some original defect in man, some obscure plight, that explains the endless striving of man and his limitations.

Thésée is a recitation of the self, an autobiography, and in many of its general lines it records the history of Gide's mind. One recognizes easily the self-deprecation in which Gide often indulged, and the life of action he advocated and tried to follow. The final portrait of man that Theseus illustrates is an absolute for Gide, the only absolute he found. It is man in his multiple traits, in the variety of his occupations and dreams, in the richness of his thought, in his defeats and in the renewed beginnings after his defeats.

12

AT GIDE'S DEATH:
1951 – 1953

The literary scene in Paris at the beginning of 1951 was very much concerned with the continuing interest in the work and, especially, in the personality of André Gide. Between his death, in February, 1951, and the beginning of 1952, four new books on him appeared, as well as an impressive volume of *Hommage*, published by *La Nouvelle Revue Française*, with which his name had been closely associated for many years prior to 1941. The small volume *Et nunc manet in te*, which Gide had arranged to have published posthumously, containing an essay on his wife and passages of his *Journal* on his wife not included in his previously published *Journal*, aroused more controversial discussion than any other book of that year.

This continuing interest in Gide was a denial of the belief that a great writer is neglected for at least a time after his death. These first publications were for the most part personal testimonials to the man, written by close friends who called upon their memories of meetings with Gide, of conversations and events. This was especially true of the *Hommage à André Gide*, in which many foreign writers as well as French writers considered some aspect of Gide's personality they believed they understood. No contemporary personality had been more complex than Gide's, and no writer had done more than Gide to stimulate controversy and contradictions about himself. During the first half of his literary career, if not all of it, he had been obsessed with how the future would judge him and his work. He never ceased following the changes that took place in his mind and attitudes and judgments, changes

that many critics have called contradictions and incon-
sistencies, but that testify rather to Gide's relentless
self-inquisition and honesty.

One of his final words, spoken on the day of his death
to the eminent physician Jean Delay, and reported in an
article of the *Hommage,* initiated a controversy. Delay was
alone with Gide and asked him whether he was in pain.
Gide announced: "It is still the struggle between what is
reasonable and what is not." (*C'est toujours la lutte entre
le raisonnable et ce qui ne l'est pas.*) Almost immediately
two Catholic writers, François Mauriac and André Rousseaux, interpreted this statement as a tragic hesitation
between faith and reason. The formula is enigmatical, and
resembles in that respect the final word of some of Gide's
books: *Les Nourritures terrestres,* for example, and *Thésée.*
But so close a friend as Roger Martin du Gard refused to
see in it anything sibylline or mystical. At his death, Gide
had two attitudes that he exposed to his friends. One was
in his words: *C'est bien. C'est très bien.* This was interpreted as meaning: "This is the way I hoped to die, lucid
up until the end. I am submitting to the inevitable." The
other attitude was more sorrowful, when tears would come
to his eyes in saying farewell. This final oscillation was for
Martin du Gard one between his acceptance of the natural
law and his sorrow at leaving his friends. And this oscillation was expressed in the phrase: *C'est toujours la lutte
entre le raisonnable et ce qui ne l'est pas.*

Before his death, Gide had received the official sign of
consecration, the recognition of his century that he was
one of its major writers. The Nobel Prize for literature,
awarded to him in 1948, indicated that his work had
attained a degree of accepted universality, and the continuing attacks of the younger avant-garde writers were
proof enough that his books were still being read by all
ages and still sufficiently vital to initiate opposition. The
miracle was that André Gide had become a "classical"
writer by the time of his death, while still remaining a
"dangerous" writer. In keeping with a great European
tradition, he uttered, at the moment of dying, a statement

so equivocal that immediately it was exploited in varying and contradictory ways.

In addition to the enigmatic sentence spoken to Jean Delay by Gide just before his death, the testimonials of those who saw him during his final illness indicate a very real resignation, a stoical acceptance of a state that he had defined himself many times during the latter part of his life as a void. All his life, Gide had suffered from insomnia, and during the period when he was forced to remain in bed, he seemed never to close his eyes. His mind remained constantly active. He reread the *Aeneid* with extraordinary satisfaction, and discussed plans for a scenario he wanted to make from his play *Les Caves du Vatican*. A few years earlier he had been astonished and grateful at being able to complete his final work, *Thésée*. The message of Gide reached in *Thésée* an unusual degree of serenity and completeness, and in this work he felt he had said all that was important for him to say. He repeated this thought to close friends just before dying, and showed in their presence a spirit of sadness or nostalgia, rather than any indication of real suffering. He seemed to give consent to this ending of his life.

The new books on Gide confirmed and completed much that was already known about him. His existence seemed to have been occupied with an extraordinary interest in life in all of its manifestations, and with an assiduous reading of literary texts. He alternated his studies of botany, his walking, swimming, insect hunting, with readings of Goethe, translations of Shakespeare and the writing of his own books. He rose early, enriched by the ideas that sleep (however intermittent it had been) had provided, and full of plans for the day. Everything offered him a subject for meditation: a page of reading, a patch of blue sky, the coloring of an insect or a flower, the beauty of a child, a conversation with a friend, a charitable gesture he had observed. In a profound sense, he was a lonely man, but he was seldom alone. He disliked social gatherings because on such occasions he felt out of place and incapable of saying anything of significance. He claimed that a writer had nothing to gain from such occasions unless he intends to write the work of a Proust. Even more than social gatherings, Gide abhorred literary groups and literary discussions, and deliberately avoided them, especially during the last years of his life.

Gide knew that he possessed nothing of the anguish of a Pascal. That trait of temperament he left to Mauriac, and appropriated to himself the characteristics of a Montaigne, of a wavering and diverse mind (*esprit ondoyant et divers*). Every moment of his day was utilized in some fashion. He remained at all times the writer who profited from every kind of experience, important or trivial. Gide was the opposite of a dreamer or a stroller. Every reflection of his mind and every object perceived were to be captured for a future use in the literary work. And yet Gide knew that this way of life was no assurance of happiness in the usual sense. At his first meeting with Claude Mauriac, in 1937, when Gide was already a very celebrated figure, he confessed to the young man that he had gone that day twice to the movies because he had felt lonely and abandoned. During 1938 and 1939, Claude Mauriac had the opportunity of observing Gide quite closely and was struck by the youthfulness of his appearance and manner. The writer had developed certain traits of distrust, certain characteristics of the tracked man under suspicion. He seemed to be haunted by a fear of boredom. Claude Mauriac believed that Gide's love for the movies came from that fear. Whatever his message was, it had become through the years indistinguishable from his character. The creation of a literary work and the creation of a personality had been continuing simultaneously for years.

On the first anniversary of Gide's death, February 19, 1952, Marc Allégret presented his film on Gide at the Cinéma Vendôme in Paris. Most of the film had been made during two months of the last year of Gide's life, in his apartment at 1 bis rue Vaneau. But there are sequences in the film dating from the time of the silent movies. Some of the most intriguing parts are Gide's own commentaries on certain of his books, and his conversa-

tions with other celebrities. In one episode he explains to
Anick Morice a Chopin scherzo that she has just played.
The scene with his two grandchildren for whom he per-
forms a trick with a box of matches was completely improvised, and filmed only once. On the occasion of the
premiere of this film, Marc Allégret was asked to describe
the personal characteristics of Gide he remembered best.
The film director spoke especially of Gide's seriousness, of
his scrupulosity in refusing a request or accepting a favor,
of the depths of his fervor, and the attentiveness with
which he spoke to friends and considered their problems.

The film, which bears the very simple title, *Avec André
Gide,* constitutes a precious document on certain aspects
of Gide's life and career. It opens with a few solemn pictures of the funeral at Cuverville and Gide's own reading
of the opening pages of *Si le grain ne meurt.* There are
pictures showing the two contrasting family origins: Normandy and Languedoc, the north and the south, the Catholic and the Protestant backgrounds. The landscape pictures of Algeria and Tunisia provide a documentation for
many of his works, from the earliest, such as *Les Nourritures terrestres,* to his *Journal* in 1941–1943. Among the
most curious episodes are the trip to the Congo, the walk
with Valéry, the home of his daughter in Brignoles, the
speech made in Moscow in the presence of Stalin, the visit
with Roger Martin du Gard in Bellême. The most surprising sequence is perhaps his role of attentive and affectionate grandfather. Of all Gide's statements, the one that has
been used the most often against him is his invective
against families: *Familles, je vous hais!* But Gide did play
the role of grandfather with his customary sincerity, and
Marc Allégret had a perfect right to include the touching
scene with the grandchildren as illustrating one of the final
roles in the long life.

Gide was probably the most photographed man of letters
of our century, and hence of all centuries. As the years
passed, his face assumed a Mongolian-like mask, with its
oblique and prominent eyebrows. One of the earliest de-
scriptions of Gide was inscribed by Roger Martin du Gard

in his journal, on the occasion of their first meeting at
Gallimard's, in 1913. The cloak Gide wore at that time
gave him the appearance of an old starving actor. "A de-
frocked priest," thought Martin du Gard, "one with an
evil conscience." His voice was, up until the very end,
rich in resonance, low-pitched, almost solemn. He enjoyed
reading favorite poems to his friends, and he did this with
the art of an experienced actor. His facial expression
revealed at all moments of attentiveness an exceptional
combination of emotion and intelligence. During his last
days, in his apartment on the rue Vaneau, when his cheeks
had grown quite hollow and his skin a parchment gray, he
wore on his head a cotton bonnet. Layers of flannel cov-
ered him because his lifelong fear of draughts had developed into a mania. The press notices of his play, *Les
Caves du Vatican,* had been on the whole quite severe.
He insisted upon reading them all by claiming that he had
grown invulnerable to attack: *Tout glisse maintenant sur
moi, je suis devenu proof.* This was far from true. No one
solicited criticism more than Gide, and no one suffered
more from it.

A possible definition of genius—and one that applies admirably to Gide—is a mind attentive to things that hold
no interest for most people. A literary genius is a man who
considers passionately what other men do not see. In the
tradition of French letters, Montaigne is preeminently this
type of genius who welcomes every occasion of pleasure,
every experience, every meeting, for the subject matter
of his writing. *Jusques aux moindres occasions de plaisir
que je puis rencontrer, je les empoigne,* wrote Montaigne.
Gide's place as an artist is precisely in this tradition, and
the magnitude of his work, of his understanding and of his
sympathy, place him beside Montaigne. The art of both
the sixteenth century essayist and the twentieth century
moralist is based upon an indefatigable curiosity and a
relentless critical spirit. Gide's enthusiasm for whatever
came within his vision was usually followed by an admirable detachment from it. Once the conquest was made,
he refused to be dominated by his conquest. The image of

the Minotaur's labyrinth, elaborately used in his last important book, *Thésée,* represents any body of doctrine that might constrict or imprison the thinking powers of man. The problem for Theseus, as it was for Gide himself, was that of surpassing his adventures. The one moral error to be avoided at all cost was immobility and fixation.

His *Journal* indicates to some degree the amount of time Gide spent in observing the world in all its manifestations. His favorite diversion was the movies, which flattered his curiosity. The pleasure he derived from reading such an author as Simenon can doubtless be explained in this way. The *Journal* is the record of his endless observations, and it will always remain the best book about him, as well as one of the best books by him. His curiosity was in its deepest sense a way of life, an appetite encouraging him toward a way of life and toward an "attentiveness" (another of his favorite words) to every manifestation of life. Each time the doorbell rang in his apartment, he would have to interrupt his work or his rest in order to eavesdrop and discover who was calling and for what reason. "My curiosity," he would say, "is my downfall." (*Je suis si curieux, cela me perd.*)

Out of this avid curiosity about everything, whether it was the coloration of a leaf or the first book of a new author, his ideas were engendered. In the manifold forms of attentiveness with which his life seems to have been spent, there are no traces of real misanthropy, of radical pessimism, of class prejudice, of fatuous satisfaction with self. But on the other hand—and this may be an inevitable trait of those temperaments which are markedly attentive to others—there was little trace of gaiety or happiness. Gide's life-long practice of consigning to paper his most intimate thoughts and his confidences caused him to be quite reserved in oral speech. In conversation, he preferred to question rather than to answer. His power of listening was so eloquent that there was little need for his verbal reply. Many have testified to this phenomenon. From a nature that was dominated by curiosity, that accepted all contradictions, and from a will to freedom as well as a sense of destiny, his mind grew into one of the most critical of our age, a mind of infinite subtlety and unexpected boldness.

During the first few years following his death, Gide seemed to survive more steadfastly than his enemies, more than a Henri Massis, for example, would have predicted. When, at his death, a writer passes into literary history, he enters a chilly domain, another kind of death. Maurice Barrès, whom Gide never liked very much, had preceded him as a discussed influential writer, a "prince" for the young, but at his death seemed to disappear very quickly as a significant literary force.

In a rather truculent way, on several occasions during the last years of his life, Gide had clearly expressed his disbelief in personal immortality. To offset this, he had articulated belief in the immortality of his work and even of his personality as a writer. The first books about Gide to appear after his death added very little about the man and his work that was not already known. The reason for this repetitiveness was in the minute care with which Gide himself had studied his own personality and built it up in page after page of his own writing. Throughout his life he had scrutinized his acts and his thoughts with the attentiveness of a historian and a psychologist.

The man André Gide, rather than the writer, received most of the critical attention between 1951 and 1953. Almost first to appear was *Hommage à André Gide,* which was in reality a homage to the founder of *La Nouvelle Revue Française* and its guiding spirit. Section III, devoted to testimonials by several men who had known Gide personally (*André Gide tel que je l'ai vu*), has the greatest value in the volume. The article, for example, by Gide's son-in-law, Jean Lambert, is a deeply moving account of the writer's last illness and death.

Claude Mauriac, in a small book entitled *Conversation avec André Gide,* published in 1951, reproduced pages from his journal in which he related his meeting with Gide soon after the break with Communism, and the visit to the home of François Mauriac in Malagar in the spring of

1939. The younger Mauriac found a momentary master in Gide (this discovery came after his earlier disappointment with Jean Cocteau) and wrote in his journal a fervent and affectionate homage to the great man. In particular, he observed the differences between his father and Gide, in their roles of professional men of letters: Mauriac, as the official Catholic writer, and Gide, as the artist free from any permanent position or point of view.

In the same year of 1951, Roger Martin du Gard published his *Notes sur André Gide 1913–1951*, most of which he had shown to Gide. This is an account of a long, intimate friendship and has special value because of the wide divergence in temperament and talent between the two writers. Both men had learned to be frank with each other in their many discussions of personal problems and of literary matters. Implicit in these "notes" is Martin du Gard's belief in the importance and genius of Gide, but he gives, on the whole, an unflattering portrait of Gide the man. He emphasizes Gide's exaggerated interest in details about himself, his indiscretion on several occasions, his lack of remorse at the death of his wife. The notes would almost seem to be an effort to correct legends about Gide, for which Gide himself was largely responsible.

The year following Gide's death, a younger man, Pierre Herbart, gave what is probably the most devastating picture of the writer's character in *À la recherche d'André Gide*. Herbart had with Gide an extremely complicated relationship. He was the husband of the daughter of Mme Théo Van Rysselberghe (the good friend who occupied one half of Gide's apartment and was in charge of the entire apartment), Elizabeth Van Rysselberghe, who was the mother of Gide's daughter Catherine. Pierre Herbart was therefore the step-father of Catherine Gide. Herbart was a close friend and admirer of Gide, but his intimate relationship led him to doubt the famous "sincerity" of Gide. The book is written in a tone close to revindication and even slander. M. Herbart does not call upon the usual criticisms of Gide's character: his egoism and pride, his concern with dress and appearance. Rather he stresses as the key to the writer's complex character his desire to please everyone, his morbid fear of disappointing friends as well as people he hardly knew. There is a long list of moral defects given in Herbart's book that provide the portrait of a man excessively emotional and callous. Gide is made out to be the type of man essentially indifferent to everything outside of himself. His political instability is explained in this way, as well as his amorous adventures that were usually swiftly begun and swiftly terminated: love affairs (although they could hardly be called that) without an aftermath. In commenting on the theory Gide himself often defined as the dissociation of the heart and the senses, Herbart builds up his own theory concerning Gide's lack of any sense of responsibility, that seems to be equated with a lack of virility. Several points in Herbart's report can be contradicted by other witnesses: Gide's untrustworthiness, for example, his lack of discrimination in friendship, his insensibility to the rights of others, the absence of any real spirituality in his nature. The litany of grievances is very long. It is difficult to understand how Herbart, with these feelings, was able to bear the company of Gide. He tries to explain this by saying he was attracted by the charm of Gide, and then declares it is impossible to define this charm.

The testimonial of "Victor" has none of the value, nor the relative importance of Pierre Herbart's testimonial. In Gide's *Journal* of 1942–1949, part of which was written when he was living with friends in North Africa, he observes this young boy he calls Victor, a member of the family. The traits he describes, the sullenness, the vindictiveness, the total lack of charm, form a very unflattering portrait. Soon after Gide's death, the same Victor, using the pseudonym of François Derais, retaliated with a vicious book, *L'Envers du journal d'André Gide*. In his effort to demean Gide and make him out to be the corruptor of youth, "Victor" succeeds only in making himself appear obnoxious. His book has its place among the trivia of literary history.

No authentic cordiality ever existed between Gide and Jean Cocteau. The principal testimony of the younger man is in a book called *Gide vivant*, in which Cocteau in his usual aphoristic style enunciates several brilliant insights, some of which are as harsh as those in Herbart's book. He compares Gide's exhibitionistic traits to those of Rousseau. He stresses in particular Gide's incapacity to write poetry, and implies that this created jealousy on the part of Gide. The English biographer, George Painter, in his book on Gide, believes that Cocteau is portrayed in the character Passavant of *Les Faux-Monnayeurs*.

Two central books of 1953 were concerned with the man and the writer, one by Enid Starkie, who had been largely responsible for the honorary degree that Gide received in Oxford, the other by Justin O'Brien of Columbia University, who has made an admirable translation of the *Journal*. Two other books are more exclusively concerned with the work of Gide and the estimate of his value as an artist: one by Jean Hytier in 1945, before Gide's death, and one in 1953 by Germaine Brée which is a brilliant analysis and which accepts no legend, no traditional view without submitting it first to close scrutiny.

It is an impressive body of testimony that appeared during the first two years after Gide's death, a time when his complete works were put on the Index, despite the official recognition and consecration which the Nobel Prize had given his work. Several of these testimonial books did raise questions concerning the consequences of his ideas. Gide himself had always disclaimed any responsibility for his ideas and had often professed distaste for disciples. The literary figure whom Gide replaced in the eyes of the young, during the twenties and thirties especially, Maurice Barrès, had cultivated more than Gide the image of a Master. His fidelity toward the land and the dead was a fulfillment for Barrès, but for Gide such fidelity would be an obstacle. Both men renounced early in their careers the possibility of being poets, and developed a prose style characterized by a classical purity tinged with preciosity.

They had a few affinities but many divergences. In their social and political concern, for example, Barrès was more nationalistic and Gide international.

The first serious studies on Gide, those in particular by M. Hytier and Mlle Brée, would seem to agree that André Gide was not a great thinker. The human experience from which he drew was not wide. The literary experience itself, the expression in words of whatever happened to him, was the principal experience in Gide's life. He took from many writers what he needed to enrich his own experience: Goethe, Nietzsche, Dostoevski, Whitman, Blake, Montaigne. A good friend of Gide, who had observed him often during the last years of his life, and who, as friend and physician, saw more deeply than most, was Dr. Jean Delay. In speaking of Gide in 1950, when the writer was eighty-two years old, he pointed out the indefatigable curiosity and open-mindedness that normally would be found in a very young man: *Il a encore d'un jeune homme la disponibilité et la curiosité infatigable.*

Among all the semiofficial eulogies made about Gide at the time of his death, the one by François Mauriac was the most harshly critical and the most moving. Mauriac did not conceal the fact that he looked upon Gide as the most dangerous enemy to Christianity of his day. He summarized Gide's moral position as that of a man who had decided to break with Christianity and to oppose Christian morality. Most men choose not to choose, and on this point Mauriac seemed to prefer the position of a Gide to the absence of a position. A Luciferian spirit is more to be desired than a spirit of indifference. Mauriac claims that the work of Gide is one of the most significant of the age, and yet he sees Gide as belonging to that category of writers whose lives are more important than their works. He mentions as comparable examples in this respect Jean-Jacques Rousseau and Chateaubriand, and opposes them to such artists as Shakespeare and Racine for whom biographical knowledge is of no importance. Mauriac speaks of the extraordinary charm and sensitivity of Gide that had been felt by so many different temperaments. He dis-

approved of Albert Camus's comment on the happy death
of Gide, a death which in the words of Camus redeems to
some extent the creation (*qui rachete un peu la création*).
As a Christian, in speaking of his old friend and enemy,
Mauriac reminds his readers that no one knows the final
thoughts, the final state of mind of a man who is dying,
and he quotes the last words of the young priest of Bernanos (in *Le Journal d'un curé de campagne*): *Tout est
grâce*. The theology of such a sentence ("all is grace") is
irrefutable: everything in a man's life, error as well as
virtue, may become instrumental in his final salvation.

13

THE JOURNAL AND
THE AUTOBIOGRAPHY

In the summer of 1939, the publication in Paris of the Pléiade edition of Gide's *Journal* was the outstanding literary event of the year. The volume contained 1,332 pages of journal writing, carried on during the fifty-year span of 1889–1939. By 1939, many theses had already been sustained on the meaning and position of André Gide in our world: writer, aesthete, humanist, skeptic, prophet, individualist, sophist, hedonist, Christian. No contemporary writer had appeared in so many different roles to so many different critics. The publication of the *Journal* confirmed all theses. In 1944, Gide published in *L'Arche*, which was appearing in North Africa, new pages of his journal. They called forth a series of violent attacks on him, and in particular an unjust article by Louis Aragon who accused him of going over to the side of the enemy.

The exacting problem of what precise position the *Journal* occupies in the entire work of Gide is one of the most debatable. Was the *Journal* written on the margin of the major work, or is it one of the fervent monuments in the work itself, the greatest perhaps? These would be the two extreme points of view. Yet, many of Gide's books are cast in the form of a journal: Alissa's journal in *La Porte étroite;* Édouard's in *Les Faux-Monnayeurs;* the "journal de route" called *Amyntas*. The need of knowing and exploring himself so motivated the writing of Gide that the concept of "sincerity" has been endowed with a new dignity because of his work. He became the man in whom the modern world has taken on an exceptional and penetrating consciousness of its perils, its dreams, its destinies. Gide proposes in his *Journal* a familiarity that is unusual in the American or English tradition. He includes not only critical judgments on readings and the account of literary conversations, but everything that can be considered search or experience or adventure. His basic preoccupation is never informational. It resembles more a warning.

Among all the great autobiographical documents (Cellini's *Vita,* Rousseau's *Confessions,* Chateaubriand's *Memoires d'outre-tombe*), Gide's stands out by its freedom from pose and artificiality. He is determined to write the truth about himself as he sees it, even if that involves, as it surely does, a formulating of contradictions. Some passages glorify desire and self-indulgence, but others appear to be apologies for an impoverishment of self, for an ascetic regimen. Pages devoted to the ethic of pleasure and expansion are counteracted by others on the belief in effort and constriction. Whatever inclination is apparent toward the gratuitous act, it is easily offset by an overwhelming abundance of good common sense. If one day Gide preaches: "Be what you are," the next day he will demonstrate how impossible it is for us to know who we are.

In the principle of contradiction, Gide found a law and an abiding creed. He and Montaigne are the two French writers who deliberately practiced a vocation of honesty, who were courageous in their willingness to reveal the contradictions of their nature. The *Essays* and the *Journal* teach that a human destiny is always complex and always on the verge of splitting apart.

The biographical value of Gide's *Journal* is very great, but the work can be considered as an authentic document only on certain limited aspects of his life and personality. He is silent on some of the most important problems. The secret drama of Gide is not examined in the *Journal,* although it is faintly adumbrated there. To sense and reconstruct a more complete picture of Gide, a reading of all his works would be necessary. He is not best characterized by wisdom or by holiness. The sage and the saint are more coherent and more easily decipherable men than Gide was. Heroism, which can be claimed for Gide, is a far more complicated quality to define. It indeed involves attributes of wisdom and goodness, but it involves especially a knowledge of what this particular man is called upon to be heroic about. Heroism implies a starting point in fear and deficiency. More fervently and tenaciously than other themes, the writer's heroism emerges from the *Journal,* the will to write as a means of self-knowledge and as a means of constructing outside of oneself a work which by its nature is permanent, even if it reflects human nature in its changes and contradictions.

Gide's life seems to have been guided and dominated by the parable of the prodigal son, even if the parable usually appears in a revised and modified version. He was consciously fearful at all times of attaching himself, of allying himself with a center or a focus. He opposed Barrès and the doctrine of racial security, of sinking one's roots into the soil of the native province. As a writer, François Mauriac deepened his vocation in an ever-increasing knowledge and study of Les Landes and Bordeaux, but Gide was rebellious against geographical and intellectual alliances. He never sought certainty or assurance except in his attempt to embrace Communism. His mind was stirred and exhilarated best by search and curiosity. His *Immoralist* knows that the hardest of all goals is to remain free. To be able at any moment in one's life to give up what one is doing, to interrupt one's preoccupation and love, to detach oneself from the closest bonds, assumed for Gide the importance of a way of life. Happiness, when it comes easily and naturally, must be refused. The forces that educate us, from which we derive the maximum good, are those that go counter to our temperament and inclinations, those against which we revolt. Gide had a profound dislike for spiritual complacency, for anything that resembled spiritual assurance and comfort. His perpetual vow was to exceed himself, to admonish, reform and reeducate himself. In his journal entry of May 16, 1905, he wrote: "Do we ever really seek happiness? No, rather the free activity (*le libre jeu*) of whatever is newest in us."

The entire work of Gide, and especially his *Journal*, is the most calculated, among contemporary writings, to disturb the reader, to startle and excite him. It is addressed to our innate and often obscured tendencies toward revolt, dissatisfaction and desire. But the form of writing is so dexterously carried out, with such precision of vocabulary, such harmony and counterpoint of sentence structure and sentence variation, with such mastery of rhetorical resources, that the work, as well as stimulating thought in the reader, sets up in him at the same time an unusual sense of voluptuousness in language. The writing of Gide is always that confluence of adventure and order: adventure of thought and experience; order of form and expression. In them we are simultaneously freed from our habitual thought and drawn close to the exact form that so liberates us.

Despite the debt younger writers, in France especially, owed to Gide and the example of his *Journal*, on the publication of the first volume in 1939, he represented a uniqueness: a temperament, a life, a fervor, that were almost no longer possible in our world. Gide may well be the last instance of a certain kind of liberty, of leisure, of *largesse*. He was never without a sense of discipline, of inner spiritual discipline, but his development was slow and meticulous. During the early years of the *Journal*, he was able and free to concentrate on his craft and his personal evolution, whereas the writers of the following generation, Malraux and Sartre, for example, addressed their first works to a much larger public. Gide had little sense of the "tragic," that Malraux was to have, and little sense of the "absurd," so characteristic of Sartre. He was more purely the writer, above the limitations of the tragic writer or the philosopher. From today's perspective, his writing is a perpetual state of dialogue. His *Journal* is a mirror for his other books which themselves

bear many reflections of the *Journal*. No matter what
degree of sincerity is reached in the writing of a journal,
it remains always, by its very nature, a compensation for
life, and records the desire to live more deeply what was
only partially or impartially experienced, or even more
simply, to live what was never lived.

From his sixteenth year on, Gide kept a journal. As
early as his thirteenth year he was a fecund letter-writer.
The autobiography, the published *Journal* and the several
volumes of correspondence form in themselves a work of
such proportions that the student of Gide can easily ask
whether it has not devoured the creative work, or whether
the creative was not absorbed into the many works of an
autobiographical nature. These works seem to us today
exercises in self-analysis and stylistic exercises, documents
and even bulletins, made ready for early publication, on
Gide's spiritual and material well-being. They are indispensable for a complete understanding of the genesis
of the creative works, of the development of Gide's style,
of the type of moral problem at the basis of the creative
works. But they do not have the definitiveness and the
universality of the major works. In 1918, Gide himself
claimed that the one valid viewpoint from which to judge
his works is the aesthetic viewpoint. *Le point de vue
esthétique est le seul où il faille se placer pour parler de
mon œuvre sainement.*

His journal writing, despite its seeming massiveness
today, is, after all, fragmentary. He wrote in his journal
when he was solicited by events, and he often published
separate volumes of his *Journal* on the solicitation of
circumstances, as if to inform his public concerning himself and his reactions to events. There are resemblances
between Gide's *Journal* and Amiel's, for example, and
Jules Renard's, but Gide's is more pervasively personal.
He remains personal even in his opinions concerning
composers and writers. He strives, as vigorously as it is
possible for a writer to strive, to keep his journal a self-
examination. One part of him instinctively tries to make
it into a work of art. The struggle against this, in the

form of hesitations and scruples, is evident from beginning
to end. To write beautifully is not the goal of the journal.
Another temptation would be to make of it a storehouse
of articles begun and abandoned, of rough sketches for
books that were never written. A clear-minded recognition
of these two temptations explains why the journal remained a journal. On its pages Gide wrote out his confessions and thoughts with the knowledge that they were
to be revealed soon or eventually to the reading public
interested in his work.

He acknowledges that often, on rereading his journal,
he adds to it or makes changes for the sake of accuracy
and honesty, always for the purpose of helping to complete a self-portrait, even if the additions are contradictory. When Gide claims that the sanest point of view
from which to judge his work is the aesthetic, he would
seem to be denying the validity or the importance of his
Journal, as well as other works, such as *Voyage au Congo*
and his *Retour de l'U.R.S.S.* Some of his ablest critics
(and among them, especially, Mr. Lawrence Thomas in
André Gide, the Ethic of the Artist, of 1950), have compared him with such figures as Montaigne and Goethe,
because his study of man does exceed the bounds of
aesthetics. Avowedly Gide had wanted to stimulate his
younger readers, if they opened his *Journal*, as he had
been stimulated at their age when he read Stendhal's
Souvenirs d'égotisme.

The entry of October 9, 1927, has been quoted by many
interpreters of Gide in an effort to define the characteristics
of the basic moral dilemma in the writer, that dilemma
which seems to have generated the moral content of many
of his books, as well as the persistent moral preoccupations
that sustain so much of the *Journal*. Gide was at Cuverville and submerged with literary projects some of which
were related to his trip to the Congo. He had just returned from Paris where evidently he had seen a good
many friends who had interrupted his work and whose
presence in his life had instigated the thoughts forming
the passage that begins: *Ne pas poser devant soi-même.*

It is a frank and profound discussion on the problem of sincerity and on the influences that form a man's character. It begins with this advice, addressed to himself, not to pose before himself. This means, for Gide, not to affect virtues and good traits that one would like to have but does not have.

But then, through the principle of human perfectibility, a man may become what he wants to be. He may end by really experiencing the sentiment that first he only pretended to feel. Gide cites the two experiences of piety and love, of men who played the comedy of being devout or of being in love (*dévots ou amoureux*) and who literally became sincerely devout or loving. If a man distrusts his sentiments, they may never develop. When a man adopts the practice of virtue in order to correspond to the opinion which others have of him, this is dangerous as long as the practice remains at this stage in insincerity. But Gide argues for the change in sentiment and belief that is always taking place, and enunciates his famous phrase: *Je ne suis jamais; je deviens.* ("I never am; I am becoming.")

From the *Journal*, Gide's life seems uneventful and even monotonous. What is recorded are the changes taking place in his inner life, in his thoughts as observer and analyst. The *Journal* follows closely the literary evolution of Gide's art. At the beginning, the idealism of *André Walter* is everywhere on the pages, where the spirit of the Platonic dialogues and familiarity with the Gospels permeate the writing. Then gradually we read of Gide's more frequent contacts with the world, his meetings with other writers, references to his conversations and notations on more and more varied readings. His powers of discernment deepen and the breadth of his interests widens. The *Journal* does show the change in Gide's character from the idealistic esthete into, not the profound thinker, but the judicious observer of humanity and of the self. During the war years, 1914–1918, his activities with the Foyer Franco-Belge are recorded. He analyzes his feelings about the conflict and about

France. His patriotism is undeniable. The spiritual crisis of 1916, when Gide felt close to the figure of Christ, is recorded in the spiritual part of the *Journal: Numquid et tu*. During the years after the war, his resentment against religion grows stronger. His brief acceptance of Communism was an effort of self-renewal. As he grew older, he began to write more frankly, in a more resigned, speculative tone, of the anomalies in his character that the general public had attached to his name.

The book is both a personal confession of a long ethical anguish and a revelation, a document on the age in which it was written. More than in the autobiography, *Si le grain ne meurt*, which in parts seems almost embarrassingly indiscreet, the *Journal* narrates a combat, a spiritual struggle to exorcise a personal devil, to adjust to a world that often appears hostile or at least inhospitable, and to educate, to widen a Puritan conscience. The wealth Gide inherited from his family, and the freedom from responsibility which this afforded him helped to create an existence where self-introspection was an indulgence. Gide acknowledges this on several occasions. He was fearful of a certain type of French mind, the penetrating critical type of mind able to construct logical arguments. He learned very early that he was no opponent for such a mind, and that it was wiser to give up an argument. Léon Blum, whose place Gide took as literary critic on *La Revue Blanche*, had this type of mind, and it reduced Gide's to impotence!

The pattern of his life remained fairly stable in the large apartment at 1 bis rue Vaneau, that he shared with his good friend Mme Maria Van Rysselberghe, and her daughter and son-in-law, Elizabeth and Pierre Herbart. Through the late forties, until a few years before his death, Gide rose early in order to write for a few hours. From nine until noon he usually worked with a secretary. He napped after lunch, and often continued writing until teatime when he customarily received friends. Whenever he traveled, he kept with him the small notebook in which he wrote the *Journal*. And he worked anywhere—in trains and subways, in unfamiliar hotel rooms and on country roads. He usually retired early, about ten, but often was up a few hours later to drink milk or to smoke. Insomnia plagued him most of his life. The theme of *les nuits blanches* is constant in the *Journal*.

The second volume in the Pléiade edition of Gide's memoirs, *Journal 1939–1949,* was published posthumously in 1954. It completes the first volume and includes several small works that are closely related to the *Journal: Si le grain ne meurt,* notably, which is the preface to the *Journal,* the book in which Gide describes his childhood and youth, the years before he began keeping a journal. The publication includes also the epilogue to the *Journal:* the journal of the last months of his life, dedicated to his daughter Catherine Lambert, and which he calls: *Ainsi soit-il, ou Les Jeux sont faits.* The Pléiade volume judiciously includes also the books of direct observation that replaced the *Journal* at various moments in Gide's life: *Le Voyage au Congo, Le Retour du Tchad, Souvenirs de la cour d'assises* and *Feuillets d'automne.* And finally, the posthumous book on Madeleine Gide: *Et nunc manet in te,* has its place as an indispensable adjunct to the *Journal.*

As the sequence to the major work, the *Journal 1939–1949* reveals similarities and developments. There are many pages of an anecdotal historical interest, especially those on which Gide describes his life in Tunis and Algiers at the time of the debarkation of the Allied Forces from North Africa. But in his notes even on the war, and on his reactions to the postwar world, the *Journal* continues to accumulate personal testimonials and confessions. There is a visible effort on the part of the aging writer to enlarge the scope of the intimate truths he wants to communicate. There are evidences of weariness, of a feeling that there is no longer any need for this striving, because the positions that the world was already calling "Gidian" were firmly established. But the idea that had become stabilized was the right never to become fixed in one pattern of life or belief, the regret to continue the search for the self and the search for pleasure.

In the journal of the last ten years, one reads not repetition exactly, but habits of thought Gide has already exposed, the rehearsal of doctrinal recipes with which his readers had become familiar. And from time to time one is inclined to wonder whether the real journal is no longer being kept. The explorer of the self now has the right to look back and to make an estimate of what has been gained, to recall the habits that have led him to the position of the moment. The prudent bourgeois background of Gide's life is more visible, and its values are more often referred to. When he is residing in Cuverville, he seems almost to be leading the country existence of a proprietor. When he is in his Paris apartment, he seems always to be receiving the famous writers of his own age and the younger men who approach him with the respect due a master. The story of Gide's innumerable relationships will one day be written, and an estimate made of the role in his life of such men as Rilke, Valéry, Charles Du Bos, Schlumberger, Ghéon, Valery Larbaud, Julien Green and Roger Martin du Gard. The influence of such writers on Gide's books is slight, and possibly nonexistent. But their work and their position in the literary world are judged by Gide almost exclusively from an aesthetic viewpoint in the *Journal*. When he judges himself, it is as a moralist.

Gide was already middle-aged when he wrote his autobiography. In it he speaks only of his childhood and early manhood, and interrupts the story just before his marriage. The writing of this book is far different from that of his memoirs, because he is trying to remember what he was and what he did, and he is fully aware that no matter how authentic a picture he is drawing, it will be incomplete. By the very nature of the book, it is selective, and every trait analyzed in it is more complicated than the analysis would indicate.

Notwithstanding the radical differences in manner of writing between the autobiography and the memoirs, some of the ideas and hypotheses in *Si le grain ne meurt* are important for an understanding of Gide the memorial-

ist in his *Journal*. He explains, for example, the need to
write, the compulsion to create a work of art, as the
means by which he may harmonize the two conflicting
elements in his background: Normandy and the Midi, the
two religions, the two families. The darker, more sullen,
more evilly motivated aspects of Gide's nature are un-
remittingly explored in *Si le grain*. He scrutinizes himself
to such a degree that at times his self-criticism would appear to be a form of narcissism. Jean Delay in his
thorough analysis of the autobiography finds in it countless
signs and announcements of a literary destiny. Even in
the boy's duplicity, in his pretended illnesses for example,
Dr. Delay finds a hypocrisy he considers implicit in art.
More than Gide himself, Delay stresses in the writer's
background the lack of compatibility between his father's
joviality of disposition and his mother's severity. These
characteristics and family dramas, as well as Gide's capacity for an absorption in nature, contribute to the
isolation of his way of life and the traits of the artist's temperament.

The personal characteristics of the younger Gide, exposed in *Si le grain ne meurt*, remain throughout his life
and deepen. His youth was not a transitory period that
can be limited by dates. The major traits are there already and will develop in time into dramas: his exalted
feelings for Madeleine Rondeaux, his insatiable desire for
experience, his love for languages, his capacity for sympathy and understanding, his interest in plants and
insects, his intimate knowledge of the Gospels and his
meditations on the figure of Christ. Gide's simple and
sometimes sophistical reading of the Bible accounts not
only for his preoccupation with religion but also for the
trace of unctuousness in his nature.

Si le grain is a major text on Gide's attentiveness, on
the concentration he was able to direct toward whatever
was happening to him. This attitude, more permanent
than others in his character, was able to convert even
the slightest experience into something significant and
revelatory. Extremes moved him equally, and he refused

to look upon them as contradictory. If one moment would be an expression of pride, the next might well be one of humility. If at one moment he might yearn for social and artistic recognition, in the next he might be overcome by a desire for solitude. Gide learned early to accept the bewildering truth that an act of sincerity on his part might be instigated by the contradictions of his nature. The very act of publishing *Si le grain* was undoubtedly prompted by a love for truth.

The mysterious and suggestive words of the book's title, taken from the Gospel, "Unless the seed die," testify, in elliptical form, to the most permanent dogma in Gide's creed: the necessity for one experience to die, so that another experience may be born. Life is a series of deaths, the disappearance of values that no longer serve. In the image of wheat, the grain itself has to die and disappear in order to reappear as fruit. The desert, in its North African setting, had been many times celebrated in Gide's writing, but in *Si le grain*, it is presented in its full value, as the richest symbol of Gide's life. The desert is, first, the site of a dispossession. Its bareness and monotony stand for the principle of impoverishment, for a needed separation from all that has become unnecessary in a life. It is evocative also of demonism and prophecy. The first visit to Algeria was his first apostasy, the first experience with the Unknown in a setting of nature and with the first indulgence in his aberration.

The experience with the exotic and the forbidden is the passage for Gide from one kind of life to another, and it is closely associated with his writer's creed. A significant work is the result of an effort to move beyond what has become a stationary position and a meaningless experience. The narrative of *Si le grain ne meurt*, in the North African episode, is clearly an effort on Gide's part to separate himself from the domination of his mother. It transcribes his determination to define himself not in terms of the familiar but to discover a new self in a new alliance with what is opposite to his nature and background.

The *Journal* gives the writer a more intense personality

than *Si le grain ne meurt*. But from the two types of writing, memoirs and autobiography, we learn that Gide's absorption in the world was never total. His real commitment was to the work of the artist in him. The picture of the timid young Huguenot of the first part of *Si le grain* is in contrast to the far less timid immoralist of the second part, but the man engaged in writing about his childhood and youth is still another figure living the artist's existence on the margin of the world.

14

GIDE'S MARRIAGE

André Gide claimed that the central drama of his existence was his love for his wife, a drama which a few months after his death was revealed in his own words in *Et nunc manet in te.* This small volume helps to complete the portrait of Gide, of the man who in our century had perhaps the deepest faculty for comprehension, the greatest lucidity in understanding ideas different from his own. During the year following his death there seemed to be more references made daily in Paris to *Et nunc* than to any other book. The picture of Gide that it gave was already, to some degree, in *L'Immoraliste,* in the character Michel, who causes the death of his wife Marceline but who also exalts her. The same man is also in Jérôme, of *La Porte étroite,* who exalts Alissa and who at the same time experiences the futility of such an exaltation.

Madeleine Rondeaux was born in 1867 and was therefore two years older than her cousin André Gide. They grew up together. Despite the deep affection that united them, both families were surprised when they announced the engagement. They were married after Gide's first visit to Algeria. Madeleine accompanied him there on his second trip. In his *Journal* Gide refers to her as Emmanuèle or as Em. Not until the posthumous work does he call her by her real name. The title is a hemistich from a line of Virgil concerning the lost Eurydice: "And now she remains in you." The work is an attempt to describe the personal drama of Gide's marriage, a drama which throughout his life was constant, secret, central. The love existing between a man and woman was replaced by a sense of purity, by an extraordinary worship. "The spiritual force of my love," Gide writes, "prevented any carnal desire." *Les Cahiers d'André Walter,* written before his marriage, analyzes this purely idealistic approach to woman.

No explanation was ever made between Gide and his wife. She seldom left the Normandy country house at Cuverville where Gide's visits became increasingly infrequent. She was pious, meticulous in the running of the large house, and devoted to the care of the poor of the countryside. Between husband and wife, the degree of silence grew as the years passed. Madeleine read few of his books, although during the first part of his career, she was an admirable critic and guide. Each of his thoughts, Gide has stated, developed through some relationship with her, because of her. The best part of his nature remained in constant communion with her. The need of expressing himself sincerely originated in the image he had of her character. Gide never rid himself of remorse for having falsified her destiny of woman. In November, 1918, at a moment of desperate sorrow over his failure to remain with her, she burned all his early letters. They were, according to Gide, his best letters, the fundamental document on his formative years, the description of his love for Madeleine. He never understood how she could have been responsible for the literary and personal loss which their destruction represented.

Gide's love for his wife dominated his entire life, but it never suppressed any part of his nature. Rather it added the element of struggle. Just at the time (1921–1922) when his love for Madeleine seemed unique in his life, he felt that she no longer believed in it, and preferred to know nothing about his sentiments. In preparing the 1939 publication of his *Journal,* Gide realized that all the deliberate omissions about his wife gave an incoherent and mutilated picture of himself. The posthumous volume remedied this in showing the inevitable drama of such a marriage and the radical differences of temperament in husband and wife. Madeleine Gide appears modest and retiring, traditionalist in taste, austere in her way of living. André Gide is practically the opposite: evasive and always capable of literally disappearing, docile to every event, incapable of refusing any kind of solicitation.

This first posthumous book on Gide contains the most tragic pages he ever wrote. On the surface, the book is an atonement, and in keeping with an atonement, Gide's candor is pitiless and devastating. He makes himself out to be, after a long period of suffering, the destroyer of the woman he married.

His marriage was an illustration of his doctrine of dissociation of love from desire. Madeleine lived for forty-three years in almost total seclusion in Cuverville. At her death, in 1938, Gide was not with her. *Et nunc manet in te* is composed of pages written soon after her death, and of fragments omitted from the *Journal*. It was privately printed in 1947, in an edition of thirteen copies. As always with Gide, a moral issue is implicit in this book: since he knew his own nature, was it right for him to impose a marriage relationship on Madeleine Rondeaux? Was it her choice as well as his? What we do know is that there was no discussion between them on this marital problem: *entre nous, jamais une explication ne fut tentée.*

Gide does not conceal the remorse he felt at having falsified his wife's destiny. She wanted a child, and yet another woman bore his child. Madeleine Gide, living quietly in Cuverville, provided the intermittent stability and peacefulness that he needed. He was throughout his life the prodigal son who always returned home. Gide acknowledges that his art owes more to Madeleine than to anyone else. The best of himself was in her. This important testimonial is stated several times, and in close association with it, the feeling that the situation was understood and accepted by Madeleine, who never complained, or rather who rebelled only once when, in 1918, she felt herself abandoned by her husband, and destroyed all the letters she had received from him. This loss was not only a sorrow for him, it was a frustration because of the value he attached to those letters: *Peut-être n'y eut-il jamais plus belle correspondance.*

He clamored uselessly and pitilessly for the restoration

of the letters, and has been judged severely by both friends and enemies for this seemingly selfish reaction. Even in the writing of such personal letters, which, according to Gide, gave the truest picture of himself, especially of his formative years, he was a literary artist, and he knew the value of such testimonials for the complete picture that ultimately the world was to have of him. There is no reason to doubt that his love for Madeleine was sincere, and there is no reason to doubt that his remorse was sincere in writing *Et nunc manet in te*. If one raises the question of whether a literary artist can be sincere, one can raise the same question about any man. Gide, more honestly than most, recorded over and over again his suspicion concerning the honesty of any sentiment as soon as the sentiment can be of any service.

The first critical commentary on *Et nunc* was on the whole so hostile, so outraged, that one of the closest friends of Gide and his wife, and a highly esteemed writer, Jean Schlumberger, published a short book on the subject: *Madeleine et André Gide*. The book was written because of Schlumberger's affection for both Madeleine and André, and because of his desire to rectify both the portrait Gide himself gives of his wife and the exaggerated interpretation of this portrait. When Madeleine burned Gide's letters in 1918, she did not destroy her own, and she left a *journal intime*, kept from January, 1891, to July, 1892, prior to her marriage, which was an important document for Schlumberger's book. His thesis is quite simple. He believes that Gide's marriage was successful. It was not in any way a mistake. In spite of Madeleine's desire for children, she was content with an etherealized love. It is true that Gide left her many times, but she had no physical strength that would have permitted her to accompany him on his voyages. She always looked upon it as a privilege to be a witness in such a life as Gide's.

She was deeply upset only once when, in 1918, her husband left for England with Marc Allégret. Madeleine was a friend of the young man's parents, and she had helped to bring about this friendship. Gide had claimed that he was stagnating in Cuverville. She was aware of the affection Gide felt for Allégret, and she realized also that she was being replaced in Paris by the Van Rysselberghes, Gide's adopted family. It is impossible to measure the degree to which Gide was aware of the sadism in his own nature. His attitude toward his mother had been markedly ambivalent, and in his marriage with Madeleine, he reversed the role he had played with his mother and became the dominant figure, the man free to come and go as he wished.

A second, very specific testimonial, closely allied with Schlumberger's, came from Pierre de Lanux. In 1908, when Pierre de Lanux was twenty, he was engaged by Gide as his secretary, and for four years lived with Madeleine and André Gide. (Pierre de Lanux was the grandson of Marc de Lanux, Gide's old music teacher.) The young man entered the service of Gide just at the time he was revising and completing *La Porte étroite*. Gide and Madeleine had been married for fifteen years, and gave every evidence to their young friend that they were united in deep affection and mutual esteem. Pierre de Lanux, in the few pages he devoted to this marriage, wanted to correct what seemed to him the excessive dramatizations of *Et nunc manet in te* and certain errors of fact and interpretation. He lived with the Gides between 1907 and 1912, and witnessed a happy marriage despite an absence of shared sexual life, despite the fairly frequent departures of Gide and the home-loving reserved nature of Madeleine.

Pierre de Lanux was unquestionably a very sympathetic observer who admired both husband and wife. In the marriage, Gide's confidence in his wife seemed limitless, and her constant solicitude, of an almost maternal nature, was cherished by her companion. Pierre de Lanux believed that the unusual pattern of this love had been accepted by Madeleine. They both seemed to believe that a total absence of sexual life was far less cruel than another type based on false hope. Up until 1917, Gide's infidelities were brief, clandestine and of little importance. Madeleine realized in 1918 that the peaceful happiness she had known in her marriage was threatened, and the burning of the letters was an indirect suicide. It took time to repair the damage and to recover what had been lost.

Jean Schlumberger's book undertakes to describe this reparation and this restitution. He has written an unusual spiritual biography, the story of a woman's soul attached to a creature who combined nobility with characteristics that some interpreters will not hesitate to define as Luciferian. Madeleine's soul reached a point of spiritual perfection that is probably never reached by a man. She lived a life in accord with the highest Protestant morality, on the confines of Catholicism to which she was unquestionably drawn in the latter years of her life. The deep sincerity of her thoughts and actions she certainly owed to her Protestant background. By contrast with hers, Gide's traits appear more than ever subtle and diverse, wavering with the skill of disguise. Madeleine knew better than anyone else the many reasons for admiring and loving André Gide.

The letters Gide wrote to Madeleine, and which he addressed at the same time to a future public, completed the portrait of himself he wished to leave. No matter what his personal relationship was with others, he remained at all times primarily the writer. His anguish over the loss of his letters was far more literary than personal, and despite the serious quarrel and momentary estrangement caused by this act of Madeleine, the story of Gide's marriage was more happy than unhappy. His genius was always manifest in his skill in bringing up to the surface, in revealing his most intimate thoughts. This skill he was able to practice on others, including Madeleine Gide. His love for her was the great love of his life. This fact is indispensable in any study of Gide because his literary work gravitated around her. This love, this devotion, because of the particular circumstances of Gide's nature and life, was his secret, and the countless commentators who have tried to understand and analyze it have reached only approximations to truth.

Gide's portrait of Alissa in *La Porte étroite* exposed to

the eyes of the curious what would seem to be the story of his marriage. This was the first of his books that Madeleine never spoke of to her husband. *Elle ne m'a jamais rien dit de mon livre.* In her letters before *La Porte étroite,* she had praised *Lettres à Angèle* and *Philoctète,* and she helped, later, to recopy the manuscript of *Les Caves du Vatican.* Certain traits and certain problems of Alissa were close to the biography of Madeleine Rondeaux. It is understandable, with her reserve and modesty, that it was difficult for her to speak of the book.

The year of 1918 was critical in every sense in the marital life of Madeleine and André Gide. Several years were necessary for a new establishment of harmony between them. But this harmony was brought back into their lives. Gide's demands for more and more freedom were granted, and Madeleine rediscovered the full force of her devotion and love. In *Et nunc* Gide comments on this rejuvenation of their marriage ties: *une harmonie nouvelle, comme surnaturelle ou surhumaine, se reforma.* They had entered upon another long period of peaceful understanding. There is a notation in a letter of October, 1928, where Madeleine states that her marriage was not an error. A few years after this, she worried over Gide's attraction to Communism, and the new kind of life he began leading with members of the party. It seemed to her a contradiction of all of her husband's most cherished beliefs. When he asked her not to worry, she replied that to cease worrying would be equivalent to loving him less: *Ne plus m'inquiéter, me demandes-tu! Ce serait ne plus t'aimer autant* (October 19, 1932). His little book on his disillusionment with the Soviet Union (*Retour de l'U.R.S.S.*) was, in a way, a homage to Madeleine's clairvoyance and understanding.

Even as a very young girl, Madeleine Rondeaux had deplored the dryness of the Protestant liturgy. She envied Catholicism its Mass and the richness of its symbols. Gide himself had little interest in such matters, and of course violently rejected the idea of a spiritual director. Each time one of his friends announced his conversion,

Ghéon, Copeau and Du Bos, in particular, Gide expressed great astonishment, and seemed convinced that the Church was stealing his friends from him. Catholicism came to mean for Gide the abdication of a man's intelligence. But Madeleine, especially during the last ten years of her life, showed an ever-increasing sympathy with the spirit of Catholicism. Fundamentally she remained Protestant in her understanding and practice of the Christian faith. The Catholic dogmas concerning the Virgin, the saints and miracles were unacceptable to her. But Gide worried about her thoughts on Catholicism and about the possibility of her conversion. In a 1926 entry of his *Journal,* he writes of the slow progress of Catholicism in her soul. Each time he returns to her, he finds new evidences of sympathy and interest, aspects of her conscience changed by what he considers Catholic influences.

When he was leaving for Senegal in 1938 (it was the year of Madeleine's death), she wrote him a long letter in order to allay his fears, and said quite explicitly that her love for him would always keep her from joining the Catholic Church. He was deeply touched by the homage of this letter, and had copies made of it to show to his friends.

The marriage of André and Madeleine Gide, despite the nature and the circumstances of Gide's life, demonstrates a long attachment, on the part of both, whose forcefulness and depth have been doubted by many. Their marriage is the story of a long passion, of a triumph, in spite of Gide's sexual anomaly and Madeleine's natural timidity. The documentation assembled by Jean Schlumberger permits this interpretation. The term used by Jean Delay in his analysis of Gide's youth—angelism—is beyond doubt one of the clues to the passion André and Madeleine felt for each other. Madeleine always clung to the purity of her innermost feelings, and led a life of the spirit. In their marriage the two cousins were brother and sister. For both of them, marriage sustained their childhood association. Gide's marriage was an application of the theory he himself expressed concerning the dissociation of sensual pleasure and the love he wished to keep pure. In a letter he once wrote to Roger Martin du Gard, Gide claimed that his love for his wife was comparable to none other: *l'amour que j'ai pour ma femme n'est comparable à aucun autre.*

Gide's marriage and his love for Madeleine are constantly examined or referred to throughout Jean Delay's *La Jeunesse d'André Gide.* The eminent psychiatrist calls his study an essay in "psychobiology," and defines his method as "parallel studies of the events in Gide's life, the evolution of his psychology and the genesis of his literary works."

Jean Delay was a close personal friend of Gide during the last years of the writer's life. At many points in his argument, he draws on this intimacy, on conversations with Gide he remembered and on which he had taken notes. He was impelled to undertake this long meticulous work—the study of Gide's life that culminates with his marriage—because of his conviction that all the important elements of a man's life and temperament are decided upon and fixed at a very early age. Gide himself shared this conviction. It is apparent in his autobiography where he tried to remember and interpret all the data of his own youth, and make out of them a coherent, recognizable character study. One of the principal methods followed by Delay in his analysis is the verification of *Si le grain ne meurt,* the correcting of points on which Gide was inexact, and the completing of the self-portrait thanks to many additional documents not used by Gide.

Among these documents, the most important and the most widely used by Delay are Gide's letters to his mother which thus far have not been published. The extracts given by Delay, especially in the second volume of the work, would indicate the great value of making this correspondence available one day. Jean Delay's scrupulosity of a scientist is visible in the way he uses this vast documentation. The childhood and youth of no other writer has been so meticulously analyzed and interpreted.

Before the publication of this monumental study, André

Gide was usually looked upon as the contemporary author who had taken the greatest care to divulge the facts of his existence, the details of his autobiography, his way of living, his thoughts and especially his contradictory thoughts. The most interesting discovery made by Delay, in his long investigation, is in his analysis of the first two books of Gide, in which he comes upon a more accurate picture of the young man than can be made out from the personal writings: journals and letters. The real writer speaks more directly about himself when he disguises himself in a character. Imaginative works of writing are more revelatory than direct forms used for self-revelation. The rigorous examination to which Dr. Delay submits *Si le grain ne meurt* is an admirable justification of this theory. Each of the two volumes of *La Jeunesse d'André Gide* bears a title: "André Gide avant *André Walter, 1869–1890*" and *"D'André Walter à* André Gide *1890–1895."* From the viewpoint of literary criticism and in the analysis of Gide's marriage, the second is more important than the first.

The principal thesis of Gide's autobiography was his effort to explain the drama of his life as the imposition of traditional morality on his nature. He emphasized the physical needs of his nature and claimed that he too had the right to happiness on his own terms. Jean Delay, in *The Youth of André Gide,* develops the opposite thesis. The drama of Gide's life, he believes, was essentially spiritual. The writer's dominant motivation was not toward the satisfaction of the senses, but it was a spiritual ambition, a drama taking place in his soul. The key word which Delay uses in order to designate this drama is "angelism."

Madeleine Rondeaux is the purest angelic figure in Gide's life. His first book, *André Walter,* is offered to his cousin as a proposal of marriage. It is also the picture of the kind of marriage which André and Madeleine were to know, an unconsummated marriage in the sexual sense, but one founded on a deep spiritual love and devotion. The "angelism" of this love is a major theme in Delay's

book. André Walter is the chaste fiancé who sings of
Emmanuèle as being his "one" love and of his presenti-
ment that his love will be devoid of carnality.

Jean Delay believes that Gide imaginatively and unconsciously established an identification between his
cousin Madeleine and his mother. The image of the cousin
and the bride was more idealistic, far more passive than
the stern maternal image. Before and after her marriage,
Madeleine incarnated virtue for Gide. This image, this
belief in an etherealized, spiritualized love was far more
real, according to the investigation of Delay, than any
physiological incapacity in Gide. The psychologist concludes that the sexual inhibitions Gide suffered from, or
believed he suffered from, could have been cured. Their
causes were not physical but moral. On this point, central
for his thesis, Delay indicates a clearer dichotomy between the physical and the moral in a human being than
perhaps other psychologists would be willing to grant.

Certain crucial sentences of Gide, quoted by Delay,
attach the sexual defeat in Gide's life to his religious
defeat. The loss of his faith—that is, the loss of his
salvation—which at one time Gide would have defined as
damnation, coincided with the failure of his marriage in
its conjugal sense. "I could have won with her," he seems
to be saying in such a phrase as: *La partie est perdue,
que je ne pouvais gagner qu'avec elle.*

15

GIDE AND CATHOLICISM

For an outsider trying to understand French civilization, one of the most puzzling paradoxes is the role of Catholicism. France is fundamentally a Catholic country, and yet the temperament of the French Catholic seems to be predominantly anticlerical. Gide came from the very small minority of French Protestants, but whenever the religious issue was raised in his life and work, it was in relationship to Catholicism. No matter what the philosophical viewpoint of the French writer is, it tends to be defined in terms of its closeness to or its distance from Catholic thought. This is as true of Rabelais's humanism, of Montaigne's skepticism, of Voltaire's deism, of Baudelaire's satanism, as it is in the twentieth century in the writings of André Gide and Jean-Paul Sartre when they analyze the concept of man's freedom.

No aspect of Gide's sensibility is more subtle and more difficult to comprehend than his sensibility to religious values. And no aspect is more important. His life and his work were marked by Christianity. The deepest and the most tenacious influence in his life was the figure and the example of Christ in the Gospels. At times in his career Gide must have been irritated by the number of militant Catholics, among his friends and enemies, who seemed to be laying siege to his soul, to be ever watchful for the slightest inclination on his part toward orthodoxy. He must have been irritated when he was not touched or amused by the expectant waiting, by the prayerful letters he received, by the close examination given by Catholics to every text he published. Gide's kind of writing was so strongly influenced by the Gospels, the texts he knew the most intimately, that by their simplicity they invited

a simple interpretation. But formal lucidity in the art of
writing is no preserver of a unique meaning.

It would be impossible to estimate the pleasure, even
the malicious pleasure, that Gide derived from partici-
pating in this game of Catholic exegesis, and of helping
to sustain the debate by offering answers that were
simultaneously negative and affirmative. He accepted
their persistence and their deep concern. Other rebels,
other nonbelievers in the world of letters—a Giraudoux,
for example—were never pursued and solicited in the
same way. But the reasons are not obscure on this point.
Gide had been a believer, a devout believer, and he was
always to some degree a religious writer. The religious
experience and belief in God were the starting point for
Gide's thought. Even when he had lost all belief in Christian dogma, he retained a love for Holy Scripture of which
he had a more intimate knowledge than any other contemporary French writer, with the exception of Claudel.

By his early twenties, he had cut himself off from any
adherence to Calvinism and from his Huguenot background. But from that time on, he betrayed an almost
emotional concern over a series of successive conversions:
Claudel, Jammes, Dupouey, Ghéon, Copeau, Du Bos,
Julien Green. Those who were most concerned about
Gide's spiritual health and about the moral effect his
writings might have on readers, were Catholics. He never
completely abandoned this problem, although during the
last years of his life he seemed to have reached an inner
state of peace in which the religious problem no longer
counted. The motives for his long involvement with
Christianity are complex. The Bible was always a source
of spiritual sustenance. He enjoyed discussion of religious
themes, and carried on with some of the eminent religious
minds of his age a subtle debate which it was more important for him to continue than to win. He freely appropriated Gospel passages in order to justify his own
moral views, and was often shocked when he was accused
of exploiting a passage for his own purposes.

On the publication of *Le Retour de l'enfant prodigue,*

Mauriac wrote an article on the work, in which he called it a "masterpiece of misinterpretation" (*un chef-d'œuvre de gauchissement.*) He used, in fact, the word "sacrilegious" (*sacrilège*), and Gide wrote to him—it was his first letter to Mauriac—in April, 1912, in order to state his displeasure with this accusation. Mauriac fully realized the seriousness of Gide's problem and the gravity with which he used Bible references. Whereas the majority of Christians never progress spiritually beyond their catechism lessons, Gide throughout much of his life meditated on the figure of Christ and the meaning of His words. If Gide did finally renounce any belief in God, he did so in full awareness of what he was doing, and in full knowledge that only God—if there be a God—can judge such an act.

In the scattered brief articles Mauriac has devoted to Gide over many years, and in the many references to Gide in Mauriac's books on other subjects, he has emphasized one theory above all. He believes that Gide's sexual concupiscence is at the heart of his spiritual drama. He believes that Gide's endless religious vacillations and preoccupations with Scripture represent an effort on his part, and not always a conscious effort, to legitimize his desires. This would be the clue to the contradictory aspirations of Gide's nature, that Mauriac was one of the first to describe as rich and profound. Christ never spoke of abnormal desires, but He condemned all concupiscence, no matter what the object of concupiscence. In Gide's case, in Gide's nature, Mauriac especially feared the act of defiance. On many occasions he tried to point out to Gide that Catholics did not feel themselves less sinful than Gide. He often quoted, before Gide had the chance to use it, the sentence from Saint John: "Our Lord came not to judge men but to save them." He realized, and other Catholic friends, who were much closer to Gide than Mauriac, also realized that their agitation and concern were usually awkward, ill-timed, lacking in profound understanding.

More than any other public event in Gide's life, and

more than the subtly phrased sentences of his books, his brief adherence to Communism in the middle thirties bewildered his religious friends and opponents. *L'Union pour la Verité*, a group of liberal intellectuals in Paris, held a meeting for the purpose of questioning Gide about his stand on Communism. The meeting hall held only two hundred people but they were largely intellectuals and professional men of letters. At one end of the table Gide was seated between his two friends Ramon Fernandez and Jean Schlumberger. On entering the hall Gide had whispered to Schlumberger, "I am sure I am going to flunk this exam." (*Je suis sûr d'être recalé.*) His adversaries, seated opposite him, were eminent and powerful: Henri Massis (whose *Jugements* had been the most virulent published attacks thus far), Mauriac, Gabriel Marcel, Jean Guéhenno, Jacques Maritain, and two younger men: Thierry Maulnier and Denis de Rougemont.

The announced subject of the debate was *Gide et son influence*, but the unannounced subject could easily have been *Gide et le catholicisme*. The exposé delivered by Massis was unequivocal. He first defined the Gidian man as the one who is formed by experience and who tries then to justify himself. With this type, Massis contrasted the classical man who is formed by dogma and who tries to develop himself in terms of dogma. Much of the exposé of Gabriel Marcel was an analysis of the deep dissatisfactions of Gide. Marcel found no trace of romanticism in these dissatisfactions, but rather an inexorable sincerity. The principal point of Marcel's thesis was that Gide's search for truth is fundamentally very different from a search for certainty.

Ostensibly, Communism was at the center of the problem as it was elaborated on by each speaker. Thierry Maulnier phrased the problem thus: "How can Gide adapt his form of humanism to the philosophy of the Soviet Union?" Maritain, who had asked to be excused from making one of the formal statements, improvised a charitable and nobly phrased homage to Gide, when he explained Gide's adherence to Communism as a sacrifice of a large part of his temperament, as an offering to his new faith. This was the most favorable comment on the reproach that most of the speakers made to Gide: his well-established negativism and vacillation that had been discussed for forty years, and this, his one affirmation, coming at the end of such a long period, in favor of Communism.

At approximately the same time when this meeting of *L'Union pour la Verité* was being held, a young man of Jewish birth, Jacques Lévy, was studying *Les Faux-Monnayeurs* which a few years later led him to enter the Catholic Church. Jacques Lévy was born in Paris in 1914 and was killed in Auschwitz in 1945. Because of bad health, he had to interrupt his studies at the École Normale Supérieure. He suffered from excessive scrupulosity, and from a persistent habit of self-accusation. In letters to his mother, of June, 1934, he speaks of finding a religious faith, and allies this faith with his study of *Les Faux-Monnayeurs*. He believed he had found in Gide's novel the clue to Gide's refusal to be converted. Posthumously his letters and journal were published in Grenoble and the volume included his study of *Les Faux-Monnayeurs*.

Explicitly Jacques Lévy states that his reading of *Les Faux-Monnayeurs* was the major event of his life and that his conversion to Catholicism dates from that study. This testimonial has greater significance than might appear at first, because Gide, in a letter to Lévy, acknowledged the clues analyzed as being accurate: *je donne mon assentiment total à ce que vous avancez*. The story of *Les Faux-Monnayeurs* is, for Jacques Lévy, the story of Gide's conscience. The characters are forces carrying on a dialogue within the writer's conscience. The action of the novel is the assault made on a soul by grace. Gide finally refused to listen to this spiritual force in order to give himself over more totally to the writing of his work. In a listing of fifty-one essential themes, Jacques Lévy offers a kind of psychoanalysis of *Les Faux-Monnayeurs*. He interprets, for example, the pregnancy of Laura as the expression on the part of Gide of the anxious expectancy of some new experience. He interprets the suicide of the boy Boris as the spiritual death of Gide himself, as the sign of a renunciation of conversion. This spiritual failure of Gide helped one of his readers to triumph in a religious sense. Jacques Lévy was baptized in 1942, two years prior to his arrest, and three years prior to his death.

By far the most moving text related to Gide's religious problem and to his relationship with Catholicism is the correspondence exchanged between himself and Claudel. This volume of letters, published when both men were over eighty, is an extraordinary dialogue, whose importance goes far beyond the immediate subject matter of the letters. At the time of the publication, in 1949, Gide and Claudel were "representative men" in France and Europe. The spiritual duel these letters carry on was implacable and at times bitter. The serene stable faith of Claudel breaks out on every page of his letters. Even when angry, he is speaking from an inner peace and joy. Gide's disquiet and restlessness are never appeased. He protects them with an almost masochistic or voluptuous care. Claudel's search had been for joy in an absolute sense, and he had found it. This joy dictates to him all the arguments he uses to chastise and help Gide. Gide's search had been for a kind of happiness that seemed to be composed of forms of meager pleasure, and for intellectual satisfaction. In this debate, the opponents were really opposite, and each, in his own way, was a match for the other. Gide used especially his dynamic suppleness, and Claudel drew upon the expansiveness of his nature dominated by his love for God.

Robert Mallet, editor of this correspondence, added all related passages from Gide's *Journal* and thereby made a striking revelation. Gide's direct reactions to Claudel are recorded in the *Journal,* and at times his resentment. The purpose of Claudel's letters was avowedly that of winning over for the Church Gide's thought and life, and often at those moments when he believed he was on the point of success, Gide was farthest away, and denying in his *Journal* entries any possible triumph on the part of Claudel.

Yet, at no point can Gide be accused of hypocrisy. He was profoundly concerned about the problems involved in the debate, although he was never affected, because of his turn of mind, by certain arguments of Claudel. As with Valéry, he was always somewhat intimidated by the physical presence of Claudel. In the writing of the letters, he was more himself, bolder in thought and expression, and yet there was always some trace of defeatism in his writing when he felt himself against the wall and disabled by any heavy barrage of arguments. His revenge was the *Journal,* and the passages chosen by M. Mallet give the impression at times that he is playing a game of hide-and-seek with Claudel.

Claudel's letters also have varying tones of sternness and gentleness. He can be difficult and obdurate, but also understanding and sympathetic. Whenever it is purely a question of Catholicism, he is majestic. Claudel was really writing in these letters a kind of catechism for his friend, and often, in explaining a dogma, he reveals a lyric enthusiasm. Some of the passages are torrential, and Gide, more reticent, more cautious by nature, must have felt overwhelmed and put off by the simple weight of Claudel's explanations and entreaties.

The correspondence was interrupted in 1926, and was not published until more than twenty years later. By that time, both men were far enough way from the controversy and the clash of temperaments to judge their letters somewhat objectively, and they must have realized, in permitting the publication, the unusual vehemence and ardor in which the letters had been written that made them a unique correspondence in French literary history. On the part of Gide, who comes off less well in the exchange than Claudel, there may have been a spiritual masochism, a further trace of defiance toward public opinion and conformity. On the part of Claudel, in giving his consent, there must have been a realization that these pages are among his strongest writings in apologetics. At every point in his letters he was fully aware of the peril to his friend's soul as Gide refused or disguised his faith.

Gide's confession to Claudel of the abnormality of his nature is the catastrophic point in the exchange. It is not the best part of the letters but it has been the most discussed. In December, 1905, Gide refers to an "enormity" he wants to write about but keeps putting off. Between that time and the letter of confession, written on the 7th of March, 1914, Gide constantly refers to this "enormity" without defining it. Claudel did not understand. The allusions in *Saül* and *L'Immoraliste* to abnormality had not contradicted the norms of morality.

Claudel insistently repeats the reason for his solicitude. He is worried over Gide's soul and wants to give it back to God. *Que ne puis-je vous aider un peu?* The offer is forthright and sincere. But Gide fears this influence and the willpower of his friend. Claudel wants to carry on a rational discussion on the articles of faith, but Gide is fundamentally untouched, unaffected by dogmatism. He dodges the implications of carefully built-up arguments, of a system of thought that offers an answer to all of man's problems. At the time when these letters were being written, Gide was working hard and successfully on his creative works, and they are based primarily on the ambiguity of man's nature. His indifference to dogma was never stronger than in those years. While he argued for the uniqueness and the greatness of the self, Claudel emphasized the opposite view that no man is great in himself but in the agreement he is able to bring about between himself and everything that surrounds him. These were the principal theses of the letters, but it would be false to claim that Gide had solely a disputatious nature, and that Claudel was peremptory and overpowering in his arguments.

There is much subtlety on both sides: on Claudel's when he argues for a total abdication in favor of faith; and on Gide's when he suspects that faith may be the most rigorous of all forms of despotism. Many of Gide's cautious, ill-articulated answers may well be ascribed to his fear of hurting Claudel. The attacks of the apologist are abrupt and direct. The withdrawals of the attacker often seem to be escapes and pretexts. Does Gide enjoy setting traps for his opponent? It is difficult to answer this, but at times there seems to be an almost demonic twist to the nature of his relationship with Claudel.

The letters on *La Porte étroite* are among the most interesting of the collection. Claudel accuses Gide of being quietistic in the book, of reviving the ancient quietist heresy and claiming that true piety has no need of reward, and that the highest form of love is the most disinterested. Gide's answer is revealing and significant. He claims that such a book could not have been written from within an orthodox viewpoint, and that in the deepest sense there is no such thing as a Catholic drama. Protestantism, because of the aloneness of the individual believer, is a school of heroism. In the discussion he gives of *La Porte étroite,* Gide shows his distrust for the "mechanics" of Catholicism, for what he calls *la mécanique admirable du catholicisme.* A *Journal* entry of January, 1912, expresses his wish that he had never known Claudel, that the man's friendship is oppressive to him: *Son amitié pèse sur ma pensée, et l'oblige, et la gêne.* Claudel must have sensed in Gide's obduracy something of the hopelessness of the struggle. In his letter of February 22, 1912, he ascribed this state of affairs to a demonic influence working on Gide and enraged at possibly losing a victim: *Vous êtes sous l'influence du diable furieux de vous voir échapper à lui.*

The beginning of the major debate over Gide's inversion came shortly after this, in March, 1914, when Claudel read in *La Nouvelle Revue Française* a passage from *Les Caves du Vatican* (the novel was being printed serially in the magazine) which he called *un passage pédérastique,* and which in a letter to Jacques Rivière he said threw light upon certain of Gide's earlier books. His letter this time to Gide was strongly worded, and he demanded of his correspondent a straightforward answer.

Gide's reply, which filled two letters, March 7th and 8th, is a moving document on his life and character. Under the circumstances there was nothing left for him to do but to confess. He first explains his long hesitation by his desire to shield his wife and to preserve her affection. His actual avowal is couched in the simplest possible way: "I have never felt desire for a woman." (*Je n'ai jamais éprouvé de désir devant la femme.*) He demands from Claudel, especially in the second letter, the secrecy of the confessional, and thereby ascribes to his friend the role of priest.

Gide's explanation of his inversion is stated as simply as his confession. He believes he was elected by God to bear the enigma he represents. He confesses that he does not know how to solve the problem that God placed on his flesh. In other words, in these two letters sent from Florence, Gide attributes his abnormality to God. Claudel was now faced with a gigantic problem which illuminated much that he had only partially understood in the preceding letters. He promised silence on Gide's secret, and even returned the two letters. Then he pointed out that nothing in his own life gave him the right to judge another. The bulk of his answer is an attack on the vice of inversion. He points out its condemnation in Scripture, and emphasizes the doctrine that this sin is an actual act, and the fear of God is sufficient to keep a man from committing it. Gide's case is all the more serious for Claudel because of the responsibility of an example. Gide could easily become an apologist for a vice that was spreading in the twentieth century. "I know," he wrote, "the inestimable value of a human soul." He asks Gide to suppress the passage in *Les Caves du Vatican,* and urges him to consult a priest to whom he had spoken about Gide: L'Abbé Fontaine.

Gide refused to subscribe to the admonition and advice of Claudel, and the correspondence ended. But the opposition of Gide and Claudel is an important chapter in twentieth century French literature. In 1963 appeared at the same time two very concise and penetrating studies of Gide and Claudel in the series *Écrivains de toujours.*

Claude Martin emphasizes the life of his author in *André Gide par lui-même,* and Paul-André Lesort studies the work of the poet in *Paul Claudel par lui-même.* Gide would seem to count especially in his meditation about himself, and Claudel in his meditation on the world. The friendship between the two men was always strained and ceremonious. In the letters he wrote to Claudel, and in much of his work, Gide tried to adapt his faith to his nature and to the nature of the world. Claudel in his letters and throughout his creative works forced all of nature as well as his own human nature to adapt to his faith. After Claudel's personal crisis of passion, of which *Partage de Midi* is the expression, his Catholic faith was consubstantial with his nature. After Gide's less significant religious crisis related in *Numquid et tu,* he accepted without serious combat the instincts of his desires and nature.

One last effort on the part of Claudel was made in 1925 when he wrote to Mme Gide to ask to see her and discuss with her the grave problems concerning her husband's salvation. She refused to see Claudel, and in the few lines of her reply spoke in unassailably sound theological terms. "Those who love André Gide," she wrote, "should pray for him. I do this every day and you do also. For his good, our best meeting place is in our prayers."

The extreme positions held by Gide and Claudel, with respect to Catholicism, and their positions in France, have now been somewhat attenuated by the passage of the years following their death. Even as old men they hurled invective against each other—Claudel with his familiar brutality and Gide with his schoolboy's maliciousness. Gide's publication of *Corydon* was a Luciferian thrust at Claudel, and as a result of this publication, Claudel showed, with respect to Gide, his nature as denouncer of heretics, and concealed the depths of affection and sympathy of which he was capable.

The character Ménalque appears in *Les Nourritures terrestres* and in *L'Immoraliste.* Of all the Gidian figures he is the most opposed to the figure of Christ to whom Gide also was deeply attached. Because of his demonlike qualities, Ménalque is totally mysterious. He has the beauty and the persuasiveness of a fallen angel. In one sense, as the critic M-R.Albérès has pointed out, the religious struggle in Gide is waged between Christ and Ménalque. As Ménalque gradually wins over Christ, the concept of personal happiness in Gide wins over the concept of religious salvation. There is no place, in the religious values invoked in *Les Nourritures terrestres,* for a transcendent God. God as the projection of our hopes and desires is proclaimed in this early book, and this seems to be Gide's permanent philosophy about the Divine. Man is discovered in God. Our desires infuse life in God. God is therefore human nature, or human nature raised to its highest power.

Before the publication of *Les Nourritures terrestres* in book form, Gide published an early version of one passage in *L'Ermitage* in January, 1896. He sent this to Francis Jammes—the two men had not met, but a cordial friendship had grown up in their correspondence where they used the familiar *tu*—in order to have Jammes's opinion. Jammes published a long vehement answer in the April issue of *L'Ermitage,* and called it *Réponse à Ménalque.* This was the first formal opposition to Gide's moral code by a Catholic friend. The pattern of the religious dispute was almost always the same: Gide initiated the dispute and then, when the arguments became too complex and dogmatic, abandoned all discussion. Gide had a more finely developed critical spirit than either Francis Jammes or Paul Claudel, but he was unable to accept the more massive, more logically ordered arguments of Catholic morality. His recourse was inevitably to personal sincerity, and here Jammes insisted on opposing a system of morality to one man's feelings about morality.

In *La Porte étroite* Gide wrote a moving story based on the morality of renunciation. His Catholic friends were sensitive to the religious austerity of Alissa and to the idealism of the work, even if they had theological reservations about it. *La Porte étroite* has remained more important in a religious sense, than the brief tract *Numquid et tu,* written in 1916, when Gide seemed to be taking a definitive step in the direction of Catholicism. Today *Numquid et tu* appears effusive and strained, and one hesitates to grant it the place of importance is has sometimes received.

The publication of *Corydon,* in 1924, represented for Gide's Catholic friends an almost definitive break on his part with the Christian tradition, an overt attack on orthodox morality. Gide had been about to publish *Corydon* in 1914, after the appearance of *Les Caves du Vatican,* but the project was abandoned when the war broke out and when Gide became affiliated with an organization caring for Belgian refugees. His religious crisis of 1916, reflected in *Numquid et tu,* induced him again to delay the publication. In 1920, twenty-one copies were privately printed and circulated among friends. Before the official Gallimard publication of 1924, Jacques Maritain called on Gide for the express purpose of pleading with him not to publish *Corydon.* Gide recorded this conversation in some detail in his *Journal.* Maritain's efforts were of no avail.

The book is cast in the form of a series of dialogues between two characters. Gide obviously wanted to avoid the form of a treatise or a tract, but the subject matter of the discussions is so complex that the dialogue form seems adequate to sustain it. Implicitly the book is Gide's public acknowledgment of his own nature and his sexual mores. Deliberately it is an apologia of homosexuality in which Gide attempts to answer the two charges that the practice of homosexuality is contrary to nature and harmful to society. He draws from scientific data on animal life, and analyzes the relationship between sexuality and art.

The importance that Gide himself ascribed to *Corydon* is granted by very few critics. In a general sense, it substantiates Gide's belief in man's need and man's right to develop his natural proclivities. The seriousness with which he confronts a tragic human problem cannot be doubted.

Even if his thesis and his conclusions left little hope to his Catholic friends that Gide would one day embrace the faith, they did acknowledge that at least Gide was not advocating inversion in the place of virtue. The general problem had already been stated in *Si le grain ne meurt* where Gide speaks of the difficulty one has in understanding the love life of someone else.

The principal weaknesses in Gide's arguments are in his insistence on zoological revelations and in his praise of "Greek love" about which actually very little is known. Many claimed that Gide was impelled to write *Corydon* because of the scandal and tragedy in the trial of Oscar Wilde. Others claimed that Proust's presentation of inversion in the first part of *Sodome et Gomorrhe* had so stressed its disgusting aspects that Gide felt urged to point out the difference he believed exists in Greek love and manifestations of inversion today. Gide stresses the naturalness of the invert's desire and, in his own case, the jubilation, the ecstasy of the senses in his sexual experiences. Charles Du Bos, who has given the most detailed Christian answer to *Corydon*, insists that sexual triumph or jubilation is that aspect of love which is of brief duration and which is the most deceptive.

From Gide's published correspondence and from the entries in his *Journal* on conversations with such friends as Claudel, Jammes, Charles Du Bos, Henri Ghéon, Jacques Copeau, Jacques Rivière, Mauriac, Maritain and Julien Green, a present-day student of Gide's thought may understandably decide that religion, after all, was not the central problem in Gide. He continued, long after *Numquid et tu,* to use Christian terminology, but such words as *dieu* and *diable* are completely secularized by him. He continues to talk about religion, but one has the feeling that it matters less and less to him. In his visit to the Mauriacs' home in Malagar, in June, 1939, a visit brought about largely by Claude Mauriac, he confides to the Mauriacs one evening that he does not believe; that there is no reason to believe and this is a certainty for him. *Je ne crois pas; je sais qu'il n'y a aucune raison de croire; c'est pour moi une certitude.* His reading of the Gospels, which had once nourished him spiritually, turned into an exercise in nostalgia, and ended by irritating him more than consoling him.

Gide's friendship with Julien Green extended over a period of more than twenty years. Many of the phases of Gide's religious belief and loss of this belief are visible in the conversations recorded in the *Journals* of both Gide and Green. More than Gide, Green is a writer tormented by the religious problem, and his faith has passed through many phases. The last three or four novels of M. Green, and the recent edition of his *Journal* of 1961 designate him as a Christian writer whose faith is tested at the very heart of an exceptionally intense form of despair. The most prevalent theme of the *Journal* is religion. In his effort to understand the meaning of his life, Green returns constantly to his experience of piety, to the subtle and often unexpected invasions of God. With such an emphasis, he is a spiritual writer by comparison with Gide, who is not essentially a spiritual writer. The many conversations between Gide and Green, related in the *Journals* of both writers, testify to this fundamental divergence in their sensibility of artists. Far less bold in its form than the Gidian confession (in such books as *Si le grain ne meurt* and *Et nunc manet in te*), the revelations made by Green in his *Journal* give a fuller and more profound explanation of the conflicts in his nature caused by religion.

It would be difficult to point out any direct influence of Gide on Julien Green, but there was in their friendship a meeting of minds and temperaments. If Gide was the type of man who had accepted himself, he was strongly attracted to that part of Green's nature that struggled against itself. He was an avid, careful reader of Green's books and discussed them with the younger man. In 1929, at the beginning of their friendship, Gide spoke on one occasion to Green about the long period of religious fervor in his life. In pointing out the number of friends who had been converted to Catholicism—Ghéon, Claudel, Laurens, Copeau—he claimed, with some degree of sadness, that their conversion had made impossible any real communication, any exchange of ideas. Gide was critical of the tendency of Catholics to see Catholicism in writers who were, for him, far from orthodox. "See what they did for Rimbaud and Rivière," he said to Green. And two years later, in 1931, he said that one day Catholics would annex Nietzsche because "everything that is tragic becomes Catholic for a Catholic spirit." (*Tout ce qui est tragique devient catholique.*) In the early thirties, before Gide's brief adherence to Communism, he felt the united efforts of men like Jacques Maritain, Abbé Altermann and Copeau to bring him into the Catholic fold. He was both moved and irritated by the effort. In speaking of it to Green, Gide called it a "flirtation."

In 1937, Gide and Green met in London where they had several serious conversations, some of which are recorded by Green. In speaking of the difficulty he had in accepting the Pauline Epistles, Gide recalled a statement that Abbé Mugnier had once made to him in which the priest called Saint Paul the bone of the fish. (*Saint Paul, c'est l'arête du poisson.*) Gide was delighted by this interpretation in which Saint Paul is the backbone of Christianity even if Christ remains the symbolic fish.

During the war years, Julien Green lived in America. In 1945 he returned to Paris and resumed his intermittent visits to Gide. These visits were not many, and they were usually brief. During the last years of his life, Gide was literally besieged by visitors. Both Gide and Green, during their last conversations, were conscious of not having time to speak as they would like. Before Green had returned to France, Gabriel Marcel had told Gide of Green's conversion to Catholicism in 1939. Gide's hostility to the Church was strong during the last years of his life, and Green interprets many of his discussions about Catholicism as a desire to weaken Green's faith and estrange him once again from the Church.

In these discussions, as partially related by Julien Green, Gide insisted on points that he writes about, especially in his *Journal*. He warned that a convert runs the risk of losing his literary talent. He deplored the fact that Catholics have an answer to everything. He explained the Catholic faith by the phenomena of autosuggestion and heredity. Green was fully aware that his conversion was looked upon by Gide as a scandal. In the arguments that Gide developed in his attack on Catholicism, Green sensed a religious zeal, the obstinacy of a missionary. The last time the two men were together, Gide asked Green if he still read his Bible every day. The answer was affirmative. Gide made no comment.

After Gide's death, his name continued to appear frequently on the pages of Green's *Journal*. It is obvious from the last entries concerning Gide, that Green admired what Gide had said to him far more than he admired Gide's writings. He made a few exceptions for *Si le grain ne meurt*, *Thésée* and the *Journal*. He was disconcerted mainly by the *récits* and *Les Faux-Monnayeurs*. Green and the Dominican priest Père Couturier were true Catholic friends who never judged Gide. Among his Catholic critics who were also friends of Gide, Charles Du Bos was the most subtle. In claiming that Gide fundamentally failed as a novelist, Du Bos develops the thesis that he was lacking in humanity, lacking in a richness of nature, despite the complexity of his nature.

Most of Gide's Catholic critics would agree that Gide was not purely the artist. More essentially he was the humanist, the man who in his writings discovered the humanity of his own nature and who tried, with intermittent success, to free himself from any religious bond. His intelligence, or the quality of his mind, in its effort to understand the religious experience, resembles Montaigne. In his efforts to liberate himself completely from any religious alliance, he resembles Diderot.

16

GIDE AND THE
VOCATION OF WRITER

Although radically different from Emerson in many ways, the thought and the example of Gide illustrate the leading points of the essay *Self-Reliance,* which Gide used to call his "morning reading" and which once he discussed with Jean Schlumberger. A sentence in the opening paragraph, for example, is easily applicable to Gide's practice as a writer: "To believe your own thought, to believe that what is true for you in your private heart is true for all men—that is genius." But especially the passage on society and conformity would seem today "Gidian" to the European reader: "Society everywhere is in conspiracy against the manhood of every one of its members. . . . Whoso would be a man, must be a non-conformist. . . . Nothing is at last sacred but the integrity of your own mind."

To a degree that dwarfed every other perspective, Gide's life was the writer's vocation. He began writing when Symbolism was triumphant, especially in the eyes of the gifted young writers in France. In early maturity he helped to found *La Nouvelle Revue Française* which quite literally he made into a kind of home for himself, a retreat and a center of literary friendships. Almost at the end of his life, he was surprised at finding enough stamina and imagination and patience to write *Thésée,* a subject that had obsessed him most of his life. Gide lived long enough not only to defend all his themes, but he had time to return to them, to recapitulate them and add to them the wisdom and the assurance which the years had brought him. He often said, half jokingly, that his own life was so interesting that it seemed pointless for him to create characters outside of himself, to create fictional characters. His work luminously reflects all the passionate interests of his life, and reflects the charm and the nobility of his nature that have been described by those who approached him.

In opposition to all the main currents of his age, Gide developed and elaborated a philosophy of optimism. He is the one optimistic thinker, who is also a major writer, in the first half of the twentieth century. In book after book, he celebrates the joyousness of his senses and of his intellect. Quite literally a half century extends between *Les Nourritures terrestres* and *Thésée,* the first and the last testaments on Gide's confidence in man, on the generosity of one man's heart that enriched through so many years the gifts of a writer.

His philosophy of optimism—but philosophy is too pompous, too academic a word, because his optimism was instinctive, born with his convictions concerning man's nature and his possibilities—was visible in the youthfulness of his spirit at no matter what age he had reached. Everyone who approached him, everyone who knew him, spoke of this youthfulness. But what was it, and how was it expressed? It is perhaps best defined in the Latin word which becomes in French *sympathie,* not "sympathy" in our sense, but a capacity to understand, a willingness to embrace and even to embody an experience or an idea not one's own. Gide's endless aptitude for *sympathie* is the clue to his many rejuvenations. These rejuvenations are marked by each of his books, by each effort to permit the youthfulness of others to pass into him. The secret of his vitality was in this understanding and absorption of others and of their ideas. He welcomed ideas as he welcomed human beings. His morning readings and his evening conversations were necessary exercises for his writer's art. The sources of his art were never exhausted.

Each of his books is an experimentation with form, and this is in keeping with the theme of each book, which is always the renewed effort to understand a moral problem. The role of Gide as an experimenter in literary forms has never been justly assessed. At Gide's death, Thomas Mann called him a "bold experimenter." He was in this domain far bolder than the experimenters of the "new French novel" in the fifties and sixties. The impulse promoting him toward a new investigation was always joined with a need to create a new form: the dithyramb of *Les Nourritures terrestres*, the story without action of *La Porte étroite*, the dialogue of *Le Retour de l'enfant prodigue*, the rich unending counterpoint of *Les Faux-Monnayeurs*.

Gide was the writer who each day of his life looked at the universe around him with an expression of solemnity and amazement. He was grateful to all the signs of the universe that offered themselves to him. He had little taste for history in its pure sense or for abstract philosophy. He was drawn to whatever he was able to see, and drawn to the daily struggle of consigning to words whatever he saw, of discovering a form into which his ideas and thoughts could be cast.

This steadfast habit of the writer was not an effort to reach simplification. It was not an effort to reach a swift clarification. The truth of the idea he was searching for was as subtle and unpredictable as the newness of the form he devised for the search. A sentence Gide ascribes to his character Saul is fully applicable to himself: "My value is in my complication." (*Ma valeur est dans ma complication.*) This *modus vivendi,* this writer's vocation, would not have worked for Gide, had it not been for the universality of his taste and understanding. He was devoted to France, and always felt himself deeply French, but he was also the great French European who read Goethe, Shakespeare and Dante as fervently as he read Montaigne, Baudelaire and Stendhal. At the end of his life he read and studied Virgil as if he were rediscovering a world.

The universality of his tastes and interests is in the variety of his books, and particularly in the variousness of their appeal to readers. In *La Porte étroite*, for example,

Gide creates a religious atmosphere which attracts some
readers as forcefully as it repulses others. (But no curious
reader of Gide stays for long with any one book.) In
L'Immoraliste he creates a drama that appears to some
readers as the epitome of courage and to others as an
example of human degradation. *Paludes* is an irritating
book for some, overprecious in its style for others, and it
has both upset and delighted readers.

When the experience derived from reading Gide is
pleasure, it is almost always an aesthetic pleasure, an
awareness of the beauty of the sentence, of the appropri-
ateness of the tone, of the subtle alliance achieved between
thought and expression. The other kind of experience, the
stimulation or the anger aroused by the ideas and the
themes of his books, is of such a nature that it serves
exactly the purpose planned and calculated by Gide.
Throughout all his writings, he is essentially the defender of freedom and individualism, of individual responsibility. This belief presides over his entire work. But
the expression given to this freedom is a search, an
ironic quest at times, an effort to reach the kind of
adaptability which will worry the reader desirous of a
succinct answer and formulation. Gide is never the contemplative, the man assured that he is contemplating the
center of existence. Neither is he the hater, because in
order to feel hate, he would have to feel certain of his
convictions and sentiments.

The searcher that Gide was never had the leisure for
contemplation nor the capacity for hate. His *Journal* will
be read in a hundred years in order to discover the real
subtleties in the structure of our age. Gide lived the life
of his times not for himself but for others, his readers of
today and tomorrow. By expressing with more and more
honesty, as time went on, his own individual conscience,
he became increasingly conscious of the world around
him. The curious way in which he fused his thinking and
his believing permitted him to write the major defense
of man in himself that we have in the twentieth century.
Curiosity in Gide always preceded the expression of his

critical faculty. But the two were indispensable to his art, indispensable to the human and the theoretical honesty of his art.

Gide, in the classical sense, is the long-range writer. When *Les Nourritures terrestres* appeared in 1897, it attracted no· attention, and was neglected for twenty years. About 1920, in the years immediately following the war, the youthful readers in France, eager to forget the tragic experiences of war, and to find their place in life with some modicum of joy, read *Les Nourritures terrestres* as a text of counsel, as a spiritual guide toward life. The book came into its own years after it was first published, and this has been true for most of Gide's books. *L'Immoraliste,* when it was first read, during the first quarter of the century, appeared to most as an example, an almost shocking example, of a complex, cruel story. Today, it is esteemed by many judicious students of Gide's work as one of the most skillfully constructed novels of the twentieth century, a document on a prevalent psychological impasse in man's search for himself and for individual freedom. *Le Retour de l'enfant prodigue,* published in 1907, was first attacked as a subversive reading of the famous parable, but today, by believers and non-believers alike, it is judged as one of the most finished examples of modern French prose, and included in an ever-increasing number of anthologies as perhaps the best single text of André Gide to present to young readers. *La Porte étroite,* of 1909, disturbed and bewildered its first readers (cf. the important letters of Paul Claudel on the religious theme in *La Porte étroite*), but today it is a classic of modern French literature, unusual in its lack of action, a forerunner in that sense of the "new novel," a story that, in its austere idealism, captivates the emotions of the reader as very few twentieth century novels are able to do.

The history of Gide's public successes, of his winning of a public, has not been written, but when this research is done, it will doubtless reveal a phenomenon different from that of other twentieth century writers. The public that reads all of Gide's work is undoubtedly smaller than the public that reads Proust's *À la recherche du temps perdu*. It would seem that each of his major books creates its own fervent public, and if these were added together they would form an impressively large segment of the reading public. Because of the degree of sincerity reached in the books just referred to, and in *Si le grain ne meurt*, *Les Faux-Monnayeurs*, the *Journal*, *Thésée*, and in the volumes of letters already published—each, in its own way is able to move a certain kind of reader. In his social relationships, Gide was able to move from one type of friend to another, to cultivate friendship with many differing temperaments and personalities. This same capacity he also realized as a writer, directing each book to a certain kind of reader whom he involves in the book's problems and whom he enchants by the style of the writing. He sensed with that infallible intuition of the real artist, that a book is the reduction of a problem, that all cannot be said, that art is a constriction, that a work of art is the result of a constraint. With Gide, the reader follows and accepts the degree of mysteriousness that is the consequence of restraint. The endings of Gide's books are the beginnings of other books which the reader can create imaginatively. The last sentence of the prodigal son is the departure from home of the youngest son, and the story of the new adventurer lies beyond the completed work. The last sentence of *Les Faux-Monnayeurs* is the possible beginning of a new episode, the new chapter in Édouard's life about which nothing is known.

The effusions of Gide's nature, his extreme emotivity, are controlled and channeled by the limitations and rules of a work of art. In a brilliant sentence in *Incidences*, Gide defines the strength and the beauty of a classical work by the degree to which its romanticism is conquered. (*l'œuvre classique ne sera forte et belle qu'en raison de son romantisme dompté.—L'Evolution du Théâtre.*) The skill with which Gide made literary virtues of his defects and limitations is the sign, the proof, of the authentic writer. Cautiously and patiently he performed this trans-

mutation with each book. Out of his narcissism he wrote
a treatise on the meaning of art. Out of his endlessly
shifting subtleties, he wrote one of the most subtle novels
of his century. Out of his sense of economy, called
avariciousness by some, he wrote *L'Immoraliste*. His version of the prodigal son is both the failure of freedom and
sensuality, and the return to the family. The story of
Alissa is both the failure of a religious life and the
heroine's return to God.

When, in 1942, Gide wrote that he considered *Corydon*
his most important book—a shocking statement that has
been used and misused—he was undoubtedly looking upon
the book as the supreme symbol of his independence, as
the work that demanded from him the most courage to
write and publish. He could easily surmise, in 1942, the
uproar which his personal evaluation of the book was
going to create. Combativeness was a part of his nature,
especially when the difficulties of human conduct and
behavior were being discussed. But always—beyond the
immediate issue at stake in whatever book he was writing or discussing—Gide's primary preoccupation was
aesthetic. His labor was the artist's: the achievement of a
form. If the starting point, the inspiration, was of a moral
order, the writer's effort was of an artistic order. In the
actual writing of the book, the moral and the aesthetic
were quickly fused. The moral quality was always there,
as the permanent bent of his nature, and the aesthetic
was the daily striving to create the suitable form and
expression.

In the labor of writing, Gide never attempted to follow
a model, to imitate any other writer. As a writer, he was
totally alone, and this is perhaps the closest we can come
to a definition of his famous sincerity. Because of this
sincerity in his writing, he establishes an intimate contact with his reader. But so strong is Gide's own lesson
of independence, that the reader, rather than electing the
writer as his guide and model, chooses himself. There are
Gidian characters in whom one senses something quite
directly from Gide's temperament: Alissa and Thésée,

for example, but there are other characters who bear opposite traits: Ménalque and Protos. The experience of
reading Gide is not for the intense reader the discovery
of Gide, but rather it is the example and the illustration
of the writer. The flattery with which Gide seems to
welcome his reader, and which has been used against
him, is not the self-portrait he offers but rather the example of naturalness he sustains and that effort toward
sincerity which is never achieved without considerable
weariness and peril.

If a repertory of Gide's interests was drawn up, some
scheme devised by which the degree of interest in each
subject could be ascertained, it would be discovered that
the repertory of real interests is very large, but that the
degree of attentiveness in each case is fairly uniform. As
the creative writer—the one steadfast role throughout
Gide's life—Gide is the anthithesis of the contemplative.
His acts of contemplation were intense but brief and he
moved easily from one subject to another. The temper of
the writer guides him to the discovery in himself of some
reaction to a person or an idea or a landscape that can
serve in the literary art. Gide is the type of man able to
examine closely, and with the full attentiveness of his
being, many subjects, and he is also the type of writer
who demonstrates in this observation patience and
honesty, a willingness to experiment, to analyze and to
recapitulate.

After the early years of fidelity to symbolism, and after
the dithyrambic style of *Les Nourritures terrestres*, the
elements in all the writings of Gide were submitted to the
close scrutiny of his intelligence, to the control of his
feelings for balance and order. The phases in his career
of writer were many. It is possible to describe some in
terms of the influence of writers who stimulated his
thought. The example of Mallarmé dominated the earliest
phases. Rimbaud, a few years later, was a veritable discovery. Barrès counted momentarily, as well as Nietzsche.
Goethe's influence was of long duration.

The central moment was the period between 1911 and

1925, when Gide devoted most of his energies to the writing of *Les Faux-Monnayeurs*. This was the midway point in his career. He was neither the young symbolist at that time, nor was he the sage who was to write *Thésée*. He wrote his novel not as a tormented moralist nor as the partisan of a belief that enflamed him. The story of this book's reception is a significant chapter in the role Gide has played of European writer. The early critics on the whole denounced the book as having no structure, no unity, no point at which all the themes converged. But today, and particularly in the light of the "new French novel" of the 1950's, Gide is esteemed as one of the true innovators in the art of the novel. The manner in which he follows his characters, watches them and listens to them, is a contradiction of the omniscient role of the traditional novelist. The way in which Gide treats action in the novel, where he never allows it to accumulate and explode in one climactic mode, is also a part of the aesthetics of the new novel. *Les Faux-Monnayeurs* is a novel, written in the present tense, in which there are multiple actions, no one of which profits from any other. The action is always taking place, and no one of the actions, not even the suicide of the boy Boris, is sufficiently dramatized or highlighted to make of it the leading catastrophe, as in a tragedy. The relationship the author establishes with his characters is that of sympathetic observer, and this encourages a similar relationship between author and reader.

This tone of intimacy and confidence is in all of Gide's books, but to an extraordinary degree in *Les Faux-Monnayeurs*, where the absence of any privileged hero sustains on the part of the reader an evenness of attention as episode follows episode and as characters succeed one another. Gide is no more in Édouard than he is in Bernard or Olivier. He does not intervene any more in the novel he is writing than the reader does. The world that Édouard observes and enters is composed of many disparate unrelated groups. It is comparable to a small world in itself, a small society that is not unlike the society that Gide the man created by his sociability, by his curiosity about different types of human beings, and by his endless adaptability to human beings different from himself. In this trait, Édouard the novelist and Gide the writer resemble each other. Gide was usually able to convert a new friend through his attentiveness and charm, but at the same time he was being converted to the new friend. The same process of enrichment was followed in Gide's reading of a new author, and the same process is followed today when a new reader begins one of Gide's books.

Of all of his books, but less subtly than the others, the *Journal* illustrates best this principle by which Gide the author creates an intimacy with his readers. But it is an emancipating intimacy without urgent or lasting ties. The *Journal* is not a mirror. Gide was not Narcissus as he wrote it. He looks at himself in order to be seen by others. The purpose of the *Journal* is to create the possibility for others to consider him, for others to surround him. The *Journal,* and all his books, were written for others. This is at the basis of their power of attraction. What we have called intimacy between writer and reader is the establishment of a dialogue, or rather of a text that will initiate a dialogue between author and reader.

Corydon, a weaker book than the *Journal* because of its strong didactic tone, is more treatise than confession, but it was motivated by the same impulse of sincerity, the same sense of honor that explains the most intimate confidences of the *Journal* and *Si le grain ne meurt.* Such an avowal was needed for the maintenance of this sociability, for the direct communication between author and public. But Gide was not motivated by a desire to separate himself from his fellowmen, to trace a self-portrait that would appear freakish or eccentric. The self-portrait visible in varying degrees in all his books is so drawn as to make him more acceptable. Whether this goal is achieved depends on the reader, but the motivation of Gide's writing is to make a place for himself in the society of mankind. There were many conversions that took place during his

life, to ideas and to people, and almost every one seemed
in contradiction to some other previous conversion. But
each was sincere. He was sensitive to those ideas and
those individuals eager to convert, because he himself was
of that very nature. Gide's ideal society has no restrictions. Rather, its limits are constantly being altered.

The desire to speak and confide is a social desire. The
writing down of this desire demands the writer's solitude
that Gide knew as well as he knew the desire for sociability. The world of his friends and the world of his
readers were for the most part composed of individuals
very different from himself. The ease with which he was
able to put himself in some one else's place is part of the
virtuosity demonstrated in his writing. He was skillful
in initiating a conversation, and this mattered far more
than the resolution of problems or the analysis of ideas
in a conversation. His social need was that of understanding rather than of winning over a new disciple. Gide
had no disciples. The effect of his social role and the effect
of his books on a reader is one of welcome. He was opposed to any emulation on the part of friend or reader.

It might seem to be a paradox that Gide was always
gratified to hear that the reading of one of his books had
affected the destiny of a reader. He was gratified especially
when the reading of his book helped reveal the reader to
himself. The progress of Gide's thought is a curious phenomenon because it is often a return to earlier positions
which are then reassembled and deepened. The explanation of this constant returning to early concepts and
themes is in itself a Gidian exercise. The serenity he
wanted from self-examination and thought was not
serenity derived from some permanent form of assurance
or dogma. It was that kind of serenity that can come
from acceptance of doubt.

Doubt was for Gide a permanent attitude, but it was
also an experience of voluptuousness, a savoring of good
and evil, an eagerness to move freely back and forth between the angelic and the demonic. The skill with which
he controlled the extremes of these experiences, of

Nathanaël and Ménalque, of the prodigal son and his younger brother, of Bernard and Olivier, creates in the reader strong experiences of astonishment and enthusiasm. Gide's books are not literary experiences separate from life. They are art forms, beyond any doubt, but they unfold almost as a life is lived, with the unpredictable and the mysterious and the contradictory as elements as familiar as the human experiences of achievement and defeat. Gide's art is not an experience alienated from life.

It is difficult to explain otherwise the closeness to Gide that so many of his readers have felt. And this phenomenon has continued to be registered and discussed since his death. His most successful works are simultaneously art forms and instruments of knowledge: divinations, intuitions concerning man's complexity and man's happiness. *Paludes* has the ironic form of a *sotie* and analyzes the ancient attraction man feels for adventure. *Saül* has the elevation of classical tragedy, and it is also one of the strongest warnings on the emptiness and endlessness of man's fantasies and desires. *Les Caves du Vatican* is a surrealist novel and a comedy of human types. *Oedipe* has the nobility of a tragedy or an ode, and it is also the study of man's free spirit in its effort to reach wisdom. *Les Nouvelles nourritures* is a hymn in prose and a celebration of joy.

It is possible for a reader of Gide to take from his books only that part which will flatter him. But the full message, the full value to be derived is always a difficult constraint, a difficult harmonization of conflicting forces and ideals. Individualism for Gide has little to do with self-adulation and self-contemplation. The development of individualism is inevitably a fusing or reconciliation of opposites, of the antimysticism in Oedipe and the blind faith of Tirésias. Oedipus is everywhere in Gide's writings the ardent spirit who tries to answer the enigma of existence. But in Gide's steady devotion to what is most personal in himself, he acknowledges faith in life. The harshest terms used against him—demonic, evasive, calculating, Machiavellian—are not the words of his readers. They are used by those who read, not the texts of Gide, but the texts of his adversaries.

In the exaltation that came to Gide from life and from works of art, he offered to those who talked with him and to those who now read him, an exchange and an alliance. If his writings appeared to some readers too removed from the pressing problems of his day, to others, more sympathetic in their judgment, they appeared the attentive testament of a man whose particular form of intelligence did not encourage the development or the expression of despair in himself.

17

GIDE TODAY

Since his death, Gide's readers have begun asking of his work the central questions: who is he and what is he offering them? The man who spent his life questioning the sphinx is now being questioned in his turn. At his death his interest in the living ceased, but the living began then, in a more subtle and significant way than previously, to be interested in him.

The real secrets of André Gide are all in his books. They are now being reread from that ultimate perspective that death provides. Every great work of literature is a self-portrait. The sole subject of Gide's books is his own adventure which he either narrated or interpreted. He never completed this adventure. He never told it all. He once said that at the end of each of his books, he would like to write: "the most important part remains to be said." Gide was capable endlessly of picking up the story where he had left it and continuing it. He was never able to trust completely what he had written the day before or published the year before. Something else had to be added, something new had to be said because the truth moved forward with him every day. This theme is explicitly developed in the last pages of his journal *Ainsi soit-il, ou Les Jeux sont faits*.

Gide began writing about 1890, at a moment of great peacefulness in Europe. He continued to write during the following sixty years, until 1950, during which time the world changed from the comparative peace of the 1890's to the chaos and imminent tragedy of the mid-century. He remained a constant and fervent witness to every ominous development in Europe and the world, from the period when a religion of science and a rational vision of the universe dominated Europe to the period after the Second World War of such deep unrest. Gide never lived isolated from the problems of his age, but he was reserved in his judgments on these problems. Essentially a moralist, Gide believed that every change in the world had to begin with a change in the individual. The way has first to be tested by the individual self. Our one way of understanding and criticizing and loving is to take ourselves as the means. Whereas the experiences of two men are never identical, there are points of resemblance between any two experiences. By being increasingly honest with oneself, by becoming more and more deeply oneself, one may discover all of human nature.

There is little doubt that Gide hoped to compose a new gospel. With his favorite themes of adolescent restlessness, revolt, escape and the gratuitous act, he was able to upset the convictions of his readers, particularly his youthful readers, and yet he never created in them feelings of terror or dismay which a Dostoevski or a Lautréamont had aroused. If he is still read today by the comparatively young, they probably do not weep over *Les Nourritures terrestres* nor aspire to be a Lafcadio. No one form of writing can be claimed as predominantly Gidian. He tried all the genres, because he was unwilling to restrict himself to any one form, and because each book, once it was well under way, became irksome to him. He would finish it off quickly in order to move on to a newer work. He had planned, for example, several more chapters for *Les Faux-Monnayeurs,* but when he wrote the sentence, *"Je suis bien curieux de connaître Caloub,"* it appeared to him such a suitable final sentence, that he felt exempt from continuing any farther. His impatience always increased when he saw the goal at hand. He preferred search to discovery.

In a moment of gratitude, Claude Mauriac once said to Gide: "You taught me and several generations intellectual honesty." As a teacher, Gide refused to formulate any dogma, but trained those who read him sympathetically in a way of learning, in an attitude toward discipline. Gide's training, if it could be called that, would culminate in the reader choosing himself rather than any teacher or any one doctrine. Whenever Christianity appeared to him in the form of a system, or a body of principles, he refused to accept it. His way was one of detachment and adventure, which would permit him the practice of what has been so often called his sincerity. His work is not only a written confession. It is at the same time a scrupulously examined code of morals. At the time of his first books, soon after 1890, Gide realized that if he lived in accordance with the accepted moral system of his society, he would live as a hypocrite. The struggle between hypocrisy and sincerity became the central moral issue for Gide, as early as his first book, *André Walter*. Between the simple although rigid laws governing his family circle and his own sincerity, his own purity as a young man, Gide sensed a troublesome dichotomy. He went against the world's morality, not because it was false for the world, but because it appeared useless and even dangerous for him. In this desire to reject the laws of his society, he was not seeking any indulgence for himself but a form and a rule for his own life, a morality that would be his own, autonomous and independent of any foreordained system.

Early in life Gide learned that advice given by someone else is of little use. The extraordinary singularity of each human being makes his particular problem unique. Gide's morality is based upon the belief that each man is elected to play a role unlike every other role. Any deviation from that role, in order to pattern oneself on the preestablished rule, represents for Gide a betrayal of oneself. This peculiar separateness of man is a Gidian theme to which Jean-Paul Sartre, many years later, was to give his own coloring and importance.

Sentence after sentence in the first books, *Voyage d'Urien, Retour de l'enfant prodigue*, and the early entries in the *Journal*, repeat the same belief that each man's way is unique. The Gospel maxim, "Whoever will save his life shall lose it," is closely associated for Gide with

the conviction that at the end of adolescence one cannot
find a set of rules, ready-made, for the conduct of one's
life. No one book, no one house, no one country can
represent the universe. The Gidian hero refuses to shut
himself off from any part of the world before he has
tested it, and he reserves the right to judge it lucidly.
Somewhere between dogmatism and total freedom, Gide
fixed his ethical ·behavior, and it was there he admonished
himself to observe everything and to try to understand
everything.

What appears as conformity to the world's law was
seriously castigated in *Les Nourritures terrestres* and in
L'Immoraliste. And yet in the two books that followed,
Paludes and *Saül*, Gide criticized the other excess of giving oneself over to one's instinct. Freedom from the
world's conventions must be won, but Gide never under-
estimated the perils of freedom. Whereas the freeing of
desire is a fairly simple thing, it is extremely difficult to
make something out of that state of freedom. It is far
easier to follow puritanism as a way of life than to make
out of joyfulness and release of spirit an ethical duty.
Gide's strictures against society follow in the wake of
an important French tradition, illustrated by the *Contrat
social* of Rousseau and *Le Rouge et le Noir* of Stendhal.
The Christian rule of doing nothing that will offend God
had gradually changed in the history of French civilization to the ethic of the bourgeoisie: do nothing that may
offend your neighbor. Gide's rule is more personal than
either of these. He is concerned with the peace that can
be found within oneself, with a rule of conduct that will
not be humiliating to oneself. This personal morality represents a turning away from religious and social morality
in order to live in sincerity with oneself. What Gide calls
"immoralism" is, therefore, an acceptance of desire, provided this acceptance be accompanied by severe demands.

After the first movement of liberation from all societal
constraints, a movement described in *Les Nourritures
terrestres*, and *L'Immoraliste*, Gide the moralist advocates
a close examination of the new freedom won. He presents

in his play *Saül* a tragedy resulting from the misuse of freedom. The very difficulty involved in living with this new freedom is the moral problem of most of his subsequent books: *Les Caves du Vatican, Les Faux-Monnayeurs, Thésée*. After learning what one's own morality consists of, there then begins the long difficulty of perfecting this morality, the long vigilance necessary not to slip back into a morality not one's own. Gide's belief about the ideal teacher is deducible from his personal morality. The real teacher will ultimately force the pupil to choose himself rather than the teacher. The value of any given lesson will therefore be the stimulation it provides to discover oneself.

Gide is no romantic, in the narrow sense of the term, and it is not difficult to distinguish between the Gidian morality of self and the romantic ego. In the volume of *Incidences*, Gide has written: "The triumph of individualism is in the giving up of individuality." Rather than offering to the public what is peculiarly characteristic and personal (as the typical romantic artist tends to do), Gide advocates a revindication of self not in order to stress its pecularity but its universality. There is unquestionably some element of Gide in many of his characters: in Michel of *L'Immoraliste*, in Jérôme of *La Porte étroite*, in Édouard of *Les Faux-Monnayeurs*, but each one represents a part of Gide he had already renounced. Whereas the romantic does not exist beyond the portrait he gives of himself, Gide is anxious to know himself in order to move beyond that self. Each of his books is therefore the extinction of one of his selves which will help prepare a more universal Gide. This conviction and his habit of writing combined to make out of a single man a literary figure of universal validity and significance. From the role of immoralist, of the young man defiant of the fixed moral standards of his day, Gide passed to the role of self-examiner and self-inquisitor, a role lasting until the end of his life, when he reached the final state of moralist.

Gide's serenity as a moralist was won after a long and often revived examination of certain basic themes that

link many of his books. Among these themes, the most
dramatically utilized is the theme of blindness, or of the
eyes that have been put out. The blind, because of their
infirmity, do not know the Law. They do not see the
consequences of sin on the faces of those who commit
sin. "If ye were blind," we read in the Gospel, "ye should
have no sin." The example of the blind was constantly
used by Christ in His preaching. He knew that desire
and all forms of concupiscence are aroused by man's
capacity to see, and He once uttered the famous admonition: "If thine eye offend thee, pluck it out." And yet
Christ often cured the blind. This paradox appealed to
Gide in his effort to understand and interpret the speech
and the actions of Christ. An innocence which does not
know the law may be less worthy. By its very name, virtue
implies a strength that is able to surmount every temptation that comes to man by means of his sight.

The early *André Walter* contained abundant quotations
from the Gospels. At that time in his career, Gide's imagination was predominantly Biblical. But the Greek myths
were to play an equally dominant role in his writings. The
theme of the eye, of the various kinds of vision, of the
ambivalent role of seer and blind man, is both Christian
and Greek. Ulysses, by piercing the one eye of Poly-
phemus with a sharp burning stake, saved himself from
being devoured. This one eye would be given a sexual
meaning by modern psychiatrists. It would be related to
the "evil eye" able to cast a spell over a man and obsess
his conscience. It is the nocturnal eye of evil obsessions,
the eye that needs to be gouged out. The symbol of the
sun is the other type of simple eye that sees everything.
It is the Greek god Apollo and a symbol of the Trinity
in Christian symbolism.

Homer is the blind poet who sees inwardly. He has lost
the sight of his physical eyes and has therefore lost all
evil desires. Tiresias is the blind priest and prophet who
can see into the evil of men's hearts. Homer and Tiresias
are ancestors of the modern *voyant*, the visionary poet
who sees beyond the ordinary vision of man. Oedipus,

for the Greek poets and for Gide also, is the man who
gouges out his eyes in order not to behold any longer the
evil of the world. Willfully he blinds himself in order
to turn away from evil and ugliness. Gide portrays this
Oedipus in his play, and also the seer Tiresias who, in
his literal blindness discerns the destiny of those around
him. He discovers the signs of evil and death in those
beings who appear living and healthy and happy. Twice,
Gide places side by side in the same work the types of
blind characters: in *La Symphonie pastorale*, with Gertrude and the pastor; and in *Oedipe*, with Oedipus and
Tiresias.

Closely connected with this theme of the eyes that see
and the eyes that have been blinded is the theme in
Gide's writings of the house, of that restricted place that
prevents a character from seeing anything outside it. The
opening of doors is similar to the power of sight. In a
scene from *Les Nourritures terrestres*, Nathanaël looks
through the window into a family scene and feels impelled to lead away from his family a boy he sees seated
in the lamplight. The theme of the house, as much a
restriction as a prison, is everywhere present in *Le
Retour de l'enfant prodigue*. The labyrinth in *Thésée* and
the several "homes" described in *Les Faux-Mónnayeurs*,
are obvious symbols for the limited horizons of a man's
life, for that place which is primarily worldly as opposed
to the limitlessness of spiritual aspiration and spiritual
renewal. The need for sincerity, with which Gide is constantly concerned, is usually transcribed into the need for
light, for the seeing of oneself and the seeing of others.
Sin, in *La Symphonie pastorale*, for example, is that force
which darkens the soul of the pastor, and it is that force
in Gertrude, when her sight is recovered, that prevents
her from seeing the innocent beauty of the world, from
seeing precisely that beauty she saw when she had no
sight in her eyes. Tiresias is at all times the priest for the
city. He wants to save Oedipus, but he wants also to
save Thebes. He alone in the play sees the needs for
salvation because he alone sees the sins of men. A

knowledge of sin for Gide, a clairvoyance into what is the darker side of human nature, is indispensable for the final accession to light, to understanding and to sincerity.

Light is the gift of innocence to man that has been obscured for him by the conventions and the machinations of the world. It is not unrelated to the theme of the natural son, of the bastard son, so frequently used by Gide. The struggle of Gide's hero against the chains that bind him is often described as the hero's opposition to his family, to all the determining factors instituted by the family in a man's existence. Gide's apology of the bastard is, in one sense, his criticism of the family. The drama of the unknown that fills the heart of the bastard is the dream of freedom. Bernard, in *Les Faux-Monnayeurs*, when he discovers the secret of his birth, discovers at the same time a new kind of happiness, an elation in the knowledge that he has broken with the past. His future stretches out before him without the usual strictures. He is free to create his future, and he moves into it with the enthusiasm of a conquering hero.

The equivocal birth of the Greek heroes used by Gide is not unlike the status of Bernard. Even if Thésée at the end of Gide's narrative, returns to his past, he first savors the thought that Egeus is not his real father and that he is doubtless a son of Poseidon. The monster of the story, the Minotaur, is a royal bastard, the son of Pasiphae, queen of Crete, and a bull. The delirium of greatness, which the bastard son by definition is more justified in cultivating than others, is an invitation of freedom in power and wealth, which the Gidian heroes, Ménalque, Michel, Lafcadio, Bernard, the prodigal son and Thésée, cultivated each in his own way.

The secretiveness of these heroes and of many others in the writings of Gide—in Marceline and Alissa, in Saül and Édouard, and even in the early Nathanaël—is precisely that element in their psychology destined to bewilder and confuse the reader. The work of a creative artist is for Gide in opposition to the clearly organized plan of society. A literary work startles by its contradictions and allusions, and especially by its reticence, by all the elements that the writer withholds. A Gidian character grows into his fullest proportions by what he conceals. The richness of his character is formed out of his secrets. The self-inflicted blindness of Oedipus is allied with his will to know all the secrets about himself. Saül and Michel are both secretive characters, and the secrets of Édouard are contained in his valise which will be stolen by Bernard. The secrets revealed by the light of day, the secrets of birth, and the deepest secrets of a man's character, are all allied in Gide's art.

What can be known, what can be apprehended concerning one individual, concerning what is called an individuality? Very little, Gide will answer. Personality, by definition, is that which is forever escaping. On the last pages of his journal, *Ainsi soit-il*, Gide returns over and over again to this disconcerting characteristic of his own personality: its fluidity, its changeableness. This accepted fact in Gide's understanding of psychology explains why, in his more purely aesthetic considerations, he clung to an attitude and a form that are close to those of Mallarmé. To offset the evasive, ever-changing forms of personality, Gide practiced as a writer the rigor and the patience of a disciple of Mallarmé. Gide deviated very little from the lessons on craftsmanship he first learned from Mallarmé, on the absolutism of the written word. The formal aspect of Gide's writing is in direct contrast to the insatiable curiosity of Gide, the man, concerning the fluctuations of his characters, their variability, their contradictions.

By the early 1940's, there already existed in Europe a large number of books and articles on Gide. Most of these testimonials were of an emotional nature, and betrayed a personal stake or ˙claim. When he died in 1951, at the age of eighty-two (it was almost the exact age of Goethe at his death), the literature about Gide grew to massive proportions. But still the emphasis in the majority of these newer books was on Gide's life, in its more complex and more daring aspects. In America the long-established tradition of judging a novelist as a craftsman, as a story-teller who deliberately omits from his stories any personal reference to himself, explains why Gide has never been fully accepted here. Americans tend to distrust in literature two traits that are Gidian: versatility, on the one hand, and intimacy, on the other. Even in Europe, where his readers are far more numerous, it has taken time for many to realize that the personal problems of the writer have to be raised to universal problems. But his best European critics, and the few in this country who have looked upon him primarily as the writer—Germaine Brée, Albert Guérard and Justin O'Brien—tend to consider him as the example of a man who won out over guilt and neurosis through the discipline of art.

The final chapter in Albert Guérard's book, *André Gide*, is entitled "Corrupter of Youth." It is obviously an allusion to Socrates's trial where the philosopher was condemned for his efforts to undermine tradition. Gide can justifiably be placed in affiliation with such figures as Socrates, Rousseau and Nietzsche, men whose purely creative powers were intermittent, and whose ideas seemed dangerous to their immediate society. But their greatness, and this is Gide's greatness also, is the power with which they modified the ideas of their age, and altered the image of their century. With *L'Immoraliste* first, and especially with *Les Faux-Monnayeurs*, his truly virtuoso work, Gide played an important part in the history of the European novel. Beyond the multiple new technical devices Gide daringly used in composing *Les Faux-Monnayeurs*, the book stands as the most brilliant example of his ceaseless search for truth. *Les Faux-Monnayeurs* is not as profound an experiment as *Ulysses*, but it demonstrates the degree to which his nature needed commitment as much as freedom from commitment. It demonstrates both his proud and his wily individualism.

To Europe, and especially to France, Gide helped to introduce Dostoevski and Conrad, as well as Whitman and Melville. He was curious about all things American, but his influence has never spread very far in North

America. Today, in world literature courses in American universities, Gide is studied as an innovator in the style of the novel and as a latter-day humanist, as the eternal observer of man. "Each man," Montaigne once said, "bears in himself the entire condition of man." (*Chaque homme porte en soi toute la condition humaine.*) André Malraux's novel, whose title comes from this sentence of Montaigne, has had a much more telling effect on American readers than any book of André Gide. The story of Gide's life is more difficult to separate from his books than Malraux's. The early discovery of North Africa, for example, is vitally important for an understanding of the way in which his thought was, temporarily at least, liberated from metaphysical and religious anguish. Even before reading Nietzsche, Gide's philosophy concurred with his. Either one might have written the sentence: "Seek to become who you are," of which there is an echo in all of Gide's books.

With Nietzsche, but in an art more subtly composed than Nietzsche's, Gide disseminated, at first to a tiny audience but one destined to grow in numbers, a feeling of unrest, of disquiet. He taught how it was possible to establish a firm equilibrium on what seemed an inevitable oscillation between extremes. After his early devotion to Mallarmé's creed, which in its deepest sense he was never to disavow, Gide turned his attention and his enthusiasm to the young Dadaists and Surrealists of the twenties. The example he had given, of escape and of liberation, had encouraged them, and at first he was accepted and published by them. Many of the more conventional elements of that generation, unwilling to participate in the noisy, boisterous manifestations of surrealism, had turned to experiences of flight and adventure. Here again, Gide was one of the precursors, one of the examples. He was the prodigal son for at least a generation, and he was beginning to be called the demonic corrupter of youth. Today, his message, if it can be called that, seems more seriously a message of detachment from limiting bonds, an appeal to spiritual courage.

In the middle twenties, and following the publication of *Les Faux-Monnayeurs*, at a time when the moral accusations leveled at Gide were the most vehement, he spent approximately a year traveling in the Congo, and there espoused the cause of the Negroes whom he saw exploited by the large colonial companies. His scrupulous notations written down day after day, with a richness of detail (because Gide had on such occasions the flair of a detective) were to serve in bringing about reform in colonial politics. The Gide whom Marc Chadourne met in Maroua, in the region of Lake Tchad, was vastly different from the Gide of Paris, famous for his long cape and his eminent literary role. M. Chadourne has described Gide the explorer as he appeared to him in the Congo, courageous, uncomplaining, his face emaciated, his head bald and uncovered.

On his return from the Congo, and for two years, Gide made an effort to understand the cause of Communism. He hoped, in this political movement and in the Russian experiment, to reconcile the rights of the individual, as he understood them, with the dictatorial demands of a collective society. In the speech he read publicly at the funeral of Gorki in Moscow, there is one sentence, typically Gidian because it can be read in more than one way, that illustrates his convictions on his visit to Russia: "In our minds the fate of civilization is bound up with the fate itself of the Soviet Union." (*Le sort de la culture est lié dans nos esprits au destin même de l'U.R.S.S.*)

The countless experimentations or disciplines in Gide's life, which are reflected in the great diversity of books he wrote—stories, novels, *récits*, parables, memoirs, investigation reports—were the efforts of a twentieth century humanist to discover who he was and therefore who man is. Guided by his permanent belief in freedom and tolerance, he espoused several causes only to abandon each in turn when it appeared perilous to his freedom of spirit. But Gide lived within disciplines and this, in the French tradition, made of him a classical writer. The first major thesis on his work, the first *doctorat ès lettres*,

was defended in the Sorbonne in January, 1953, exactly
one year after the famous *soutenance de thèse* on Rimbaud
by Étiemble. M. Pierre Lafille wrote his major thesis on
"Gide as novelist" (*André Gide romancier*), and argued
that the Gidian themes that might appear as immoralisms
or as dangerous poisons were always transmuted into
serums of wisdom, into toxic medicines for humanity.
(During the *soutenance*, M. Lafille insisted several times
that Lafcadio of *Les Caves* is Apollinaire.)

The published letters exchanged between Gide and
Valéry (*André Gide et Paul Valéry: Correspondance
1890–1942*) is a major critical document not only on the
wisdom of Gide but on his intellectual limitations as. well.
The bulk of the letters published (the important preface
and notes for this edition were prepared by Robert Mallet)
were written between 1890 and 1900, and it would be
difficult to find a more literary correspondence. Obviously for Gide and Valéry, literary speculation was second
nature, and yet they remain "human" at all times, and
their investigations of art and poetry are often sparked
with humor.

The origin of their friendship is an important detail in
French literary history. Pierre Louÿs had met Valéry in
May, 1890, at Palavas. At that time, Valéry was in mili-
tary service in Montpellier. Louÿs was somewhat surprised to discover that the young provincial who lived
far from Paris was already an admirer of Huysmans,
Verlaine and Mallarmé. Gide first learned about Valéry
in the letters he received from Louÿs, and in December
of 1890, when he visited his uncle, Charles Gide, in
Montpellier, he was able to meet Valéry. Gide was
twenty-one and engaged on writing *André Walter*.
Valéry was a year or two younger, and trying to give up
the study of law.

The first three hundred letters of the collection evoke
the entire climate of symbolism. Huysmans and Mallarmé
form the background for the exuberant exchange of ideas
and judgments and theories. The language of the two
young men is affected. They both seem to be imitating

the rich convoluted style of Mallarmé, but the subject matter of their letters hardly justifies the ornate style. It is clear from the beginning of this exchange that each one has seen in the other not only a new friend but a mind and sensibility of great value. From the beginning of their friendship, Gide venerated Valéry's intelligence. In Gide, Valéry sensed the nature of an authentic artist and a sensitivity keenly aware of aesthetic problems that preoccupied him. At this time in their lives both young men were seeking in artistic creation a way of life, a reason for living. Their appearance and manners designated them as youthful esthetes scornful of the type of bourgeois inattentive to the power of art.

The richest letters in this correspondence are the earliest, and they reveal enduring traits in both men. Valéry's tone is total cordiality and directness and unabashed confidence. Later in his life, with other correspondents and other friends, he showed himself less expansive and more skeptical. Gide seems more reserved, more secretive, although in his early books he was to be overflowing with verbosity, lyrical in his effusions. M. Robert Mallet points out this difference in his preface to the correspondence. Although Valéry was the more optimistic about literature as a way of life, he was soon to renounce the professional practice of literature for twenty years, whereas Gide, more cautious about his judgments on the literary life, was to embark upon it avidly. Literature was at the basis of this friendship, although the two friends were to follow diametrically opposed literary vocations, and evoke through the years two opposing theories of literature.

The generation of Gide and Valéry, which includes Claudel and Proust, was the last to use the art of letter writing as a means of expressing not only personal problems but philosophical and political problems. When such problems have been raised by subsequent writers—by Mauriac, Cocteau, Sartre—they tend to be published in open letters printed in newspapers or periodicals. The letters of Gide and Valéry are personal, first, and then they are analyses of methods of knowing, of ways to be fol-

lowed in order to reach truth. By contrast, in the history
of French literature, the famous letters of Voltaire would
seem to be editorials, and the letters of Mme de Sévigné
would seem to be the daily column of a newspaper, a
chronicle of events.

Three of the last most important collections of letters
are those exchanged between Gide and Valéry, Gide and
Claudel, and Gide and Francis Jammes. In his letters to
Valéry one feels in Gide a certain sense of intimidation
of an intellectual order. Each of the two men tries to
understand this friendship that binds them. In a letter
written from Biskra, in March, 1894, Gide defines it as "a
relationship between two incommensurables" (*un rapport
entre deux incommensurables.*) He was always to acknowledge that Valéry eclipsed him in intellectual nimble-
ness. With Jammes, Gide was far more sure of himself,
and revealed some degree of brio and aggressiveness. The
jokester, the teaser in Gide, comes out in his letters to the
poet of the Pyrenees. With Claudel the zealous con-
verter, Gide shows the most complex sides of his nature
and his mind. But the letters to Claudel are probably the
most important he wrote.

The Valéry-Gide friendship existed without any profound affinities of temperament. It seemed to hold together by a thread, but the thread was unbreakable. In
the earliest very lengthy letters, characterized by excessive literariness, it is difficult to distinguish one correspondent from the other. As soon as Valéry comes to
Paris and settles there, a sharper distinction becomes
apparent. Valéry's letters are more interesting in themselves. He writes as if to himself, and quite soon begins
to elaborate on the aspects of his life which plague him,
the difficulties he encounters, the stupidity of the world.
His temperament as a man is revealed in the letters, but
it is totally absent from his major work. When he felt in
the presence of Gide, in the writing of these letters, a
spirit of liveliness and frankness came over him and he
was able to write directly of his feelings, his disappoint-
ments, his projects.

Early in his career Gide was adviser, and he cultivated this role effortlessly throughout his life. In August, 1956, several years after his death, *La Nouvelle Revue Française* published an article of advice to a young writer, *Conseils au jeune écrivain*. This piece was probably written about 1925, and earlier than Rilke's famous *Lettres à un jeune poète*. But whatever the exact chronology is, the two works are very different. Rilke's work emphasizes the education of the poet's soul and sensibility. The program is one of an almost spiritual initiation and the cultivation of affinities. Gide's short piece is more incisive and practical. With an ironic touch, he characterizes the profession of the writer, the snares and pitfalls and ways of overcoming such difficulties. Gide's tone has the dryness of a La Bruyère. He makes point after point, almost in the style of a Chamfort or a Joubert, in advising the writer to beware of easy success, and to distrust all forms of journalistic writing. Any kind of writing that will be less interesting tomorrow than today is to be avoided. Gide reminds the novice that the masterpiece does not appear beautiful at first.

Originality is a literary trait not too difficult to acquire, but the only sound originality, Gide claims, is that which comes from sincere feeling. Virtuosity is a danger for the young writer. Gide allows his novice to write at moments of great enthusiasm provided that he is in a state of sobriety when he begins the rereading of what he wrote. *Écris, si tu veux, dans l'ivresse; mais, quand tu te relis, sois à jeun.* Throughout the article it is Gide the technician who is speaking. His advice is Cartesian and antiromantic. One should write only what seems indispensable. This means that one should write less than what one wants to write. The one point that resembles Rilke's treatise is the need to perfect not one's craft, but oneself. This point, however, is left somewhat vague by Gide. He knows that the way of perfection, even for the writer, will ultimately lead to silence. The page written for oneself will always testify to some compromise with vanity. Gide never ceased trying to join the two towers in his literary inheritance: the ivory tower of Flaubert and Mallarmé, where the artist writes for himself in order to write better for all men, and the Tower of Constance, which is the sign of some practical mission. "If you set out into the world," Gide writes, "see to it you are dressed as a deep-sea diver." (*Si tu t'aventures dans le monde, que ce soit en scaphandrier.*)

It was a curious coincidence that the year 1947, in which Gide was awarded the Nobel Prize for literature, was also the fiftieth anniversary of *Les Nourritures terrestres*. This was the volume with which a generation of young readers was introduced to the work of Gide. Of all of his books, *Les Nourritures terrestres* had the strongest effect on a generation or two of French adolescents who found in it a program of freedom from scruples and family morality, a way of diminishing the severity of God's law and man's law. The first generation to be startled by *Les Nourritures terrestres* turned away from symbolist idols: from the mistresses of Baudelaire and the jeweled turtle of Des Esseintes, toward a fresh conquest of personal truths. They were first incited toward a search for freedom, and then severely warned about the perils of an ethic of pure pleasure.

Les Nourritures terrestres was the real beginning of a long work which, at the very start, was destined to elicit a variety of interpretations. The art of Gide is essentially reticent, even such a book as *Les Nourritures terrestres*, which seems to be written in an uncontrolled lyric expansiveness. All is crystalline, but all is not clear. By the time of the Nobel Prize, Gide had reached something very close to his real stature as a major contemporary writer, whose ideas were never clearly stated in any one book, and whose ideas were not possible to join from book to book in anything comparable to a coherent system. Writers like Voltaire and Anatole France were victims of their own clarity of thought. Gide, like Valéry, knew that the so-called obscure or difficult writers are better assured of literary survival.

It was fairly clear, by 1947, that André Gide was the most classical of twentieth century French writers. Proust was already being looked upon by that time as the arch-romantic, the writer lost in details and intoxicated with sensations. Claudel had very early found his position in terms of his faith, and he never moved from that central position. In his own way, Gide too was incorruptible. He was too intelligent to be simple. But he was unseizable, a multiple personality in his quests, always changing, always revising, always accenting a new value. And he, who had never solicited the slightest honor, because honors bind one to the benefactor, was given the one literary honor in the world that does not categorize the incumbent.

Gide's death, four years after the awarding of the Nobel Prize, created a second pause for stocktaking and estimation of what his work had accomplished, of what his work might possibly signify. Most of the well-worn clichés were revived, but some deeper views, some enduring prophecies also were articulated. The profile of the man honored suddenly became clearer, and what he represented in literary achievement appeared more free of personal indictment.

Here was a writer, a major writer, who had not played the literary game in the usual way, who had cut himself off from all opportunism, who had never compromised himself for any academic honor, who had never dreamed of campaigning for a *fauteuil* in the *Académie Française,* who had never participated in Paris in social life where literary fortune is strengthened. Gide's honor, Gide's triumphant virtue is the French language. This was first mentioned, in unequivocal terms, in the homage of Saint-John Perse, and this belief, among all the tributes paid at Gide's death, has continued to be justified since 1951, during these last thirteen years.

Gide's language is his survival. Whatever his life was, its value as well as its dramas, its weaknesses as well as its courage, are at the very source of his literary creation,

and are important simply because they have been transmuted into the work. He testifies to what is, what has
been for centuries, the very essence of French genius:
quality, first, that highest component demanded by the
aesthetic experience; then the necessity for writing, which
is an urgency coming from the writer himself and from
his relationship with the world about him; and third, a
will to articulate the truth, as the writer understands it,
to add one more measure of truth to the totality of truth
that mankind has reached in the imaginative productions
of its greatest artists. The quality of the writing, the impatient need to write a given book, the human truth
which this book will reveal are traits characterizing the
French genius: a Pascal, a Mallarmé, as well as, to a
preeminent degree, a Gide.

Genius cannot be explained in any satisfactory or
absolute way. Each example is different from all others.
The ways by which Gide's work reached these traits of
his nation's literary masters, are unique to him and honor
him in a purely personal way. His lack of complacency
has been referred to by countless friends and admirers,
but it is important to remember that Gide's lack of
complacency existed without any trace of arrogance. This
absence of satisfaction with self was maintained through
and by a fervor of spirit, through and by a sense of values
felt and safeguarded by a rare combination of instinct
and judgment. His intuitive powers were as strong as
his analytical powers.

Any work of such dimensions is bound to be uneven,
and Gide's is no exception. But his has the unity of a
self-portrait, of the man sensitive to the unpredictable,
of a man guided by a fundamental honesty of thought,
by a curiosity for what was new. He judged himself with
the same rigor with which he judged others, but always
with the motivation for knowing and learning. Most men
are influenced by events occurring in their lives and in
the world. Gide was never influenced by events to the
degree that his conduct was modified by them. In the

simplicity and also in the artfulness with which he composed his sentences, he continued to analyze and study his great theme of how a man justifies his human conduct when he is not guided by any outside force or doctrine. In the irony of his *récits*, he treated his grave subject as an artist. In his extended study of man and his behavior, he served the cause of literature all his life. In his opposition to social morality and to Catholicism, it would not have been enough merely to have been sincere. He forced himself to be sincere over the hardest problems of human nature.

Once Gide had become a public figure, his need to expose his thoughts became all the more acute and all the more perilous. Any attempt at self-definition was repellent to Gide, and yet this was inevitable in his program. The definition had to be constantly rewritten. What seemed to be sincere one day would be revealed the next day as the boasting of a conviction. His definitions had to be constantly reduced and banished. He was equally scornful of any adhesion to a group and any adhesion to a self-portrait. The *Journal* was not a mirror. He examined himself for the sole purpose that others might see him. The *Journal* was written for readers, and in it there is no trace of a desire on the part of Gide to make himself into an exceptional or an unusual person. He wanted at his death to be accepted for what he was. His friends and his enemies defined themselves at his death in contradistinction to him.

In the lives of countless young readers, Gide was the first vibrant contact with literature, the first irruption of literature. Many have testified to this fact. They began with Gide, and it was he who encouraged them to read others: Mallarmé, Racine, Stendhal. The books of Gide serve as invitations to go beyond them, to explore the ways leading to honesty and truth. His courage and his independence of spirit, and the form in which he gave expression to these virtues, were sensed by those readers who learned to love him as he taught them to love freedom of inquiry and to hate arbitrariness and falsehood. Many learned first in reading Gide that freedom is destiny, and that the spirit of contradiction is as vital as the spirit of freedom. Man's impatience to reach freedom must be cherished as much as his hope to reach freedom.

SELECTED

BIBLIOGRAPHY

WORKS OF GIDE IN FRENCH:

Oeuvres Complètes, 15 volumes, edited by Louis Martin-Chauffier. Gallimard.
Romans. Édition Pléiade, Gallimard, 1958.
Journal 1889–1939. Pléiade, Gallimard, 1939.
Journal 1939–1949, Souvenirs. Pléiade, Gallimard, 1954.
Les Cahiers d'André Walter, 1891.
Le Traité du Narcisse, 1891.
Paludes, 1895.
Les Nourritures terrestres, 1897.
Le Prométhée mal enchaîné, 1899.
L'Immoraliste, 1902.
Le Retour de l'enfant prodigue, 1907.
La Porte étroite, 1909.
Les Caves du Vatican, 1914.
La Symphonie Pastorale, 1919.
Corydon, 1924.
Incidences, 1924.
Si le grain ne meurt, 1926.
Les Faux-Monnayeurs, 1926.
Journal des Faux-Monnayeurs, 1926.
Voyage au Congo, 1927.
Les Nouvelles nourritures, 1935.
Retour de l'U.R.S.S., 1936.
Théâtre, 1942.
Thésée, 1946.
Et nunc manet in te, 1951.
Ainsi soit-il, 1951.
Claudel-Gide: Correspondance 1899–1926. (1949)

Gide-Jammes: Correspondance 1893–1938. (1948)
Gide-Valéry: Correspondance 1890–1942. (1955)

WORKS OF GIDE IN ENGLISH:

Marshlands, tr. by G. Painter. New Directions, 1953.
Fruits of the Earth, tr. by D. Bussy. Knopf, 1949.
Prometheus Misbound, tr. by G. Painter. New Directions, 1953.
The Immoralist, tr. by D. Bussy. Knopf, 1930.
Strait Is the Gate, tr. by D. Bussy. Knopf, 1924.
Return of the Prodigal Son, tr. by Wallace Fowlie. *French Stories.* Bantam, 1960.
The Vatican Swindle, tr. by D. Bussy. Knopf, 1925.
The Pastoral Symphony, tr. by D. Bussy. Knopf, 1931.
Later Fruits of the Earth, tr. by D. Bussy. Knopf, 1949.
Corydon, tr. by Hugh Gibb. Farrar, Straus, 1950.
If It Die, tr. by D. Bussy. Random House, 1935.
The Counterfeiters, tr. by D. Bussy. Knopf, 1927.
Travels in the Congo, tr. by D. Bussy. Knopf, 1930.
The Journals of André Gide 1889–1949, tr. by J. O'Brien. Knopf, 1952.
Pretexts, ed. J. O'Brien, tr. by A. P. Bertocci and others. Meridian, 1959.
Return from the USSR, tr. by D. Bussy. Dial Press, 1937.
Theseus, tr. by J. Russell. Knopf, 1950.
Madeleine, tr. by J. O'Brien. Knopf, 1952.
So Be It or The Chips Are Down, tr. by J. O'Brien. Knopf, 1959.
Claudel-Gide: Correspondence, tr. by J. Russell. Pantheon, 1952.
My Theatre, tr. by J. Mathews. Knopf, 1951.

WORKS IN FRENCH ON GIDE:

Albérès, R.-M., *L'Odyssée d'André Gide.* La Nouvelle Édition, 1951.
Brée, Germaine, *André Gide, l'insaisissable Protée.* Belles-Lettres, 1953.

Davet, Yvonne, *Autour des Nourritures terrestres*. Galli-
     mard, 1948.
Delay, Jean, *La Jeunesse d'André Gide*. 2 vols. Gallimard,
     1956–1958.
Du Bos, Charles, *Le Dialogue avec André Gide*. Corréa,
     1947.
Fernandez, Ramon, *André Gide*. Corréa, 1931.
Hytier, Jean, *André Gide*. Charlot, 1938; 1945.
Lafille, Pierre, *André Gide romancier*. Hachette, 1954.
Lang, Renée, *André Gide et la pensée allemande*. Univ. de
     Fribourg, 1949.
Martin du Gard, Roger, *Notes sur André Gide 1913–1951*.
     Gallimard, 1951.
Pierre-Quint, Léon, *André Gide, sa vie, son œuvre*. Stock,
     1952.
Schlumberger, Jean, *Madeleine et André Gide, leur vrai
     visage*. Gallimard, 1956.

WORKS IN ENGLISH ON GIDE:

Ames, Van Meter, *André Gide*. New Directions, 1947.
Guerard, Albert, *André Gide*. Harvard Univ. Press, 1951.
Ireland, G. W., *André Gide*. Grove Press, 1963.
Mann, Klaus, *André Gide and the Crisis of Modern
     Thought*. Creative Age, 1943.
O'Brien, Justin, *Portrait of André Gide. A Critical Biog-
     raphy*. Knopf, 1953.
Painter, George, *André Gide, A Critical and Biographical
     Study*. Roy Publishers, 1951.
Starkie, Enid, *André Gide*. Yale Univ. Press, 1954.
Thomas, D. L., *André Gide, The Ethic of the Artist*.
     Secker & Warburg, 1950.

ARTICLES OR CHAPTERS ON GIDE:

Blanchot, Maurice, "Gide et la littérature d'expérience."
     L'Arche, Jan., 1947.
Brée, Germaine, "Form and Content in Gide." *French
     Review*, May, 1957.

Fowlie, Wallace, "The Fountain and the Thirst." *Accent*, winter, 1948.

"Gide's Earliest Quest: Les Nourritures terrestres." *Essays in Criticism*, July, 1952.

"Who Was André Gide?" *Sewanee Review*, winter, 1952.

Hoog, Armand, *André Gide et l'acte gratuit*. Nef, May, 1946.

Peyre, Henri, *The Contemporary French Novel*. Oxford, 1955. pp. 67–100.

Sypher, Wylie, "Gide's Cubist Novel." *Kenyon Review*, spring, 1949.

INDEX

Alain-Fournier, Henri, 5, 41
Albérès, M.-R., 169
Allégret, Jean-Paul, 103
Allégret, Marc, 77, 89, 103, 124, 125, 150, 151
Altermann, Abbé, 173
Amiel, Henri-Frédéric, 17, 138
Amyot, Jacques, 113
Anouilh, Jean, 73, 116
Apollinaire, Guilaume, 200
Aragon, Louis, 101, 134
Augustine, St., 2

Bach, Johann Sebastian, 104
Balzac, Honoré de, 82, 89
Barrès, Maurice, 8, 19, 36, 101, 128, 131, 132, 136, 182
Baudelaire, Charles, 35, 42, 158, 177, 204
Bavretel, Armand, 15
Beaunier, André, 63
Beckett, Samuel, 41
Bennett, Arnold, 77
Bergson, Henri, 6, 7, 16, 73
Bernanos, Georges, 7, 48, 133
Berrichon, Paterne, 36

Bertrand, Aloysius, 35
Blake, William, 105, 132
Blanche, Jacques-Émile, 20, 25
Blanchot, Maurice, 35
Blum, Léon, 141
Boccaccio, 69
Brée, Germaine, 74, 131, 132, 197
Brummel, Beau, 27
Byron, Lord, 27

Camus, Albert, 48, 133
Cellini, Benvenuto, 2, 135
Chadourne, Marc, 199
Chamfort, Nicolas-Sébastien Roch, 203
Chateaubriand, François-René de, 56, 80, 132, 135
Claudel, Paul, 7, 20, 22, 24, 34, 42, 57, 64, 76, 77, 85, 101, 106, 159, 163-69, 171, 173, 179, 201, 202, 205
Conrad, Joseph, 100, 105, 197
Constant, Benjamin, 53, 56
Copeau, Jacques, 57, 68, 69, 154, 159, 171, 173
Corneille, Pierre, 9

Couturier, Père, 174
Cravan, Arthur, 71

Dabit, Eugène, 102
D'Annunzio, Gabriele, 30
Dante, 177
Defoe, Daniel, 69
Delay, Jean, 12, 17, 29, 122, 123, 132, 144, 154-57
Démarest, Albert, 15
Démarest, Claire, 15
Derais, François, 130
Desjardins, administrator, 105
Dostoevski, Fedor, 3, 32, 70, 72, 132, 189, 197
Douglas, Lord Alfred, 22, 27
Dreyfus, Alfred, 99
Drouin, Marcel, 16
Du Bos, Charles, 26, 51, 105, 143, 154, 159, 171, 174
Dupouey, 159

Ehrenburg, Ilya, 102
Eliot, T. S., 99
Emerson, Ralph Waldo, 175
Emmanuèle. See Gide, Madeleine
Étiemble, 200

Fargue, Léon-Paul, 20
Fernandez, Ramon, 101, 161
Flaubert, Gustave, 89, 204
Fontaine, L'Abbé, 167
France, Anatole, 204

Gauguin, Paul, 20
Ghéon, Henri, 57, 77, 143, 154, 159, 171, 173
Gide, Catherine, 89, 129, 142
Gide, Charles, 13, 16, 26, 29, 200
Gide, Madeleine, 12, 13, 15-17, 21, 26-31, 45, 56, 63, 104, 142, 144, 147-57, 168
Gide, Paul, 11
Gide, Mme Paul, 10, 12-15, 27-29
Gide, Tancrède, 11
Giraudoux, Jean, 116, 159
Goethe, Wolfgang, 20, 31, 32, 56, 104, 105, 123, 132, 139, 177, 182
Gorki, Maxim, 102, 199
Green, Julien, 48, 101, 143, 159, 171, 172, 174
Greene, Graham, 7, 41, 48
Guéhenno, Jean, 101, 161
Guérard, Albert, 197

Herbart, Pierre, 102, 129, 130, 131, 141
Heredia, 20
Hérold, poet, 22, 25
Huxley, Aldous, 48, 97
Huysmans, Joris-Karl, 200
Hytier, Jean, 131, 132

Ionesco, Eugène, 73, 97

James, Henry, 77, 86, 99

Jammes, Francis, 29, 55, 57, 58, 77, 106, 159, 169, 171, 202
John, St., 28, 160
Joubert, Joseph, 203
Joyce, James, 85, 97, 98, 100

Kierkegaard, Sören, 105

La Bruyère, Jean de, 1, 203
Lafille, Pierre, 200
Lambert, Jean, 128
Lanux, Marc de, 151
Lanux, Pierre de, 151
Larbaud, Valéry, 68, 143
La Rochefoucauld, 86
Last, Jef, 102
Laurens, Jean-Paul, 16
Laurens, Paul, 16, 20-22, 24, 173
Lautréamont (Isidore Ducasse), 45, 189
Lawrence, D. H., 5, 7, 48
Lawrence, T. E., 5
Leconte de Lisle, 11
Leo XIII, 69, 73
Lesort, Paul André, 168
Lévy, Jacques, 162, 163
Louÿs, Pierre, 16, 17, 20, 22, 25, 27, 200
Luke, St., 3, 59, 60, 65

Mallarmé, Stéphane, 19, 20, 23, 24, 36, 85, 98, 182, 196, 198, 200, 201, 204, 205, 207
Mallet, Robert, 163, 164, 200, 201

Malraux, André, 5, 101, 105, 137, 198
Mann, Klaus, 25
Mann, Thomas, 85, 98, 100, 104, 177
Marcel, Gabriel, 101, 161, 173
Mardrus, Dr., 11
Maritain, Jacques, 101, 161, 170, 171, 173
Martin, Claude, 168
Martin du Gard, Roger, 105, 122, 125, 126, 129, 143
Massis, Henri, 76, 101, 108, 128, 161
Maulnier, Thierry, 161
Mauriac, Claude, 124, 128, 171, 189
Mauriac, François, 101, 105, 122, 124, 128, 129, 132, 133, 136, 160, 161, 171, 201
Melville, Herman, 197
Mérimée, Prosper, 80
Miller, Henry, 48, 86
Molière, Jean-Baptiste, 73
Montaigne, Michel de, 1, 2, 63, 86, 100, 124, 126, 132, 135, 139, 158, 174, 177, 198
Moravia, Alberto, 48
Moréas, Jean, 19
Morice, Anick, 125
Mozart, Wolfgang Amadeus, 104
Mugnier, Abbé, 173

Nerval, Gérard de, 20

Nietzsche, Friedrich, 3, 6, 7, 32, 36, 45, 47, 52, 104, 132, 173, 182, 197, 198

O'Brien, Justin, 131, 197

Painter, George, 131
Pascal, Blaise, 1, 3, 124, 205
Paul, St., 28, 78
Pauly, Jean de, 68
Péguy, Charles, 7
Pirandello, Luigi, 48
Pitoëff, Georges, 109
Plutarch, 113
Prévost, Marcel, 69
Proust, Marcel, 20, 69, 85, 91, 98, 100, 124, 171, 180, 201
Psichari, Jean, 5
Pushkin, Alexander, 105

Rabelais, 69, 110, 158
Racine, Jean, 110, 113, 119, 132, 207
Redon, Odilon, 20
Régnier, Henri de, 23
Renan, Ernest, 5, 101
Renard, Jules, 138
Rilke, Rainer Maria, 143, 203
Rimbaud, Arthur, 6, 22, 35, 36, 40, 41, 45, 173, 182, 200
Rivière, Jacques, 5, 105, 166, 171, 173
Rolland, Romain, 102
Rondeaux, Édouard, 10

Rondeaux, Émile, 12
Rondeaux, Henri, 10
Rondeaux, Jeanne, 16
Rondeaux, Juliette. See Gide, Mme Paul
Rondeaux, Madeleine. See Gide, Madeleine
Rondeaux, Mathilde, 12
Rousseau, Jean-Jacques, 2, 3, 36, 52, 86, 131, 132, 135, 191, 197
Rousseaux, André, 122
Rysselberghe, Elizabeth, 89, 129, 141
Rysselberghe, Maria (Mme Théo), 89, 129, 141

Saint-Exupéry, Antoine de, 5, 100, 103
Saint-John Perse (Alexis Saint-Léger Léger), 205
Sartre, Jean-Paul, 48, 52, 137, 158, 190, 201
Scheffer, Ary, 56
Schiffrin, Jacques, 102
Schlumberger, Jean, 143, 150, 151, 152, 154, 161, 175
Schopenhauer, Arthur, 16
Schwob, Marcel, 36
Sévigné, Mme de, 202
Shackleton, Anna, 10, 12, 15, 63
Shakespeare, William, 123, 132, 177
Simenon, Georges, 127
Socrates, 197
Sophocles, 110
Soupault, Phillipe, 103

Stalin, Joseph, 125
Starkie, Enid, 131
Stendhal (Henri Beyle), 52, 69, 71, 86, 139, 177, 191, 207
Strauss, Richard, 104
Sue, Eugène, 72

Tagore, Rabindranath, 76
Taine, Hippolyte, 5
Thibaudet, Albert, 91
Thomas, Lawrence, 139
Tolstoi, Léon, 69

Unamuno, Miguel de, 6

Valéry, Paul, 1, 2, 17, 18, 20, 23, 25, 36, 55, 85, 105, 125, 143, 164, 200, 201, 202, 204
Verlaine, Paul, 200
Vilar, Jean, 109
Virgil, 147, 177
Vuillard, Édouard, 20

Wagner, Richard, 104
Wharton, Edith, 77
Whistler, James A. McNeill, 20
Whitman, Walt, 6, 76, 104, 132, 197
Wilde, Oscar, 20, 22, 27, 36, 55, 99, 171
Witt, François de, 15